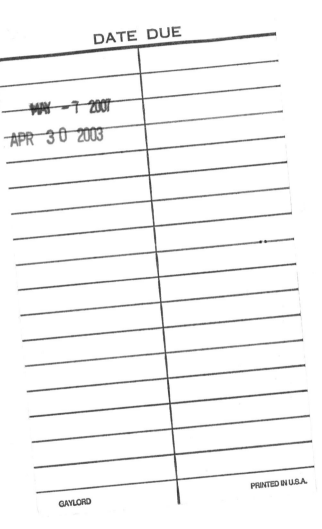

A Club Manager's Guide

to Private Parties and Club Functions

A Club Manager's Guide

to Private Parties and Club Functions

Joe Perdue
Rhonda J. Montgomery
Patti J. Shock
John M. Stefanelli

John Wiley & Sons, Inc.

New York   Chichester   Weinheim   Brisbane   Singapore   Toronto

Copyright © 1998 by John Wiley & Sons, Inc. All rights reserved.

Published simultaneously in Canada.

This publication is designed to provide accurate and authoritative information in regard to the subject matter covered. It is sold with the understanding that the publisher is not engaged in rendering professional services. If professional advice or other expert assistance is required, the services of a competent professional person should be sought.

Library of Congress Cataloging-in-Publication Data:

Club manager's guide to private parties and club functions / Joe
   Perdue . . . [et al.].
      p.   cm.
   Includes index.
   ISBN 0-471-02978-5 (cloth : alk. paper)
   1. Clubs—Management.   2. Hospitality industry—Management.
I. Perdue, Joe.
TX911.3.M27C584   1998
642'.4'068—dc21   97-41087

Printed in the United States of America.

10 9 8 7 6 5 4 3 2 1

To Mick Montgomery, whose tireless work and commitment to this project
made this book possible.

Contents

Preface

The primary objective of this book is to provide club catering professionals, as well as aspiring professionals, with an in-depth, one-stop source of generally accepted club catering principles and practices. In it you will find considerable discussion of the organization and administration of catering in the club industry, major club catering activities, marketing procedures, and club catering production and service techniques.

The many topics covered in this text will give you a general perspective on the catering and special event business in private clubs, as well as specific information that can be used to plan, develop, implement, supervise, and follow up on a catering function. This book can also be a valuable, concise desk reference. For instance, it will help you determine the approximate number of servers to schedule for a particular type of event, how to price meal functions, and how to develop catering proposals. There is a great deal of valuable, hands-on, reality-based information that will give you a clear and comprehensive view of the club catering activity, as well as its relationship to the management of a successful club operation.

Shortly after the publication of Patti Shock and John Stefanelli's *Hotel Catering: A Handbook for Sales and Operations* (Wiley, 1992), a club manager remarked that it would be good to have a similar reference book for private club managers. The authors agreed that this would be a significant contribution to the industry. There are similarities between hotels and private clubs, but many of the most critical, subtle details can be learned only from someone who has been in the position of club manager. So the race was on to find someone who could help convert a book on hotel catering to one focused exclusively on catering within private clubs. The obvious choice, Joe Perdue, was approached and was asked to join the team. He immediately agreed, but, as Vice President of Education for the Club Managers Association of America (CMAA), his time was limited. So another expert in the field, Rhonda Montgomery, was asked to lend a hand. She eagerly enlisted in this growing army.

Each of the authors brings something unique to the project. Any one of us working alone probably could not have developed an acceptable book on catering and special events for the private club industry. Together, we think we have created the very best possible book. We are confident that you will enjoy it and will profit from it.

During the writing of this book, the authors have benefited from the thoughtful and constructive feedback of colleagues who continually reviewed our efforts. We would especially like to acknowledge our expert reviewers who diligently corrected our errors and oversights.

The appropriate methods used to organize a memorable catering function are subject to a certain amount of discussion, opinion, and interpretation. We realize that often there are no right or wrong ways of doing things—just different ways. Also, since a book of this type is a living document, subject to revision as the club industry changes, we welcome your ideas and suggestions for the next edition.

While no book can claim to be the last word on any subject, we feel that the material presented in this volume provides a thorough view of club catering. It is a synthesis of generally accepted club industry practices and our personal experiences and judgments. We hope that our discussion of this exciting and rewarding field will be a worthy contribution to the club management profession and a significant boost to each reader's professional career development.

ACKNOWLEDGMENTS

Special thanks to Haissam Baityeh and Cathy Gustafson for their keen insight and reviews of the manuscript. Our sincerest gratitude to Joy Cook, whose research efforts on this project are greatly appreciated.

Our heartfelt gratitude to Claire Thompson Zukerman, our editor, whose gentle prodding and encouragement gave us the strength to finish.

We would also like to thank the following individuals for their contributions to this work:

Ron Bartnett

John Jordan, CCM—Cherokee Town and Country Club

William A. Schultz, MCM—Houston Country Club
Peter K. Oldfield—The Granite Club
Terry L. Gilmer, CCM, CFE—Indian Hills Country Club
Micah Schachinger—Kinston Country Club
Susan W. Cascio—Petroleum Club of Shreveport

Joe Perdue
Rhonda J. Montgomery
Patti J. Shock
John M. Stefanelli

A Club Manager's Guide
to Private Parties and Club Functions

1

Special Events in Private Clubs

. . . .

Private club managers address many issues in their role as chief operating officers for their clubs. Special events within a private club are probably the most challenging, rewarding, and creative parts of a private club manager's duties. With special events, the club manager has the opportunity to showcase his or her facility and staff. Whether hosting a theme party or a wedding, the private club manager can create a special and memorable occasion for members and guests.

Special events, private parties, or catering—depending on what your club calls these events—both on and off the premises, are becoming big business for private clubs. In the United States, it is estimated that catering revenue exceeds more than a billion dollars annually. Within private clubs, this category of business is estimated to be 25–50 percent of the average club's overall food and beverage revenue mix. Special events at a private club range from small VIP receptions of ten or less to parties or social events for the entire membership.

Catering is one of the fastest-growing segments of the foodservice industry. It offers the clients the opportunity to impress their families, friends, and business associates. Holding functions at their club makes sense—the member is free to enjoy the event along with the guests, instead of trying to handle the myriad of details and chores personally. Many clubs are sharing in the trend toward larger and more frequent special events being hosted in their facilities. Club catering is a major revenue generator and contributes significantly to the club's responsibility to operate food and beverage departments more profitably. Virtually every club is capable of hosting special functions, preparing special menus, and providing amenities and accompaniments to generate additional revenue. Even with facility layout and size limitations, most clubs can expand their catering/special event business to reach additional markets outside of the club membership. Although many private clubs are nonprofit, they still must function profitably. Effective marketing of catering/special event services can substantially increase sales revenue and generate a positive net income before depreciation.

U.S. foodservice sales equal about 5 percent of the U.S. gross national product (GNP). This is expected to increase throughout the late 1990s. Today, over 40 percent of all money spent for food in the United States is spent in a foodservice operation. In 1950, less than 25 percent of the food dollar was spent away from home. On the average day, almost 50 percent of the U.S. population will spend money at a foodservice establishment. About 60 percent of them will eat in a foodservice operation, while the remainder will purchase food for off-premise consumption.

The on-premise and off-premise catering segments of the U.S. foodservice industry have enjoyed similar success and growth over the years. Every day thousands of business and social groups get together to enjoy each other's company and the refreshments that are usually found at these gatherings. Some of these events are catered by the group members themselves, but, since time is a precious commodity, more and more groups are demanding professionally prepared and served food and beverages. This allows participants to concentrate solely on their personal, social, and business activities while simultaneously enjoying the events. And, as a bonus, they can leave the cleanup to someone else. Private club members view their club as an extension of their homes; therefore, it makes sense that they would look to their club for their catering or special event needs.

TYPES OF CATERING OR SPECIAL EVENTS WITHIN PRIVATE CLUBS

Catering within private clubs can be classified several ways. The most common method is to categorize catering into social catering and business catering. Social catering includes such events as wedding receptions, bridal showers, reunions, society balls, birthday parties, charity benefits, member/guest functions, business functions, themed holiday parties, bar mitzvahs and bas mitzvahs, and golf, tennis, or pool functions.

Private clubs also have a category of functions called *club functions* or *club events*. These are functions planned by club management and the social committee for all club members and guests and are generally subsidized by the club. Examples of club events include club tournaments, pool parties, Christmas parties or dances, Fourth of July celebrations, and New Year's Eve dances.

Business catering includes such events as business luncheons and dinners, civic meetings, corporate meetings, service awards banquets, recognition banquets, and educational training sessions. It is estimated that business catering accounts for about 75 percent of all catering sales within the public sector of the industry; within private club business, business catering is a much smaller part of the special event business.

Catering can also be categorized into off-premises catering and on-premises catering. Off-premises catering usually involves production at a central kitchen with delivery to and service provided at a client's location, although at times the caterer may do on-site production as well as service. Off-premises catering also includes fewer complex functions and can be as simple as a halfway house on the golf course, a refreshment cart that roams the property, carryout party trays, or take-home meals.

Club catering is a form of on-premises catering. All production and service are handled at the club, with the club controlling all aspects of the catered event. Members usually receive a one-stop shopping opportunity from the typical private club. Most club catering departments specialize in providing the ultimate service experience to their members by taking care of all details.

Although the majority of catering or special events done by a private club take place on the premises, there is a growing trend toward providing off-premises catering in order to maintain revenue flow during slower business times. Some private clubs have made their sponsorship guidelines for nonmember business less restrictive to encourage the use of their facilities during times when member usage is slow. Although this practice may be excellent for the club's bottom line, a good balance must be maintained to ensure that members do not feel neglected or that their club is no longer available to them.

CLUB CATERING DEPARTMENT FUNCTIONS

Although the management structure will vary within each private club, the person in charge of the club catering department must perform the normal management functions. The title given to this person may vary from club to club, but some of the most common titles are assistant manager, banquet manager, social director, catering manager, and food and beverage director. As the head of a major club department, he or she must engage in the following:

1. *Planning.*   Planning is the most critical component of this job. The department must accomplish its financial and nonfinancial objectives. To do so, it must develop appropriate marketing, production, and service procedures. It also must ensure that the department's operating budgets and other functions are consistent with the club's overall objectives. Every single special event takes advance planning. These events run the gamut from simple beverage breaks that can be planned over the phone to extensive wedding receptions, which require numerous lengthy meetings and may be planned up to a year in advance. Special events are detailed productions, and advance planning is crucial to the success of the club's catering department.

2. *Organizing.*   The department must organize the resources needed to follow the plan. Management must recruit and train staff members, prepare work schedules, and administer performance evaluations.

3. *Directing.*   Employee supervision is an integral part of every supervisor's job. Supervisory style will emanate from top management. The catering department's supervisory procedures must be consistent with club policies. Directing an event is usually the most challenging part of the job since every function is unique and themes will dictate different directions from management. It is important that the host of a function doesn't feel like it's "just another function"; hosts must feel that their function is very special—not only to them but to the club as well.

4. *Controlling.*   The catering department manager must ensure that actual performance corresponds with planned performance. Effective financial controls ensure that actual profit-and-loss statements are consistent with pro forma budgets, while effective quality controls ensure that production and service meet club standards.

5. *Evaluating.*   The management of each department needs feedback from its members and guests to aid in evaluating the event. Adjustments to future events should be made, if appropriate, with this information.

CLUB CATERING/SPECIAL EVENTS
DEPARTMENT OBJECTIVES

Club catering departments have a variety of objectives. The weight and priority given to each will depend on club policy. Some of the most common objectives are:

- Meet and exceed club members' and other hosts' needs and expectations regarding private parties, special events, and catered functions.
- Generate consistent contribution to the overhead for the club within legal guidelines determined by club status (profit/not for profit) and within club bylaws.
- Exceed member satisfaction. This will lead to repeat patronage as well as positive membership referrals. Any foodservice operation thrives on repeat patronage, and this is especially true for the club catering department because it is dealing with a finite number of members and because of the restrictions generally placed on advertising and solicitation of business.
- Provide consistent quality and service. The best surprise is no surprise! Members are happy when the actual quality and service received parallels or exceeds what was promised. Punctuality and consistency are hallmarks of the well-run catering department.
- Meet the club's mission statement.
- Convey a particular image. Private clubs want to be known as providing outstanding products and services. They strive to be unique because they want members and guests to think of them whenever a specific atmosphere or ambience is required. Special events, private parties, or catered events are often the club's most visible characteristics.
- Develop a reputation for dependability. Regardless of the pressure that any event places on the catering department, clubs want members and guests to feel confident that their needs will be met. The catering department must adequately fill the liaison role between members and all special-event-related services, such as the provision of cakes and flowers and recreational coordination.
- Develop a reputation for flexibility. To be dependable, the typical club catering department must be flexible. The department must be able to react on a moment's notice. Members and guests will remember fondly the service that bailed them out at the last minute. In addition, successful catering managers must be able to foresee potential

flaws in the plan and prevent potential conflict. *Remember, at a private club, the rules are made to be bent.*

CLUB CATERING DEPARTMENT ORGANIZATION

Club catering departments are organized according to the needs of the individual club. Usually a club's primary focus centers on meeting the specific needs of its members. These needs generally include the ability to host private parties, special events, and catered business functions at the club. Occasionally members will also request off-premises catering in their homes or businesses as well as catering for golf, tennis, and other related recreational business.

Catering department organization depends on the size of the club and the percentage of food and beverage revenue generated by catering. In the case of a very small club, the department consists of a general manager who books all functions and then coordinates with the chef and dining room manager to execute the function (see Figure 1.1). In the case of a larger club (see Figure 1.2), there may be a director of food and beverage or a social coordinator who books all functions and has a staff that organizes the functions and works closely with the chef and wait staff. Regardless of the size of the club, the catering department should be designed to provide:

1. *Efficiency.* Members work with one designated person who has the authority to oversee the event from greetings to good-byes. Last-minute requests and changes must be addressed quickly and with a smile.

2. *Isolated responsibility.* Responsibility should be assigned to one person. Management and hosts need to know who to contact if questions arise. This contact person occupies a key role in that he or she is the sole liaison between a host and all special event services. It is a very critical position in that the contact person is responsible for transforming the member's needs and wishes into reality.

3. *Job enrichment.* A person in charge of an event enjoys more variety than does a person involved with only one or two aspects. When the event is a success, the person in charge can rightfully take a bow.

4. *Repeat patronage.* When members deal with one person, there are additional opportunities to solicit repeat patronage and referrals because of the trust that is built between the contact person and the member.

5. *Improved communications.* Centralizing contact between the host and one staff member reduces ambiguity and misinterpretations.

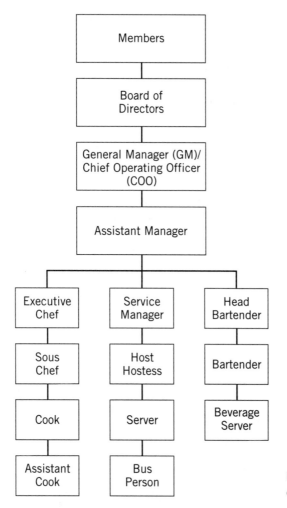

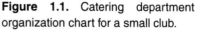

Figure 1.1. Catering department organization chart for a small club.

STAFF

Catering Staff Positions

Depending on the size of the club, catering departments require a variety of staff positions in order to operate effectively and efficiently. However, clubs need less staff than larger operations such as major hotels and convention centers. Depending on the type of catered event, a club also depends on other club departments' employees to handle special details of larger func-

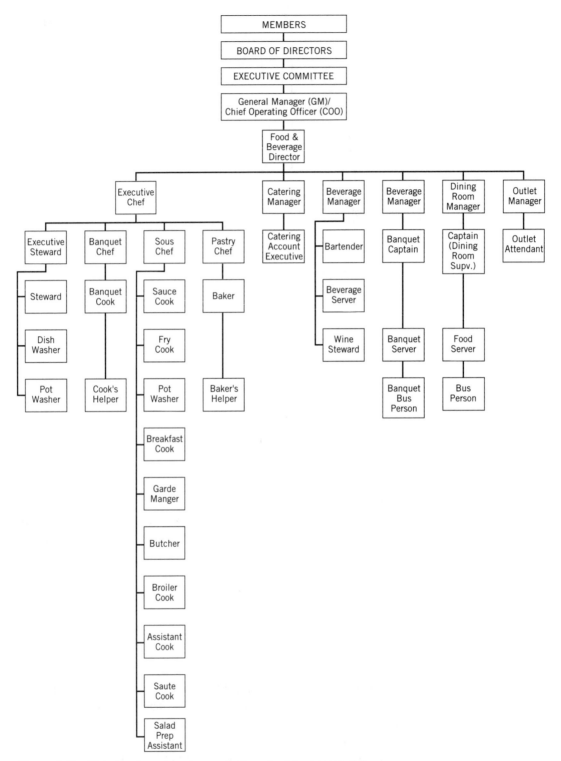

Figure 1.2. Catering department organization chart for a large club.

tions. In a large club, the typical positions needed to service members and guests are:

General manager	Busser
Clubhouse manager	Food handler
Chef	Bartender
Sous chef	Sommelier
Pastry chef	Houseman
Cooks	Attendant
Food and beverage director	Engineer
	Steward
Social coordinator	Doormen
Banquet manager	Valet parkers
Banquet setup manager	Security
Maitre d'	Golf cart drivers (to transport guests from their parked cars to the front door and back)
Captain	
Server	

Job Specifications of Catering Employees

A job specification contains the qualities sought in a job candidate. Before hiring an employee, a superior generally looks for several major qualities.

1. *Technical skills.* Ideally, catering employees will have food and beverage knowledge and preparation or service skills. At the very least, they must have the aptitude to learn these skills. All catering employees must be familiar with the products so that they can respond adequately to customer inquiries.

2. *Communication skills.* The ability to effectively communicate with members and their guests is absolutely essential for catering staff members. Each function is a unique undertaking. There is no standard pattern. Consequently, open and intelligible communications are critical to the success of a catered event.

3. *Conceptual skills.* As much as possible, catering department staff members must be able to view the entire catering function and not see things exclusively from their particular job perspectives. For instance, a banquet chef must appreciate the ceremonies involved with a wedding function and not ignore them when preparing and coordinating food courses.

4. *Human (interpersonal) skills.* Customer-contact skills are extremely important in the hospitality industry, but they are even more so in the private club. Getting along with people, along with satisfying them while simultaneously making a profit, is a challenge that must be met and overcome by all catering staff members. Unlike technical and conceptual skills, basic human skills generally cannot be taught by the club's training program. As Ellsworth Statler, the great hotelier, once said before the turn of the century, "Hire only good-natured people."

5. *Other qualities.*   Other characteristics that superiors look for in job candidates depend on the type of position and club policies. For instance, if the club has a policy of promoting from within, a manager would seek a job candidate who has the ability and desire to advance and grow with the club.

6. *Appearance and good grooming.*   Personal appearance is extremely important in private clubs. Remember the staff *is* the club to members and guests.

Job Descriptions

A job description contains a list of duties an employee must perform. It also includes the job candidate's superior, job performance evaluation criteria, the job objectives, and a career path. It is usually prepared before, or in conjunction with, the job specification. Example abbreviated job descriptions for the staff positions involved directly or indirectly with catering are:

1. *Catering manager.*   (Depending on the size of the club, this position may be called the food and beverage director, clubhouse manager, or the general manager.) Assigns and oversees all functions; oversees all marketing efforts; interacts with members and other club departments; creates menus; usually reports to the food and beverage director, but in some clubs may report to the general manager.

2. *Assistant catering manager.*   Oversees much of the actual operations side of the catering events and is the key communication liaison between the host and back- and front-of-the-house staff.

3. *Banquet floor manager.*   Implements the special event plan; oversees captains; supervises all functions in progress; staffs and schedules servers and bartenders; coordinates all support departments; provides the charge information to the controller after the event.

(This person is the operations director, as opposed to catering executives, who handle primarily the selling and planning chores.)

4. *Banquet setup manager (sometimes referred to as housekeeping supervisor).* Supervises the banquet setup crew; coordinates the movement of tables, chairs, and other room equipment from storage; supervises teardown of event.

5. *Assistant banquet manager.* Reports to banquet manager; supervises table settings and decor. (There may be two or more assistants depending on the size of the club and banquet operations).

6. *Maitre d'.* The floor manager; in charge of all service personnel; oversees all aspects of member/guest service during all catered events, seated receptions, and meal and beverage functions.

7. *Captain.* Room or section manager; is in charge of service at meal functions; typically oversees all activity in the entire function room or a portion of it during a meal; supervises service personnel.

8. *Server (food and cocktail).* Food servers deliver foods, nonalcoholic beverages, and utensils to tables; clear tables; attend to guest needs. Cocktail servers perform similar duties, but concentrate on serving alcoholic beverages. Servers are sometimes backed up by buspersons, whose primary responsibilities are to clear tables, restock side stands, and serve ice water, rolls, butter, and condiments.

9. *Food handler.* (Sometimes referred to as a food steward or expediter.) Prepares finished food products noted on banquet event orders (BEOs); responsible for having them ready according to schedule.

10. *Bartender.* Concentrates on alcoholic beverage production and service; sometimes assisted by bar backs, whose primary responsibilities are to initially stock and replenish the bars with liquor, ice, glassware, and direct operating supplies.

11. *Sommelier.* Wine steward; usually used only at fancy, upscale events; responsible for wine service and, in some cases, the selection of wines.

12. *Houseman (sometimes referred to as a porter).* Physically sets up rooms with risers, hardware, tables, chairs, and other necessary equipment; reports to banquet setup manager.

13. *Steward.* Delivers the proper amounts of china, glass, silver, and other similar items to function rooms, kitchens, and bar areas.

CLUB CATERING DEPARTMENT POLICIES

The club must establish policies to guide the catering department's relations with members. The typical policies include:

1. *Food and beverage prices.* These must be clearly listed. It is a good idea to note that any listed prices are subject to change; in other words, the club should not assume responsibility if potential hosts are viewing outdated menus. Usually clubs note that published menu prices are subject to change until firm price guarantees are negotiated and noted on the contract. All menu pages should be dated to avoid members using outdated menus or prices.

2. *Gratuities (often labeled as service charges in clubs) and taxes.* These are mandatory charges for service added to the catering prices. Some clubs do not automatically add these to a special event, leaving the gratuity to the member's discretion. When clubs automatically add a gratuity into the bill, this charge is no longer a gratuity and becomes a service charge. Service charges vary, but generally are 15–20 percent. You cannot assume that members are aware of these traditional charges; they must be informed about them up front. Hosts must also be informed of the amount of taxes imposed by state and local governments.

3. *Deposits.* The deposit procedures must be spelled out clearly and may only be required in the event of nonmember business. The host must be informed of the amount that must be paid, when it must be paid, and how it will be applied to the final billing.

4. *Refunds.* While no one likes to broach a negative subject, it is important to detail your refund policies and procedures in advance.

5. *Guarantees.* Usually a host must give a firm guarantee of the number of guests to attend one to three days in advance of the event. The club will prepare for that number, plus, for larger events, a stipulated percentage to handle any guests who decide to attend at the last minute. For instance, most clubs will agree to handle the guaranteed number of guests and to overset about 5–10 percent. If the function is very large, the club usually will use a sliding-scale guarantee. For instance, while it may agree to a 5-percent overage for parties up to 50 persons, it may agree to accommodate only a 3-percent overage for parties in excess of 500. Negotiating guarantees is a very tricky undertaking. The wise catering executive makes sure that members understand clearly the

club's position. However, if the event is relatively small—less than 35 guests—it is customary to set for only the guaranteed amount. The issue of extra seating should be discussed in advance, as some hosts prefer to have the exact amount so that it does not appear that there were some who did not show up for the party. Hosts must be made aware that, if actual attendance is less than guaranteed, they are still responsible for the guaranteed amount.

6. *Setup charges.*   If these are not included in the food and beverage menu prices, the host must be told in advance about these extra charges. Most clubs do not charge members a setup charge, but these charges may be assessed for nonmember business.

7. *Room rental rates.*   The typical club will usually charge members rent for function rooms only if they are used for meetings and other functions that do not include significant food and beverage sales. However, in the case of nonmember business, room rental charges are always assessed, as that individual does not pay dues to the club to assist in its upkeep.

8. *Other extra charges.*   Depending on the size of the function, the club may add on extra charges for bartenders, coat-checking facilities, and security. If members require additional labor because their functions are scheduled to last longer than normal, they usually will be assessed an additional charge to cover the extra payroll cost.

9. *Outside food and beverage.*   Clubs generally will not allow members to bring in their own food and beverage supplies (with the exception of wedding cakes and related items). In most situations, the club's liquor license, health permit, and/or business license forbids the use of personal products. The same restrictions may apply to other materials, such as paper products, decorations, and equipment.

10. *Setup service charges.*   If the law and the club allow members to bring in their own products, there usually will be a charge for setup service. For instance, if a member is allowed to bring in his or her own liquor, beer, or wine, there may be a standard, one-time corkage fee for the service. Alternatively, the club might charge a standard fee for each drink prepared or each bottle opened.

11. *Underage guests.*   The club must ensure that members realize that the pertinent liquor laws will not be suspended during their catered events. For instance, wedding hosts may not see anything wrong with serving champagne to an underage guest at a private

party. However, the law does not make this distinction. The same thing is true for service to visibly intoxicated guests; they cannot legally be served by the banquet or bartending staff. If members request self-service bars, some clubs will require them to sign a waiver of liquor liability so that the club will not be held responsible for guest actions. This type of waiver is necessary because, in the case of self-service, the club does not have bartenders and cocktail servers on site to monitor underage drinking and service to visibly intoxicated guests. For this reason, many clubs will not allow self-service bars on premise.

12. *Responsibility for loss and/or damage.* Personal property (such as personal china or silver platters used to display food) brought into the club by members and guests usually will not be covered by the club's insurance policies. Consequently, hosts need to be informed of this policy and agree to it before receiving permission to use their own property.

13. *Indemnification.* The club usually expects members to agree to indemnify the club against any claims, losses, and/or damages, except those due solely to the negligence and/or willful misconduct of the club staff. The club also wants protection from claims made by outside service contractors, such as florists, decorators, or audiovisual firms engaged by members. Furthermore, members are expected to stipulate that, by paying the final bill, they agree that there are no disputes with the products and services received. Members who sponsor nonmember business are responsible for assuring full and timely payment for nonmember business to the club.

14. *Uncontrollable acts.* There are times when the club will be unable to perform through no fault of its own. For instance, strikes, labor disputes, power outages, or acts of God could hamper the club's ability to service its members. Consequently, members must agree to hold the club harmless under these types of conditions.

15. *Substitutions.* This is similar to the uncontrollable acts policy. Occasionally, supply problems may force the club to substitute menu products. Or it may be necessary to move a function from one meeting room to another. For instance, an outside event may have to be moved indoors at the last minute because of inclement weather. While few of us want to think about these potential problems, the member must be advised in advance that they could happen.

16. *Security.* A club may require a member to provide additional security for his or her event.

17. *Licenses and permits.* Some functions may need to be approved and/or licensed by the local government licensing agency. The club should reserve the right to refuse service to any member who does not hold the appropriate licenses and permits prior to the event.

18. *Cancellation policy and penalty charges.* Clubs generally have cancellation charges for events canceled within a certain time period before the event. These charges generally differ for member versus nonmember business and may vary depending on the season. For example, many clubs have a cancellation clause for Saturday and holiday-season events that requires a 15-percent penalty charge if the event is canceled within 60 days of the event and a 50-percent charge if the event is canceled within 10 days of the event.

MAJOR CHALLENGES

There are many challenges to be faced when a club gets into the special-event business. Among these are:

1. *Marketing the club's catering services.* A great deal of time must be spent in the effort to distinguish your club's products and services from other venues that can host special events and catered functions. Having a good personal relationship with your members goes a long way in giving you a leg up on your competition, but in today's competitive market you may need more than this.

2. *Difficulty with costing and pricing.* Special requests and last-minute needs will cost more because of the specialized circumstances. Since the demand for these needs cannot always be predicted in advance, function hosts usually must wait until a final accounting is made by the club, for a complete overview of all function costs. This can cause ill will, especially with those who are on a tight budget and who would appreciate price guarantees.

3. *Ethical traps.* Sometimes the club may encounter conflict-of-interest dilemmas. For example, hosts who need outside contractors such as decorators, entertainers, or bakers (wedding cakes) may ask the club for a recommendation. The club, always mindful of its image and reputation, will tend to recommend only a few outside contractors that can fill the bill adequately. However, such favoritism could

be perceived by some as shady dealing. This situation is best handled by providing a written list recommending three or four vendors within each category with a bold disclaimer on the same page. Most clubs will recommend, but will never contact, an outside contractor on behalf of members/hosts.

4. *Responsibility greater than authority.* It is very important to determine in advance who is responsible for each part of the event. For instance, a member may want to hire his or her own band, but simultaneously may expect the club to coordinate the details. This can easily lead to misunderstanding and unhappy members unless everything is spelled out clearly.

5. *Time pressures.* The club catering department is a pressure cooker. It seems as if everything must be ready yesterday. Catering personnel must learn to work well under time constraints and with last minute surprises.

6. *Working and coordinating with others.* Proper advance planning is necessary to avoid service glitches that could cause guest dissatisfaction. It is crucial that the chef, maitre d', banquet captains, and staff all be informed of the details associated with an event in advance. Obviously, the chef may need more notice to enable proper handling whereas the banquet staff would be notified in the service meeting prior to the event.

7. *Lack of experience.* Due to the rapid growth of the hospitality industry in many communities, there are fewer and fewer experienced catering professionals and trained servers to go around. Lack of experience often leads to lack of planning and potential error. It is important to train all catering staff in the club's standards prior to working an actual event.

2

Identifying and Reaching Your Markets

....

The number and types of potential special events are limited only by the imagination. Club catering departments, especially those in large clubs, can expect to service the smallest social function to the largest wedding reception, golf outings, and social or corporate functions. Just as with membership, catering is a member-driven market, stimulated by members who demand exceptional quality and excellent value for a reasonable price. Value is determined by the member, not by club management. *Member perceptions are the club manager's realities.* This means that the impression a member has of your club's catering or special event business, whether positive or negative, is reality for them and will influence their decision. Since most of your members will comparison shop when they are considering the location of their event, your club must be perceived as the best choice because you are reliable and consistent and can create the best-quality event and most memorable occasions.

Clubs can no longer assume that they have the lowest prices in the area or that they can offer the best deal. Hotels, restaurants, and professional catering firms located around the community view your members as an opportunity to expand their catering business. With increasing frequency, they are seeking and contacting your members and soliciting their business with extremely competitive offers. You must know the strengths and weaknesses of your competition (prices, furnishings, skills of the banquet staff, and so on). You must also be aware of the strengths of your own catering operation.

What products and services should your catering department offer? A critical first step is to review previous bookings to identify which menus, services, and types of functions were most frequently booked. These historical data serve as the primary basis for determining product and service selection. Which products and services does the club do best in terms of quality, cost, and presentation? Remember that it is better to offer a limited number of products that are done well than to offer many items without the ability to guarantee that the club will provide quality preparation, presentation, and service. Generally speaking, clubs can handle most types of food and beverage functions and can provide, under one roof, all the room space needed by the function. Its ability to offer one-stop convenience to the club member suggests that it can cast its marketing net far and wide with members. Usually the typical club catering department is in the enviable position of deciding whether it wants to specialize and concentrate on certain markets, or it can strive to service any legitimate type of event a member needs.

Our society has a never-ending love affair with meetings, celebrations, ceremonies, and various other special events, and the majority of these events revolve around food. The purpose of this chapter is to outline the opportunities that exist for the private club wishing to expand its special events business.

THE BUSINESS MARKET

The business market represents approximately 75 percent of total catering sales in the United States. Within the private club industry, this figure varies depending on the type of club. City clubs will see a larger percentage of their catering functions addressing the needs of business, whereas country clubs will most likely do a smaller percentage of their special events in the business market. The business market is generally divided into three segments: shallow, midlevel, and deep.

The shallow segment is characterized by low-budget functions. These events usually involve a short lead time for the club. An example is a business meeting that needs a few deli platters and salads delivered to the meeting room. Hosts in this segment usually shop around for the best price. This does not mean that they ignore quality and service; however, they normally are on a limited budget and do not want to spend a great deal to provide food and beverages for the function attendees. The shallow customer of today, though, can very easily be the member who brings a large piece of business to the club in the future because of his or her previous experience. As a result, the club that does a good job with this group is apt to win repeat business as well as gain an inside track on securing potentially more profitable functions in the future. There is also the opportunity to introduce your club to nonmembers who are attending the function.

The midlevel segment usually involves a sit-down meal function. For instance, an executive luncheon for a few persons, complete with all the trimmings, is a typical midlevel catering opportunity. These events usually are planned well in advance. While price is important, members will not quibble over a few dollars; it is imperative that the event be memorable and consistent with the members' status in the business community. The midlevel function often leads to repeat business. For instance, the executive business luncheon can easily become a monthly affair. The club providing excellent value will more than likely become the favored provider for these members. Business persons are trained to shop around for the best value; however, when it comes to their personal pleasures, they will not switch loyalties on the spur of the moment. Furthermore, these small functions can lead to bigger and better things in the future. This segment can also be expanded by seeking out community or civic groups that have monthly luncheons, such as the Rotary Club or Chamber of Commerce.

The deep segment involves especially fancy business meal functions. These are expensive events where cost takes a back seat. Furthermore, these functions oftentimes represent repeat business. Meeting planners for businesses will often have clients who belong to a number of clubs and will go to the club that meets and exceeds their expectations. Even though most large business events are booked months in advance, the club specializing in the deep segment must be prepared to service a member at a moment's notice. Loyal club members expect this and are willing to pay for it.

Business Market Events

Companies have several catering needs. Since most clubs are capable of servicing many demands, they could enjoy a competitive advantage. The clubs that can handle a variety of business functions will earn considerable catering and food and beverage revenue. Business functions range from small meetings to lavish receptions. Some of the typical events that clubs cater are:

1. *Meetings.* These events represent the bulk of the business market. Some, such as sales meetings, can be rather routine affairs easily

serviced by the typical club. Others, though, such as annual stock-holders' meetings or large company parties, can severely test a club's catering department.

Probably the biggest advantage of working with the corporate/business market is that these types of clients can give you more accurate predictions. They usually can give you a precise number of attendees. For instance, if a company plans a meeting for 100 persons, it usually will have 100. If a person cancels, normally he or she will be replaced by someone else in the company. A business group also tends to allocate more money per attendee than do other types of markets served by clubs. As a general rule, corporate events are usually attended by business persons accustomed to judging overall value without concentrating solely on price. This market is also considered to be more stable than other markets. Often its events are scheduled months or even years in advance. Furthermore, there are many events, such as sales meetings, that must be held periodically.

Another advantage of this market segment is the general level of professionalism that exists among those who plan and organize their events. These persons tend to know exactly what they want. They also are in business, so they can understand and appreciate the club's capabilities and problems much better than someone who has never been in the business world.

2. *Incentive events.*   The purpose of these events is to encourage company employees to meet or exceed sales and/or production goals. When the goals are met, a celebration is planned to honor those who contributed to their successful achievement. These events tend to be high-budget events and may often involve a club for recreational activities such as a golf tournament. Although these types of events may not account for a large percentage of the club business market, they still should not be ignored.

3. *Recognition events.*   These are similar to incentive events, although generally less elaborate. Typically they involve awards dinners and other types of ceremonies intended to recognize several employees at many levels of performance. For instance, many companies and associations will hold an annual recognition luncheon to recognize long-term employees and to honor the employee of the year, as well as those retiring from the company.

4. *Training sessions and seminars.*   If an education event is expected to last one day or more, the company usually will want to hold it at a place where food and beverage are readily available. The typical club

fulfills this requirement. Furthermore, the club will often be able to provide the necessary basic audiovisual equipment that the average catering company may not have.

SPECIAL EVENTS MARKET

According to Joe Jeff Goldblatt, "A special event recognizes a unique moment in time with ceremony and ritual to satisfy specific needs." In his book *Special Events: The Art and Science of Celebration* (1995), he states that all human societies celebrate, privately and publicly, individually and as a group. This segment generally accounts for the largest percentage of catering business done by country clubs.

To some extent, every catered event could be considered a special event, at least for some clients and their guests. To that end, functions scheduled by the business market could involve some ceremonial and/or ritualistic elements. Special events differ from daily, ordinary events in at least three ways. A daily event generally occurs spontaneously, while a special event is always planned in advance. A daily event does not necessarily arouse expectations, but a special event always does. And while a daily event usually occurs for no particular reason, some type of celebration is the motivating force behind a special event.

Types of Special Events

Most special events are life-cycle events. Birthdays, bar and bat mitzvahs, weddings, anniversaries, reunions, and so forth mark time in our lives. They are usually celebrated with specific ceremonies and rituals.

Many of these events are celebrated privately, and, because the club is viewed as the extension of one's home, a club is more likely to play a part in these private affairs than, say, a public restaurant, hotel, or catering company (Figure 2.1). Other events are small celebrations that the club may cater at the member's home or other locations. And some are larger affairs that would be of interest to the typical club. Some of the special events that clubs handle are:

1. *Weddings.* Weddings today are longer and more expensive than ever before (Figure 2.2). Many women are marrying later in life and have more time and money to devote to this special day. Clubs that can provide one-stop service are apt to have a competitive edge among women who have many demands on their time. Clubs

Figure 2.1. A function room, ready for a party. (Courtesy Terry Blackburn Photography)

that have unique surroundings, picturesque views, and/or romantic settings are especially preferred by wedding planners. Many clubs generate a significant portion of their catering dollars from weddings and focus on being wedding specialists. Many weddings have specific religious requirements; for instance, the Jewish wedding requires a canopy and the breaking of glass. The club will need to be aware of these types of traditions or else it might disappoint and/or insult guests. Ethnic weddings, such as Italian and Greek weddings, are quite often very extravagant affairs. Guests normally come from all over the world. The club manager is ex-

Figure 2.2. Weddings hold out endless possibilities for producing a beautiful club event. (Courtesy Terry Blackburn Photography)

pected to be a protocol specialist and to be familiar with all of the traditions associated with the weddings being hosted at the club.

2. *Wedding anniversaries.* These are usually surprise celebrations hosted by adult children on milestone years. The silver wedding anniversary is especially popular. The children of the anniversary couple generally need a good deal of advice when putting together their celebrations. The club should be there to advise them.

3. *Reunions.* The reunion market encompasses everything from high school classes to military units. Reunions require a lot of

preplanning. A successful event usually needs a one-year lead time. Usually there are a few faithful alumni who shoulder the bulk of the planning burden, or they will engage a professional reunion planner. Many reunion organizers will benefit from any advice the club can offer. This type of host usually has no experience in planning and organizing these events. Consequently, the club representative must be able to recommend little things that will be a big hit with attendees. For instance, one very popular technique is to put each school reunion attendee's original yearbook picture on a name badge. Another strategy sure to please the school reunion attendee is to recreate the yearbook using the attendees' current pictures. It will also be necessary to arrange for a professional photographer for a group photo.

4. *Bar and bat mitzvahs.* A bar mitzvah is the traditional ceremony celebrated on a Jewish boy's 13th birthday. It marks the coming of age in the Jewish faith. During the ceremony, the young man publicly recites benedictions from the Torah (the Jewish scripture) and accepts personal responsibility for observing the commandments set down in the Torah. The bat mitzvah, for young Jewish girls, is similar to the bar mitzvah. The celebrations of these events traditionally are very serious and glamorous, similar in scale to large wedding receptions. Important elements include the blessing of the bread and wine and the lighting of candles. Menus and food preparation and service may follow kosher dietary restrictions. Jewish clubs and other clubs with Jewish members thrive on these events and know the dollar value they can produce.

5. *Baptisms.* A baptism is the Christian rite that results in the acceptance of the baptized person into the faith. The reception or luncheon is most often held at the parents' home or club after the ceremony. (The ceremony itself usually takes place at the church.)

6. *Confirmations.* A confirmation is the Christian rite confirming a child's infant baptism into the faith. The ceremony allows the young person to confirm that he or she knows right from wrong and that Christ is the chosen savior. Receptions usually are very popular, with the confirmed receiving several gifts and a considerable amount of attention.

7. *Graduations.* This can be a very attractive market segment these days especially given the fact that many older persons are graduating from college. They have fulfilled lifelong dreams and are usually very anxious to celebrate. The club is an obvious choice to service these types of events.

8. *Proms.*   These are high school affairs that are not high on the priority list of the typical private club. Underage adolescents, coupled with tight budgets, do not normally result in profitable affairs for the private club. As with high school graduations, though, if you impress these guests today, they may remember it and become members tomorrow.

9. *Birthdays.*   The large expensive birthday celebrations tend to be surprise parties. The club must be involved in a considerable amount of preplanning and subterfuge.

10. *Gourmet/wine clubs.*   More and more club members are becoming involved in gourmet and/or wine clubs that host very large upscale events. Choosing one's own club makes sense to the participants. There are also many clubs that organize such clubs as an added member service.

11. *Holiday/theme parties.*   Holiday, costume, and theme parties represent an excellent and profitable business segment for the private club. Many clubs specialize in providing outstanding holiday parties that become a standard part of the members' holiday celebration. Theme parties are often used as club parties to encourage members to come together as a whole. If the club bylaws allow the club to do in-home catering for members, the club can do a great deal of business for their members during holiday times.

12. *Teas, coffees, and brunches.*   These types of parties have become very popular among private club members and are used to host bridal showers, baby showers, birthday parties, and other similar social events. They provide the member with the opportunity to gather friends or family together for a special event without the larger expense of an evening function.

13. *Cocktail receptions.*   Although not as popular as they once were in the 1970s and 1980s, they still can be a popular function for club members to host. These receptions almost always include food in the form of hors d'oeuvres or a dinner following the reception.

DEVELOPING A MARKETING PLAN

In the past, most club managers paid less attention to marketing than they do today. Historically, there was only one club per metropolitan area, so the club tended to be the only game in town for its members' special events. Club managers at that time concentrated almost exclusively on production management and member service. We assumed that members would always have their special events in the club.

These good old days, though, are not with us any longer. The club industry, especially where special events are concerned, is a battleground. Club members have a myriad of choices when planning special events. Some members may believe that one caterer is as good as another. To dispel this image and stand out in a crowded field, the successful club catering department must develop a competitive edge. Members do not buy a meal; they buy an experience, or fantasy, as well as fun, service, ambience, entertainment, and memories. They also buy food and beverage, but only incidentally.

As a result, much of what a club sells is intangible. The member cannot touch or feel an event before it occurs. The club is selling something that has yet to be produced and delivered. It cannot be resold, restocked, or returned. Members and guests purchase what they *think* will happen. It is a gamble for them. They are understandably nervous and need to be reassured that they have made the correct decision.

Clubs that consistently achieve their revenue goals are those that understand their members and what they are buying. They develop marketing procedures that meet their members' needs. In today's business environment, a strong price/value relationship must prevail in order to attract a profitable share of the market. The club's services must be equal to or better than the competition's. The club's staff must be very familiar with the services offered, their costs and benefits, and their impact on the club's overall performance.

It is said that *sizzle sells the steak,* and for many clubs the sizzle may be their excellent banquet and club facilities. Statistics show that the type and quality of cuisine offered, ability to accommodate groups, entertainment attractions, and variety of services offered are the major factors a member considers when selecting a caterer. The successful club catering department will ensure that these aspects are clearly defined and articulated to potential clients.

Michael Roman, president of the National Institute for Off-Premise Catering, thinks that the successful caterer develops a well-defined marketing plan and follows it closely. He feels that the marketing plan must include three major aspects:

1. Getting the job
2. Performing well
3. Following up

This marketing plan must be adapted to fit the private club because many clubs, prior to getting the job, must identify their catering goals and then create awareness of the club's catering program among the members.

Identifying Catering Goals

Before a club can market its catering function, it must clearly define its catering/special events goals and objectives. The club management should ask and answer the following questions:

1. Why does the club want to provide catered events for its members?
2. Is the club interested in attracting nonmember business?
3. What bylaws and governmental regulations pertain to the amount of member versus nonmember business and what do they stipulate?
4. What is your members' perception of the club's ability to cater special events?
5. What has the club done successfully in the past?
6. What are the club's physical limitations?
7. What are the club's staff limitations?
8. What are the financial goals for the club's catering department?
9. What effect will this have on the club's tax status?
10. How will these catered events impact member services?
11. What are the financial goals for the catering department?

The typical club is not large enough to mix and match several markets; it is more likely to have a specific focus. This affords the opportunity to maximize revenue and profit. Specialization can lead to increased efficiency as well as a unique reputation and image in the marketplace. Clubs should closely examine desired markets to determine the extent of their catering needs. For example, if a club wishes to cater for the wedding market, it should examine closely and quantify the supply (i.e., other competing caterers) and the demand (i.e., potential wedding clients) to see if it is economically feasible to concentrate on this segment. A close review of membership is required. This might also be ascertained through the use of a member-needs assessment designed to gain insight into your membership's needs for catered events.

After determining the desired market(s), the next step is to set financial goals. There should be revenue and profit goals. There also should be some attention paid to other income that can be generated indirectly from catering; for instance, if a club has rooms, a wedding party could generate sleeping-rooms business as well as revenue from the use of other facilities such as parking, room rental, recreational facilities, and so on.

Revenue and profit goals must be reasonable. It is useless to set unrealistically high goals because the certain failure to attain them can negatively impact the board's perception of the club's ability to provide this service to its members. However, the club manager must be willing to take some risks when setting these goals. He or she should not be overly conservative or else the club's overall performance will suffer.

Creating Awareness

Getting the job—booking business—also includes the need to create a particular image. If, for example, the club wants to specialize in weddings, it may develop logos, menus, decorations, room layouts and designs, employee uniforms, and so forth to complement and enhance that image. For example, one club that specializes in weddings has gone to great lengths to stage the first meeting with the prospective bride so that it sets the mood for the entire event. The club has an extremely elaborate bride's room where the bridal party will dress and freshen up throughout the event, and the first meeting is held in this room where light refreshments (small tea cakes with a bridal flair and punch) are served, and picture albums of former weddings are viewed while talking about the bride's dreams of her wedding.

Whatever your focus, it is important that you create an awareness of your services among club members and the community at large. You should develop standardized procedures to:

Internally market your services to your members. Focus on highlighting the selling points of your club. Emphasize

Location

Decor/architectural features (possibly a large staircase perfect for bridal photos, for example)

Competitive pricing

Excellent food

Exceptional service

More member-friendly terms on the agreement (contract)

Identify and meet with club members who might have a need for your catering services.

Be able to clearly define the services your club is prepared to offer.

Finalize agreements with club members and guests wishing to host catered events at your club.

As you know, a satisfied member is the best advertisement for your catering operation, but you cannot rely only upon word of mouth to increase your catering business. You should also develop internal publicity and advertising materials to generate additional awareness and sales. These may include but are not limited to:

Direct mail. This may consist of a specially prepared flyer or a mini-brochure describing the availability and advantages of using the club for catered events. The club can mail these only to its members.

Daily bulletin. Short, to-the-point reminders about your catering services that can be posted throughout the club on bulletin boards or in locker rooms or included in member billing statements, and so on.

Posters and flyers. Professionally designed posters and flyers placed at entrances of high-traffic areas that will heighten community awareness of your catering operation.

Club telephone recording. If the club uses an answering machine or voice mail for after-hour messages, a brief, friendly invitation can be extended to callers suggesting that they consider holding their next special event in the club. An example may say something such as:

> *We invite you to host your special event at the club. We will make your function a most memorable occasion. For information about our catering program please call (Name) at (Phone Number).*

Inserts. Attractive inserts can be prepared for enclosure with monthly statements, menus, dues notices, or calendars of activities mailings.

In-house opportunities. During member events, dinner theater, Sunday brunches, or live entertainment or in member dining, use table tents and high-quality flyers to promote increased awareness of your catering services.

Club newsletters and calendars. Use both of these to include small segments about the services provided by the club. Pictures of events hosted by members (obviously with the member's permission) also serve as a reminder of the club's ability to provide for members' catered needs. Always keep your messages short and simple. Enhance your message with borders, photos, graphics, and such.

Promotional tie-ins. Your catering program can be promoted by spot announcements at club events. Prepare complimentary bite-sized samples of your club's catering signature dishes. If your club has a Sunday brunch, feature some of your catering specialties and make note of the availability for catered events. Serve members a complimentary item featured on your catering menu as an appetizer or dessert during their meal, with your wait staff briefly encouraging them to consider the club for their next special event.

Employees. Employee recommendations can result in additional bookings. Make sure your employees know about your catering program and offer them an incentive (for example, a $50 award) if an event is held based on their recommendation.

Members. Encourage member recommendations about your catering program. Offer members an incentive, such as complimentary dinner for two, if someone books a function based upon their recommendation.

Word of mouth. Never underestimate how powerful and effective word of mouth is in generating additional business. For private clubs, sometimes this is the most productive form of marketing they have. A successful event will often result in repeat business and positive recommendations to others by the sponsor and his/her guests. However, this can also work against you if the word of mouth is negative. A less-than-successful function will produce negative comments and possibly a loss of future business. After-event follow-up is critical.

Performing Well

Once members or hosts have booked special events with you, the emphasis shifts from sales to service. Hosts and their guests want to be treated with care. They want to be handled in a professional manner. Function hosts want the event to enhance their image. Performing well involves standardized procedures designed to ensure that:

1. Service is punctual
2. Foods, beverages, presentations, sanitation, cleanliness, and ambience meet established quality standards
3. Professional attention will be paid to all details
4. The function host will be made to feel like a guest at his or her event

5. All last-minute requests and/or crises will be handled calmly, professionally, and to everyone's satisfaction

Performing well is the bottom line. Members have entrusted their events to the club. They have relinquished control. Consequently, they will be understandably nervous and anxious. The club that can satisfy members and make them look good will enjoy several benefits. Referral business is an obvious benefit, as is repeat patronage, but perhaps the biggest benefit of satisfying a member's catering needs is that of providing one more opportunity to be an integral part of your member's life whether the event is business or social.

Following Up

Following up is another very important part of the marketing plan. Clubs need to develop standardized procedures to ensure that:

1. Thank-you calls are made
2. Individual, personalized follow-up letters are sent
3. Event assessments are performed, one with the member and one with the catering staff, wherein all aspects of the function are evaluated and critiqued
4. Referral business is solicited
5. Appropriate souvenir gifts are presented to hosts (when appropriate and in line with club policy)
6. Accounts are settled

The following guidelines were developed by one general manager of a private club for follow-up once contact had been made with the club:

1. The social director/catering professional immediately writes a letter to the host thanking him or her for wanting to use the club for the event and confirming the reservation. This letter also informs the host of the necessary details and possibly includes some menus. The focus of this letter, though, is to assure the host that the function will be tailored to his or her specific wishes.
2. One week after the letter is mailed, the club makes a follow-up phone call to arrange an appointment.
3. Then there is a face-to-face meeting to discuss all details. Again, this meeting is designed to give the host confidence in the club's ability to provide a very special event.

4. After the meeting, the club sends a letter critiquing the event and verifying all information and details for the function.

5. During the function, the staff must handle all details professionally, including last-minute changes, according to the host's wishes. During the event, the catering manager should make continuous contact with the host to ensure his or her complete satisfaction with the event.

6. Within 48–72 hours after the event, the general manager or assistant general manager should phone the host to discuss the event and to solicit his or her feedback.

7. Finally, the club should send a letter to the host thanking him or her for selecting the club for the function and inviting the person to use the club again. Of course, this letter should include a request for payment.

Many industry experts feel that the follow-up stage is the most critical part of the marketing plan. The club and host have been working together for some time. It is inappropriate to simply give the member an invoice at the end of the event and say good-bye. The relationship should not be ended abruptly; it must be continued. The time spent with the host during the follow-up stage will pay huge dividends.

The follow-up time is the time during which the club can learn something from the member that can be used to improve future functions. Long-term relationships are cemented and memberships are sealed or lost, the seeds of referral and repeat business are planted and cultivated.

The club staff, including general manager, assistant general manager, social coordinator/catering professional, executive chef, housekeeping supervisor, banquet manager, maitre d', dining room manager, and banquet captain, should meet weekly to discuss all special events. This debriefing session should be used not only to provide positive encouragement for a job well done, but to openly discuss any challenges the club may have experienced with its special functions.

Sales Analysis

A thorough sales analysis is critical to determining the success of a marketing plan and should include the following items:

1. *Total revenue.* Monthly revenue totals should be evaluated with an eye toward establishing trends. This can help ensure that mar-

keting dollars are directed to the season of the year with the most sales potential.

2. *Average revenue per function.* This statistic will reveal average productivity per function. If there is a consistent shortfall between the actual average revenue and potential average revenue, marketing dollars can be devoted to reconciling this inequity.

3. *Average revenue per type of function.* This figure will indicate which functions carry the greatest sales potential. Marketing funds can therefore be allocated appropriately, and sales in this area may increase (for example, a cocktail and hors d'oeuvre reception may generate more profit than a seated dinner).

4. *Average guest count per function.* Some functions have few guests. Unless the host is paying a large amount per guest, it may be profitable to concentrate on larger groups. More guests mean more exposure for the club. However, most clubs cannot be this selective.

5. *Average check.* The per-person price for different types of functions is a good measure of labor productivity—cocktail receptions consume much less labor than seated dinners and other functions. It also can reveal opportunities where marketing dollars can be spent in an effort to increase the average revenue per guest.

6. *Average contribution margin.* This is similar to the average check. The difference is that this is the amount of money available from the average check after the club pays the cost of food and beverage used to serve a guest. Most foodservice experts feel that the average contribution margin per guest (sometimes referred to as the *menu score*) is more important than the average check because it represents the amount of money left to cover all other expenses and a fair profit.

7. *Number of functions.* A monthly analysis can indicate how well the club manages and sells its available space. Trends will reveal where marketing dollars should be used; for instance, if February is a slow month, perhaps a slight change in the marketing plan can significantly improve sales and profits during this time period. More suggestive selling to members may give the club that extra boost.

8. *Space utilization percentages.* This analysis can indicate periods of time when certain function space is underutilized. For example, if a particular room is vacant every Wednesday and Thursday, the club should consider some changes in the marketing plan to locate and encourage functions for this time and space.

9. *Popularity of different types of functions.* These statistics can indicate the club catering department's strengths and weaknesses. If, for instance, weddings are the most frequently scheduled function, members must view the club as a good place to hold weddings. This gives the club a competitive edge for this type of business, but it may eliminate the club from consideration for other types of events. The event mix is important to full utilization of the property.

10. *Percentage of repeat business.* It takes much more time, money, and effort to create a new customer than it does to retain an old one. Turning a customer into a repeat patron is a significant goal. Clubs thrive on repeat business and must strive for it.

11. *Percentage of referral business.* You know a product is good when you can recommend it to your friends. The club catering department that receives a considerable percentage of referral business is obviously doing something right. Since membership is limited, it is most important to a private club that members recommend their club to nonmembers.

The primary purpose for performing this type of sales analysis is to determine the success rate of the current marketing plan. If the results of the analysis suggest that changes should be made, then future marketing efforts will need to be altered to reflect a new direction.

For instance, the club may find that there has been a steady decline in the business-related functions handled by the club. If business-related functions are not a profitable sales item, marketing dollars might be wasted trying to increase this particular segment of business. On the other hand, a bit of research into the business market might indicate that there is a good deal of potential in this segment and that a few adjustments in the marketing plan could make the club very competitive.

If the marketing plan requires significant alterations, the club manager should ensure that the club can accommodate the changes. An analysis will reveal feasible opportunities and suggest profitable changes that should be considered. This analysis should include an evaluation of:

1. The club's capabilities
2. The types of markets available
3. Potential sales trends in these markets
4. Number and types of competitors

5. The club's strengths and weaknesses as compared to its competitors

6. Trends in sales efforts and sales revenue

Do not make alterations in the marketing plan hastily. Once a plan has been established, give it a fair chance to work. Just as we should not dig up the earth every few days to see how seeds we have planted are doing, we should not make a habit of second-guessing our marketing efforts.

Consider changes in the marketing plan only after evaluating past trends and future opportunities. Make changes only if there is a reasonable expectation of improving sales revenues, profits, and/or reputation.

Record Keeping

Group History File   A group history file is created whenever initial contact is made with a prospective host. Eventually this file will include all facets of the host's business relationship with the club. To a certain extent, the file involves a "cradle-to-grave" synopsis of all relevant aspects of the catered event, from initial inquiry to final disposition.

Usually the club uses a predetermined, standardized format to record function information. In the case of nonmember business, information is gathered only after contact with a member-sponsor has been established. Generally, no concrete information or dollar quotes are made in advance. When a potential host calls the club for price quotations and space availability, the important details are recorded. A club representative (social coordinator, clubhouse manager, assistant manager, director of catering, general manager) follows up on the inquiry after studying these details. If the initial inquiry results in a booked function, the appropriate entries are made in the function book and also in the group history file. A word of caution is included here to ensure that the general manager is adhering to the bylaws and to the club board's wishes concerning nonmember events.

The group history file should be complete if it is to be useful. It should contain all relevant information, such as correspondence, decision-maker information, attendance figures, contracts, potential for future business, membership number, address of member or sponsoring member, credit history (if nonmember), business referrals, and other relevant data.

Group history files represent the club's major source of repeat patronage. The wise club manager will ensure that the function decision makers noted in these files are not forgotten. He or she will personally maintain some sort of communication link with them or will assign this responsibility to another member of the catering staff. For instance, birthday cards, direct mail flyers, and/or holiday greeting cards should be sent to these individuals.

Lost-Business File If client inquiries or sales solicitations do not lead to booked business, the group history file will be transformed into a lost-business file. These files must be evaluated periodically in order to determine why potential business did not materialize. If certain patterns—space unavailability, high prices, or inadequate menu offerings, for example—are discovered, perhaps the club can do something to ameliorate the underlying problems. For instance, if there is a consistent problem with space availability, the club could use this information to support a proposal to construct additional function rooms. Future marketing plans highlighting the additional space could lead to a significant increase in business.

Some lost-business files will be created after the catering event is booked. For instance, the event could be scheduled, but the host may cancel at the last minute. The club manager would want to know why the host canceled. It is inappropriate merely to retain the host's deposit (in the case of nonmember business); some further contact with the host must be made to determine if the cancellation was due to any action of the club's management or staff. Determining the problem will help the club correct any problems it may be having in its catering department.

A lost-business file that has to be created after the event is over is probably the most unfortunate one as far as the club is concerned. This generally occurs if there was some dissatisfaction with the quality of food, beverage, service, and so forth. In this situation, the host's final billing usually must be credited, in part or in full. The major problem created by an unhappy incident like this is not so much the loss of revenue, but the fact that an upset member is liable to share his or her disappointment with other members or potential members. The club manager must do whatever is reasonable to minimize any negative publicity.

Tracer File Tracer files (sometimes referred to as *tickler files*) are similar to a manager's personal things-to-do-today list. For instance, if a current member books catering business on a fairly regular basis, the manger's tracer file will include this information. The file will also note when the host should be contacted, how he or she should be approached, any special considerations that must be offered, and so forth.

A tracer file should be established for tentative bookings so that space is not held more than, say, two weeks without a deposit or definite option (members are generally not charged a deposit). Similarly, a tracer file can be developed that will trace the number of bookings per market segment. A market segment that provides 5 percent or more of the club's total catering business should be monitored closely for trends and other indicators of future business. Furthermore, if the club has, for example, 18 separate market segments, it should consider developing a specific marketing plan for each one.

Lost-business files should be part of the club's tracer filing system. Lost business should be coded according to the reason why it was lost. Perhaps the business was lost because you did not have a function room available.

The individual lost-business events should be placed in a tickler file, so that the club's catering staff will be able to go back to the file the same time next year and attempt to solicit the member's business.

Catering representatives usually check and update the tracer files daily. They will add pertinent information to them as it is obtained. They also will use a system whereby the group history files will be traced and reviewed a few days before function decision makers are contacted.

Marketing Research

Marketing research is an ongoing activity. It involves a continuing analysis of the potential catering needs of your club members and the competition that resides in the club's surrounding community. The club's competition is not easy to define. Theoretically, it could be the entire community's offerings of upscale restaurants or other clubs; realistically, it is a lot closer to home.

Retain records of members' comments concerning the event, as well as any personal information, in their files. If members chose to have a catered event someplace other than the club, ask them what factors influenced their decision. Always know your major competitors. Remember, with club members, the private club has a huge advantage over its competition in that it sees its members often and has an opportunity to develop a relationship that spans beyond that of just caterer. It can provide service above and beyond that which is offered by its competitors for this very reason.

Market and Competition Surveys

Market and competition surveys consist of detailed descriptions of potential members and current and potential competitors. The typical sourcing procedure usually involves studying consumer trends, member desires, and other similar data. The best way to obtain these data is to conduct a market and competition survey.

A market survey can be a simple questionnaire sent to members asking them about their catering needs and the amount of money they would be willing to pay for these services. More elaborate surveys are costly, but they do reveal considerably more information.

A competition survey should be an ongoing effort. Catering executives must know as much as they can about the competition. The club's marketing plan cannot be completed without some knowledge of competing products and services. A competition survey should include the following information for each competitor:

1. Competitor name and address
2. Space available and quality of space
3. Guest capacity
4. Major markets serviced
5. Number of catering employees
6. Average checks or other similar data (pricing)
7. Main products and services offered

When gathering data on competitors, you must be careful not to violate the pertinent federal, state, and local antitrust laws. For instance, you cannot get together with a competitor and discuss your pricing strategies. Nor can you agree with a competitor to charge the same prices. You should unearth and utilize only those nonproprietary data available to the general public.

The competition survey will reveal any unmet market niches. For instance, if the director of catering learns that no one seems to be specializing in the civic-events market segments, he or she may decide to explore the possibility of targeting this pool of potential business.

The competition survey also lets the catering executive know what he or she is up against. In today's competitive hospitality business, it is necessary to carve out a unique reputation, image, and/or specialty. However, any attempts to do this should be initiated only after analyzing the competitive environment.

The Four Ps of Marketing

An effective marketing plan includes a description of the club's four Ps:

1. Place
2. Products and services offered

3. Prices charged

4. Promotion policies and procedures

The director of catering, either alone or in conjunction with other management personnel, must develop and implement these four Ps of marketing.

Place   Place refers to the club's location, amount of space available, and the type of environment and ambience provided. This is very important to the host and must be emphasized. Members are very interested in the number of persons that can be accommodated as well as the speed with which they can be served. Detailed information on space should be readily accessible.

A club's environment and ambience include its sanitation, cleanliness, decor, view, and other related factors. The catering manager cannot do anything about the club's location, but he or she can ensure that the controllable variables meet established quality control standards.

Products and Services Offered   The club's products and services are probably the most flexible part of the marketing plan. The large club usually has the ability to provide an unlimited number of food and beverage menus (Figure 2.3), meal service styles, and other ancillary services. The property that offers members a one-stop shopping opportunity will usually have a significant competitive edge in the marketplace.

Prices Charged   Price is perhaps one of the most important and troublesome parts of the marketing plan. It is a major concern to the host, and it can present several problems for club caterers, particularly because it is risky to quote prices too far in advance. Food costs fluctuate widely, undergoing seasonal price changes.

The club catering department has several costs that must be covered. In addition to food and beverage costs, it will incur costs for payroll, payroll benefits, direct operating supplies, music and entertainment, internal marketing, utilities, administrative and general costs, repairs and maintenance, and so forth.

Appropriate prices must be charged in order to cover the fixed and variable costs, as well as to leave a fair profit for the club. The director of catering also must ensure that prices are competitive and that they represent a good price/value ratio. It is a delicate balancing act.

Usually the total price quoted for a catered event is the sum of several prices for individual function needs. For instance, a wedding's total price

(Text continues on page 48)

Figure 2.3. Club banquet menu.

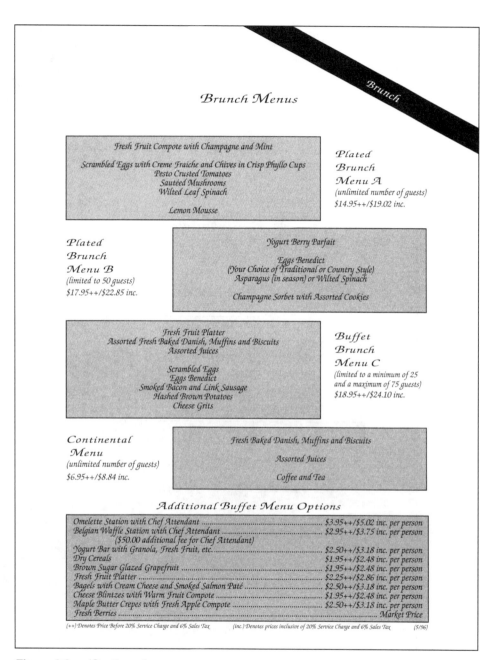

Brunch Menus

Brunch

Fresh Fruit Compote with Champagne and Mint

Scrambled Eggs with Creme Fraiche and Chives in Crisp Phyllo Cups
Pesto Crusted Tomatoes
Sautéed Mushrooms
Wilted Leaf Spinach

Lemon Mousse

Plated
Brunch
Menu A
(unlimited number of guests)
$14.95++/$19.02 inc.

Plated
Brunch
Menu B
(limited to 50 guests)
$17.95++/$22.85 inc.

Yogurt Berry Parfait

Eggs Benedict
(Your Choice of Traditional or Country Style)
Asparagus (in season) or Wilted Spinach

Champagne Sorbet with Assorted Cookies

Fresh Fruit Platter
Assorted Fresh Baked Danish, Muffins and Biscuits
Assorted Juices

Scrambled Eggs
Eggs Benedict
Smoked Bacon and Link Sausage
Hashed Brown Potatoes
Cheese Grits

Buffet
Brunch
Menu C
(limited to a minimum of 25
and a maximum of 75 guests)
$18.95++/$24.10 inc.

Continental
Menu
(unlimited number of guests)
$6.95++/$8.84 inc.

Fresh Baked Danish, Muffins and Biscuits

Assorted Juices

Coffee and Tea

Additional Buffet Menu Options

Omelette Station with Chef Attendant	$3.95++/$5.02 inc. per person
Belgian Waffle Station with Chef Attendant	$2.95++/$3.75 inc. per person
($50.00 additional fee for Chef Attendant)	
Yogurt Bar with Granola, Fresh Fruit, etc.	$2.50++/$3.18 inc. per person
Dry Cereals	$1.95++/$2.48 inc. per person
Brown Sugar Glazed Grapefruit	$1.95++/$2.48 inc. per person
Fresh Fruit Platter	$2.25++/$2.86 inc. per person
Bagels with Cream Cheese and Smoked Salmon Paté	$2.50++/$3.18 inc. per person
Cheese Blintzes with Warm Fruit Compote	$1.95++/$2.48 inc. per person
Maple Butter Crepes with Fresh Apple Compote	$2.50++/$3.18 inc. per person
Fresh Berries	Market Price

(++) Denotes Price Before 20% Service Charge and 6% Sales Tax   (inc.) Denotes prices inclusive of 20% Service Charge and 6% Sales Tax   (5/96)

Figure 2.3. *(Continued).*

Luncheon Menus

C herokee offers a wide range and variety of luncheon selections. Some of these menus are limited to a certain number of guests which is listed beneath each menu heading. We have also listed a style of wine which will complement the item. Please refer to the appropriate wine page for current selections. Wines are not included in the listed food price, and therefore are available at an additional cost.

Curried Cauliflower and Apple Soup

Chutney Chicken Salad with
Premium Lettuces, Couscous and Toasted Almonds
(Off-Dry White Wine)

Florida Lemon Tart with Seasonal Berries and Raspberry Sauce

Luncheon Menu A
(limited to 75 guests)
$18.95++/$24.11 inc.

Luncheon Menu B
(limited to 75 guests)
$22.95++/$29.20 inc.

Butternut Squash Soup with Ginger Cream and Spiced Pecans

Barbecue Grilled Boneless Quail on Bed of Greens with
Sesame Orange Vinaigrette
(Light, Fruity Red Wine)

Chocolate Cheesecake with Caramel Sauce

Baby Leaf Spinach Salad with Georgia Peanut Dressing

Roasted Tenderloin of Pork with Blackberry Glaze and Sweet Potato Puree
(Light, Fruity Red Wine)

Old Fashioned Pecan Pie with Chocolate and Caramel Sauces

Luncheon Menu C
(limited to 75 guests)
$21.95++/$27.92 inc.

Luncheon Menu D
(limited to 75 guests)
$21.95++/$27.92 inc.

Lemon Chicken Soup with Orzo

Grilled Tuna Niçoise Salad
(Full-Bodied, Complex White Wine)

Angel Food Cake with Berry Compote and Sweet Cream

(++) Denotes Price Before 20% Service Charge and 6% Sales Tax   (inc.) Denotes prices inclusive of 20% Service Charge and 6% Sales Tax   (5/96)

Figure 2.3. *(Continued).*

Luncheons

Luncheon Menus, continued

*T*he following luncheon menu selections are available to an unlimited number of guests. Please note that the listed style of wine is at an additional cost. Please refer to the appropriate wine page for current selections.

Premium Lettuce Salad with
Oven Roasted Tomatoes and Creamy Basil Vinaigrette

Breast of Chicken Stuffed with Spinach and Crab
(Dry, Medium-Bodied White Wine)

Sweet Potato Pie with Whipped Cream

Luncheon
Menu E
(unlimited number of guests)
$19.95++/$25.38 inc.

Luncheon
Menu F
(unlimited number of guests)
$26.95++/$34.28 inc.

Smoked Salmon Salad Bouquet with Herbed Dressing

Grilled Tenderloin of Beef with
Golden Oak Mushrooms in Cabernet Wine Sauce
(Rich, Classic, Full-Bodied Red Wine)

Chocolate Almond Fudge Tart with Tahitian Vanilla Sauce

Tomato Basil Bisque with Prosciutto and Parmesan Chips

Grilled Marinated Chicken Breast
on Caesar Salad with Black Olive Foccacia
(Dry, Medium-Bodied White Wine)

Key Lime Pie

Luncheon
Menu G
(unlimited number of guests)
$17.95++/$22.84 inc.

Luncheon
Menu H
(unlimited number of guests)
$22.95++/$29.20 inc.

Roasted Eggplant Soup with Red Pepper Cream

Grilled Salmon Fillet on Soft Polenta
with Tomato Endive Relish and Basil Oil
(Full-Bodied, Complex White Wine)

Florida Lemon Tart with Seasonal Berries and Raspberry Sauce

(++) Denotes Price Before 20% Service Charge and 6% Sales Tax   (inc.) Denotes prices inclusive of 20% Service Charge and 6% Sales Tax   (5/96)

Figure 2.3.   *(Continued).*

Receptions

Reception Menus

The Grant Collection
$24.95++/$31.74 inc.

Cold
Caramelized Bacon Crisps
Assorted Canapés
House Smoked Trout Fillets with Rye Bread and Horseradish Cream
Vegetable Crudité in a Basket with Dipping Sauces
Domestic Cheese Board with Breads and Carr's Wafers
Hot
Spicy Sausage and Kalamata Fig Skewers with Sweet Mustard
Corn Fried Seafood Bites with Caper Aioli
Tiropitas (Baked Cheese Filled Phyllo Pastry)
Almond Breaded Chicken Tenderloins with Dipping Sauces

Cold
Crabmeat Stuffed Cherry Tomatoes
Imported Cheese Selection with Breads and Carr's Wafers
Smoked Salmon Mousse in Puff Pastry Crescents
Melon Wrapped with Prosciutto Ham
Steak Tartare with Rye Toast Points
Hot
Asian Style Chicken Satays with Spicy Peanut Sauce
Black Bean Cakes with Barbecued Shrimp
Lobster Sausage Baked in Puff Pastry
Roasted Creamer Potatoes with Smoked Salmon, Sour Cream and Chives

The Cherokee Collection
$28.95++/$36.82 inc.

The Chastain Collection
$22.95++/$29.19 inc.

Cold
Domestic Cheese Board with Breads and Carr's Wafers
Smoked Salmon Mousse with Bagel Crisps
Vegetable Crudité in a Basket with Dipping Sauces
Assorted Finger Sandwiches
Hot
Sliced Smoked Turkey on Sweet Potato Biscuits
Artichoke Dip with Hazelnut Crust
Pecan Battered Chicken Tenderloins with Honey Mustard Dipping Sauce
Veal and Sun-Dried Tomato Meatballs with Basil Sauce

Cold
Assorted Canapés
Endive with Boursin Cheese and Spiced Walnuts
Stuffed Eggs with Smoked Salmon and Caviar
Pepper Seared Beef Carpaccio and Watercress Wraps
Imported Cheese Selection with Breads and Carr's Wafers
Hot
Seafood Strudel
Marinated Beef Teriyaki Skewers
Tortilla Taquitos with Salsa and Sour Cream
Baked Mushroom Caps Stuffed with Chicken and Herb Mousse

The Phoenix Collection
$26.95++/$34.28 inc.

(++) Denotes Price Before 20% Service Charge and 6% Sales Tax   (inc.) Denotes prices inclusive of 20% Service Charge and 6% Sales Tax   (5/96)

Figure 2.3.   *(Continued).*

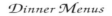

Dinner Menus

*C*herokee offers a wide range and variety of dinner selections. Some of these menus, depending on the difficulty of preparation, are limited to a certain number of people, which is listed beneath each menu heading. We have also listed a style of wine which will complement the item. Please refer to the appropriate wine page for current selections. Wines are not included in the listed food price, and therefore are available at an additional cost.

**Dinner
Menu A**
(limited to 75 guests)
$34.95++/$44.46 inc.

> *Barbecue Grilled Quail Salad with Sesame Vinaigrette*
> *(Light, Fruity Red Wine)*
>
> *Almond Crusted Salmon Fillet with Beurre Rouge and Sautéed Leaf Spinach*
> *(Full-Bodied, Complex White Wine)*
>
> *Warm Blackberry Charlotte with Vanilla Bean Ice Cream*

> *Chilled Soufflé of Lump Crab and Roasted Peppers*
> *(Dry, Light-Bodied White Wine)*
>
> *Roasted Rack of Domestic Lamb with Rosemary and Dijon Mustard Glaze*
> *(Rich, Classic, Full-Bodied Red Wine)*
>
> *Chocolate Macaroon Terrine with Seasonal Berries*

**Dinner
Menu B**
(limited to 75 guests)
$40.95++/$52.09 inc.

**Dinner
Menu C**
(limited to 75 guests)
$41.95++/$53.36 inc.

> *Poached Fillet of Salmon with Cucumbers and Oysters in Dill Cream*
> *(Dry, Light-Bodied White Wine)*
>
> *Belgian Endive and Watercress with Roquefort Dressing and Roasted Walnuts*
>
> *Roasted Rack of Veal with Cracked Pepper and Black Currant Jus*
> *(Robust, Very Full-Bodied Red Wine)*
>
> *Grand Marnier Tira Misu with Assorted Berries and Chocolate Sauce*

> *Chicken Consommé with Wild Mushrooms*
> *(Dry Sherry or Dry, Medium-Bodied White Wine)*
>
> *Caesar Salad in Toasted Parmesan Basket*
>
> *Grilled Medallions of Beef and Salmon with Sun-Dried Tomato Choron*
> *(Rich, Classic, Full-Bodied Red Wine)*
>
> *Seasonal Fruit Cobbler with Vanilla Bean Ice Cream*

**Dinner
Menu D**
(limited to 75 guests)
$39.95++/$50.82 inc.

(++) Denotes Price Before 20% Service Charge and 6% Sales Tax   *(inc.) Denotes prices inclusive of 20% Service Charge and 6% Sales Tax*   *(5/96)*

Figure 2.3.   *(Continued).*

Dinners

Dinner Menus, *continued*

The following dinner menu selections are available to an unlimited number of guests. Please note that the suggested styles of wine are at an additional cost.

Dinner Menu E
(unlimited number of guests)
$36.95++/$47.00 inc.

Gulf Shrimp Bisque with Dry Sherry and Dill Cream
(Dry Sherry or Dry, Medium-Bodied White Wine)

Premium House Salad with Chardonnay Dressing

Grilled Filet Mignon of Beef with Sauce Bearnaise
(Rich, Classic, Full-Bodied Red Wine)

Praline Pecan Cheesecake

Chicken Consommé with Wild Rice and Roasted Garlic Flan
(Dry, Medium-Bodied White Wine)

Ashland Farms Lettuces with Creamy Herb Vinaigrette

Baked Fillet of Smoke-Enhanced Salmon with Grain Mustard Beurre Blanc
(Full-Bodied, Complex White Wine)

Florida Lemon Tart with Seasonal Berries and Raspberry Sauce

Dinner Menu F
(unlimited number of guests)
$33.95++/$43.18 inc.

Dinner Menu G
(unlimited number of guests)
$39.95++/$50.82 inc.

Smoked Duck Breast with Duck Liver Mousse
(Off-Dry White Wine or Light, Fruity Red Wine)

Premium House Salad with Chardonnay Dressing

Roasted Strip Loin of Veal with Shallot Confit and Natural Jus
(Rich, Classic, Full-Bodied Red Wine)

White Chocolate Mousse and Marinated Strawberries in a Chocolate Tulip Cup

Atlantic Salmon and Maine Lobster Terrine with Tarragon Mustard Sauce
(Dry, Medium-Bodied White Wine)

Supreme of Chicken Stuffed with Wild Mushroom Mousseline
(Full-Bodied, Complex White Wine)

Souffléed Berry Tart with Raspberry Sauce

Dinner Menu H
(unlimited number of guests)
$30.95++/$39.37 inc.

(++) Denotes Price Before 20% Service Charge and 6% Sales Tax   (inc.) Denotes prices inclusive of 20% Service Charge and 6% Sales Tax   (5/96)

Figure 2.3. *(Continued).*

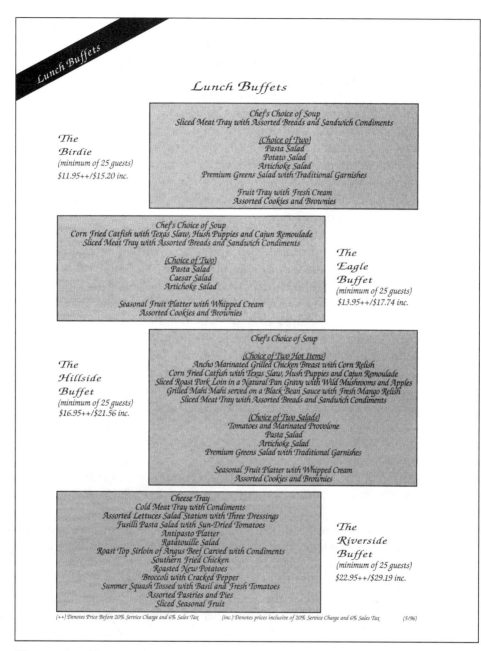

Lunch Buffets

The Birdie
(minimum of 25 guests)
$11.95++/$15.20 inc.

Chef's Choice of Soup
Sliced Meat Tray with Assorted Breads and Sandwich Condiments

(Choice of Two)
Pasta Salad
Potato Salad
Artichoke Salad
Premium Greens Salad with Traditional Garnishes

Fruit Tray with Fresh Cream
Assorted Cookies and Brownies

Chef's Choice of Soup
Corn Fried Catfish with Texas Slaw, Hush Puppies and Cajun Remoulade
Sliced Meat Tray with Assorted Breads and Sandwich Condiments

(Choice of Two)
Pasta Salad
Caesar Salad
Artichoke Salad

Seasonal Fruit Platter with Whipped Cream
Assorted Cookies and Brownies

The Eagle Buffet
(minimum of 25 guests)
$13.95++/$17.74 inc.

The Hillside Buffet
(minimum of 25 guests)
$16.95++/$21.56 inc.

Chef's Choice of Soup

(Choice of Two Hot Items)
Ancho Marinated Grilled Chicken Breast with Corn Relish
Corn Fried Catfish with Texas Slaw, Hush Puppies and Cajun Remoulade
Sliced Roast Pork Loin in a Natural Pan Gravy with Wild Mushrooms and Apples
Grilled Mahi Mahi served on a Black Bean Sauce with Fresh Mango Relish
Sliced Meat Tray with Assorted Breads and Sandwich Condiments

(Choice of Two Salads)
Tomatoes and Marinated Provolone
Pasta Salad
Artichoke Salad
Premium Greens Salad with Traditional Garnishes

Seasonal Fruit Platter with Whipped Cream
Assorted Cookies and Brownies

Cheese Tray
Cold Meat Tray with Condiments
Assorted Lettuces Salad Station with Three Dressings
Fusilli Pasta Salad with Sun-Dried Tomatoes
Antipasto Platter
Ratatouille Salad
Roast Top Sirloin of Angus Beef Carved with Condiments
Southern Fried Chicken
Roasted New Potatoes
Broccoli with Cracked Pepper
Summer Squash Tossed with Basil and Fresh Tomatoes
Assorted Pastries and Pies
Sliced Seasonal Fruit

The Riverside Buffet
(minimum of 25 guests)
$22.95++/$29.19 inc.

(++) Denotes Price Before 20% Service Charge and 6% Sales Tax   (inc.) Denotes prices inclusive of 20% Service Charge and 6% Sales Tax   (5/96)

Figure 2.3. *(Continued).*

could include charges for food and beverage, room rentals, deposits, security, florists, lighting, entertainment, and printing. With so many aspects to consider, there is ample room for variable pricing depending on the type of food and beverage and amenities wanted.

Computing the total price can be somewhat complicated. Fortunately, the catering executive can tap the resources offered by the club controller when confronted with this task. The director of catering for the club must have a good understanding of costs in order to compute competitive and profitable prices. For instance, when computing food menu prices, the manager must precost the menu; factor in other variable costs such as payroll, payroll benefits, and direct operating supplies; and factor in an allowance for overhead and profit.

Menu precosting involves costing out each food recipe item in order to compute the food cost per serving. This cost is then multiplied by the number of servings needed. The amount of other variable costs needed to service the particular type and size of event must be added, as well as the additional charge needed to cover overhead and profit. If applicable, charges for room rental, security, setups, and so forth must be included. The total price can then be divided by the number of attendees to obtain a per-person price quotation, or the manager can quote the total price for the event.

If applicable, the director of catering also must determine room rental rates and other similar charges. The basic pricing format is the same as the one used for setting menu prices. The total price is a compilation of variable costs, fixed costs, and profit. For instance, when setting room rental rates, one would consider the variable costs and provide a sliding scale dependent on how much money is being spent. It is common to charge room rentals to nonmembers and either lower or no room rentals for members. Private clubs usually have policies sometimes set in the bylaws regarding room rental charges.

Usually the fixed-cost portion of any price is calculated only once in a while. For instance, the director of catering generally will have a good idea of the amount of fixed charges he or she will incur whenever a particular banquet room must be opened and readied for service. When calculating a price quotation for a meal function, the catering sales manager will divide these fixed charges by the number of guests to get a per-person overhead charge. To this charge, he or she will add the variable costs needed per person to determine a tentative price quotation.

The same pricing strategy can also be used when determining menu prices for a standardized menu. You can compute the variable costs for one serving and add to it the standard set charge to cover overhead and profit. For example, some menu items' prices are set to reflect a 25- to 30-percent food cost. The remaining 70 to 75 percent (referred to as the contribution margin or gross profit) is usually sufficient to cover all other costs, plus leave a fair profit for the club.

Before quoting a tentative price for a member, you may want to revise it in light of competitive pressures. For instance, if your direct competitors are selling the same product for one dollar less than your price estimate, you may need to meet this competitive price or, alternatively, convince the host that you provide additional value to justify the extra cost.

The profit margins for catered events generally are greater than are those in member dining. However, the catering department has many slow days—even days when there is no business—with which to contend. As a result, even though the director of catering may sympathize with hosts' budgetary constraints, the price cannot be lowered, at which point, a less expensive menu item, served buffet style, may be suggested. This keeps the business, yet reduces costs to the club member.

Deposits, guarantees, cancellation fees, gratuities, tips, and refund policies also need to be detailed by the director of catering and reviewed by senior management. Again, in many private clubs these policies are set by the board of directors.

MARKETING BROCHURES

Promotion Policies and Procedures

A brochure is a promise of excellence. It serves as a vehicle of communication. It is also a representation of you, your facility, its goods, and its services. Your brochure is your primary sales tool (see Figure 2.4 for an example of a club brochure). It should help your members understand what products and services the club offers, as well as the skills and capabilities of the staff.

The brochure should convey an image of style, quality, and professionalism. The underlying message should be that the club understands the members' needs and that the member can be confident that the club will handle each aspect of the event with professionalism and accuracy.

Your competition will seek through its brochures to convey an image of skilled catering personnel and experienced staff of support personnel, giving the assurance that the event will be done correctly. You cannot afford to do any less.

A catering brochure must emphasize what your club can and will do for the member, not what a member *must do* or *cannot do*. Make it user-friendly. Keep *will not, cannot, prohibited,* and other negative words out of the copy. Avoid the use of the term *club policy* in your brochure. Keep in mind that

Figure 2.4. Club catering brochure.

COLD & HOT HORS D'OEUVRES
BANQUET PUNCHES
DELI ITEMS
PLANNED PARTY ITEMS
THEME PARTIES & DINNER BUFFETS
DINNER SUGGESTIONS
LUNCHEON MENUS
OTHER SERVICES & PLANNING CHECKLIST
BREAKFAST MENU
PARTY & BEVERAGE ARRANGEMENTS
PARTY ROOMS & WEDDINGS
BOOKING & BILLING ARRANGEMENTS
GENERAL INFORMATION

FORWARD

We are pleased that you have selected Fort Gordon Club System for your next social event. This brochure has been designed as a guide to assist you in planning your special occasion.

SERVICE PHILOSOPHY

Our mission is to provide the best service possible for our customers as outlined in the following mission statement:

> Our catering operation is committed to growth within our military markets via an aggressive marketing and sales program. Both the management and staff are well trained, responsive to client needs, and committed to excellent service. We provide a quality product with special detailing for each individual client. The operation is run by a strict code of ethics within a fair pricing structure. We operate efficiently allowing for maximum profits which ultimately contribute to our overall goal of improving the quality of life.

To achieve this mission, we practice the following service ideals:

1. Customers are the most important part of our business.
2. Customers are not dependent on us, we are dependent on them.
3. Customers never interrupt our work, they are its sole purpose.
4. Customers bring us their wants, our job is to fill those wants.
5. Customers deserve the most courteous and attentive treatment we can give.
6. Customers are the life blood of our business.

We are proud to serve you, whatever the event may be. You will find our staff helpful, attentive, and cordial. Our goal is to provide you and your group excellent food and gracious service in a pleasing environment. Please feel free to discuss your particular needs with us and we will do our utmost to provide the services while at the same time, taking into consideration your own special needs.

Figure 2.4. *(Continued).*

the brochure is a sales vehicle, not a policy document. Policies and restrictions can be discreetly conveyed to the member later, by including them on the agreement or on a separate handout. You may also wish to refer members to the club's bylaws and rules and regulations for various related club policies.

Your brochure should reflect the quality of your catering program. Its purpose is to create interest and sell! Use descriptive words, brand names, or geographic locations to highlight items on your menus. Examples include:

1/2 pound	Fall	Natural
14-ounce	Florida oranges	New Original
16-ounce	Free-range	Prime
Black Angus beef	Fresh	Rainbow
Boston baked beans	Gulf waters	Seasonal
California strawberries	Hägen-Dazs ice cream	Spring
Chef's	Harvest	Summer
Cherrystones	Idaho baked potato	Virginia baked ham
Corn-fed	Jumbo	Whole
Created	Little necks	Winter
Extra-large		

These words can be highly effective when describing a service, product, skill, or special decor. However, use these words sparingly so that your message has greater impact. Avoid overused cliches, such as *chef's choice* or *cooked to your liking, cooked to perfection, old world style,* and so on.

Keep truth in menu in mind. Don't call a steak *prime* if it is *choice* or identify large eggs as jumbo. Don't say that you have Virginia baked ham or Maine lobster if the products do not come from these locations. Never use the term *starch* on your brochure or when talking to a client—that is a dated term with a negative connotation in today's health-conscious climate. Starch goes in shirts.

Components of a Great Brochure

Remember, your brochure represents you and your club. The following elements greatly affect the design and image of your brochure.

- The size of the brochure is important. Brochures should not be so lengthy as to confuse potential clients or members, but long enough to provide all pertinent information.
- The colors used have an impact on the member. Use classic colors, such as deep greens, burgundies, and blues, as opposed to trendy fuschia or lime.
- The paper stock selected should be durable and of good quality. Whether it is coated or not depends on your budget. Coated paper costs more, but lasts longer and conveys quality. The texture of the paper adds to the image and feel of the brochure. Textured paper is only slightly more expensive than normal stock. The decision to use textured paper will depend on the theme of the brochure and the budget.
- The print depends on the type size and the font. There are hundreds of fonts from which to choose. Selecting the right style of type is important to the overall theme and visual impact of the brochure. Be sure the type is readable. Use at least a 12-point font.
- Highlight appropriate photography, including pictures of your function space and perhaps previous events in action. It is best to have people in your photos, even if it is the staff. People add life to a photo and create a point of identification.
- Graphics are important. A well-designed brochure should contain visually appealing and attractive layouts. Graphics can be designed professionally or in-house—there are computer programs that give you graphics capabilities and contain clip art that you can use for illustrations.

If your brochures contain prices, be sure you date every page with prices. Some members may have old brochures in their files, and it is important to establish that you are looking at the same information.

Clubs should consider producing the brochure. With a computer, the correct software program, and laser printer it is possible to print a professional, highly attractive brochure. Many clubs have done this with excellent results. The cover or brochure folder should still be professionally printed, but the catering material in the inside pockets can be done quickly and easily if the club has the correct hardware and software and someone who knows how to use them. There are few investments that pay off as handsomely as a professionally prepared catering brochure. A good catering brochure doesn't cost, it pays!

Once printed, be sure all members receive a copy of the brochure for promotional and reference purposes. Updates in the menus or prices should be made available to anyone who uses the brochure regularly.

Priced Versus Nonpriced Brochures

Should the menu portion of the brochure be printed with or without prices? Priced menus include prices on the same page as the item descriptions. Nonpriced menus have the prices on a separate page from the item descriptions and are often referred to as *bingo menus*. This is a club decision, based upon aesthetic and budgetary considerations. Most of your public competitors have elected to print prices as part of their menus. There are some factors to consider before making your decision.

Advantages of priced menus

- The brochure looks more professional with prices.
- It is easier to gain an understanding of the cost and is more user-friendly.
- It eliminates the necessity and inconvenience of having the client search for a code on a supplemental price listing, having to refer to two documents simultaneously.
- Because prices and menus will change, this gives management the opportunity to review other sections of the brochure that may need updating or changing. When only the supplemental price list is updated, the normal tendency is to keep the brochure as is. Your primary merchandising tool may become dated and stale.
- The separate price list can be lost or misplaced.

Disadvantages of priced menus

- It groups menu items together and reduces the club's ability to interchange food items without complete repricing.
- The club is locked into the menu, prices, and procedures until the brochure is republished.
- It is costly to change and republish the brochure, while the cost to reprint the supplemental sheet is inexpensive.
- It assists the host in price shopping instead of menu shopping.

Hints for Developing Great Menus

You should establish your credibility by emphasizing your points of difference such as:

- Skill and training level of your service staff
- Skill of the chef and kitchen staff
- Knowledgeable and accommodating catering manager
- Pleasant and attractive decor and ambience
- High-quality food, preparation, and presentation
- The availability of ancillary services, such as bakers, florists, or photographers
- The attention to detail the club will give to the event
- Positive testimonials
- The willingness and ability of the club to accommodate custom-designed arrangements
- The inclusion of local specialty foods in your menu suggestions

Brochures generally include a considerable amount of information that potential hosts can evaluate. The brochure notes the club's logo, slogan, catering policies, room availabilities, suggested menus, prices, credit information, and service procedures. Be sure that you include your telephone and fax numbers and e-mail address. Again, make sure that the typeface chosen (12-point minimum) is attractive and easy to read.

3

Member/Host Relations

....

The initial member contact sets into motion a series of events that one hopes will lead to a completed and successful catered function. The catering executive will be involved throughout this process.

When a potential host indicates a serious interest in using the club for a catered event, the catering staff should find out as much as it can about the host's needs before proposing various alternatives. The staff also must have some idea of the host's minimum and maximum spending limits. Usually this type of information is obtained during an initial meeting with the potential member host.

Once these preliminaries are taken care of, the host relations cycle shifts into high gear. Generally, the major aspects of this cycle are:

1. Provide information
2. Exploration of alternative menus and space (negotiations)
3. Communications with the function host
4. Problem resolution

Woven throughout this cycle are protocols to which club staff members must adhere in order to please the host while simultaneously achieving the club's goals.

FUNCTION NEGOTIATIONS

Before entering into serious negotiations, the club's catering sales representative must evaluate the host's needs. The catering executive should determine for each function:

1. Estimated attendance
2. Audiovisual needs
3. Meal service requirements
4. Ceremonies performed during the event
5. Lighting needs
6. Sound needs
7. Display needs (banners, flags, and such)
8. Entertainment requirements
9. Required platforms and table setups
10. Decorations needed
11. Timing of events
12. Rehearsal time needed
13. Special diets and other unique requests
14. Head table requirements
15. Budget constraints

Before, during, or just after gathering this information, the club's catering executive must see to it that the host is informed about the club's production and service capabilities. A good motto to have during this stage is "Undercommit and overdeliver."

All potential hosts, even long-term members, need some amount of education in this area. A club's catering executive expects to provide a different kind of learning experience to, say, the parents of the bride planning a wedding reception than to the professional meeting planner for someone wanting to do a corporate function. However, all hosts must understand early on what types of services the club can provide and the size of functions it is able to accommodate.

The club's catering executive must also educate hosts to prevent them from making any obvious mistakes. According to Barbara Nichols, editor of *Professional Meeting Management*, the most common mistakes made by function planners that you should caution them to avoid are:

1. Selecting heavy foods for breakfast and lunch. Sink-to-the-bottom entrees will make guests drowsy and unable to fully appreciate the program to follow.

2. Not taking into account some guests' special dietary restrictions.

3. Failing to accommodate guests who prefer a wide selection of non-alcoholic beverages.

4. Scheduling an excessively lengthy reception before a dinner function. Guests are liable to become exhausted and/or inebriated if the reception stretches on too long.

5. Booking inadequate room space.

6. Paying scant attention to room ambience, comfort, attractiveness, and suitability for the event.

7. Failing to rehearse the event. This can cause unnecessary problems that are apt to embarrass the host as well as the club.

8. Saving money by skimping on sound and lighting. For instance, if the speaker cannot be properly heard, guests will become anxious and are liable to embarrass the function host.

9. Lack of familiarity with the audience. Function planners must know their guests or else they will be unable to select appropriate food, beverage, entertainment, and other services.

10. Failing to include head table guests in the guest count. For instance, it is sometimes easy to overlook guest speakers and presenters as well as VIPs who are not processed through regular channels.

Once this groundwork is settled, the club's catering sales representative can begin planning the major aspects all catering functions share—prices, special needs, and guarantees.

Prices

Potential hosts must be aware of all relevant charges. You should quote them the total charge for all products and services purchased. For instance, some clubs quote separate prices for meal and beverage functions, room rentals, room setups, taxes, gratuities, costs for continuing service beyond the scheduled cutoff time, license fees, insurance costs, and outside contract services. Club personnel involved with selling the event must ensure that the price quotation lists all these separate charges as well as the grand total; last-minute surprises will seriously harm the club's professional image.

Some clubs are willing to quote prices three to six months in advance. Since their costs of doing business tend to fluctuate (particularly food costs), anything over the six-month period usually calls for a price-range quotation. For example, the club may agree to quote a tentative price, subject to a range of percentages that will be used to increase or decrease the final price.

The short-term booking (less than 1 month out) puts the club in the driver's seat. The short period of time usually precludes the function planner from pulling out of the deal. A host would have to pay a cancellation fee and take the chance of finding another suitable location for the function. Furthermore, the host may have printed invitations or other materials that would have to be redone.

While price is a key consideration in the selection of a facility to host catered events, statistics show that quality of food and beverage is another very important criterion evaluated by hosts when deciding which caterer to use. On the one hand, hosts are very price sensitive. But, on the other hand, they want good-quality food and beverage products. In effect, they want to maximize the price-value relationships received. This is where a club can beat out most local competition.

Functions with unlimited budgets are the most fun to work with. In this case, price negotiations may consist of nothing more than weighing the pros and cons of French service.

Many function hosts, however, want filet mignon at peanut-butter-and-jelly prices. This is particularly true of some members in the club. The extent to which the club chooses to negotiate will be directly impacted by the season in which the event is being held.

Price negotiation is a game. There are many options the club's sales staff can offer. If the club and host choose wisely, the catered event will be profitable for the club and memorable for the member. The successful club will try to find some common ground whereby the club and member can achieve their personal objectives.

For example, the club can ask the member to allow the club to be creative. Instead of haggling over a lower price for something on a standardized food menu, maybe it would be better for everyone if the member allows the club to work with the chef and create something unique within the client's budget.

The club could suggest food items that are in season as well as those that are not labor intensive, allowing the member who is willing to make a few minor menu changes to enjoy a lower price.

If there are other similar events in the club that day, perhaps the host would be willing to accept the same menu as another group (a process known as *ganging menus*). This option can reduce production costs and increase labor productivity. A function host willing to do this may be rewarded with a lower price quotation.

Since payroll, employee benefits, and payroll-related administrative costs can exceed 40 percent of revenue, a host could save money by selecting a menu that is easy to produce and serve. For instance, you may be able to reduce the number of servers if guests would be satisfied with self-service options or with standard American service, where foods are preplated in the kitchen and served quickly and efficiently to guests. Payroll can also be reduced if the host allows you to preset some courses, such as salad and dessert, on the dining tables. Preplated and preset food is a very functional and quick type of table service. If the club member is booking a function for personal/family needs such as a birthday party, remember that he or she is paying dues to support the club and that the club should try to give members a break where possible—for example, free doorman service, free room rental, reduced setup charges, or lower service charges.

If beverage is a major part of the catered event, there are some money-saving ideas that the catering sales representative could suggest to the function host. For instance:

1. Bars could be wedded toward the end of the event. Wedding a bar means closing one or more portable bars down about half an hour before the end of the function and using the partial bottles at those bars remaining open. Alternatively, if your banquet rooms have permanent bars, you could offer to close one early. Under both strategies, the client should be able to reduce labor expenses. Wedding bars usually is a viable alternative only when a host purchases liquor by the bottle. However, in some parts of the country, purchasing full bottles for on-premises consumption may be prohibited by local liquor codes. Furthermore, the codes may not allow you to move beverage from one bar to another during a catering function. You must ensure that your local liquor code allows you to offer this form of cost-saving alternative.

2. Avoid letting guests prepare their own alcoholic drinks. If all drinks are prepared and served by bartenders or prepared by bartenders and passed by cocktail servers, liquor consumption will decrease significantly. People tend to drink much less when they are served. Even though there is a higher labor cost when liquor preparation

and service is controlled by the club, the product cost savings obtained with reduced consumption could more than offset the extra payroll charges.

3. Offer the use of low-cost house brands instead of call or premium brands.

4. Serve large quantities of food. The more people eat, generally the less they drink. Cheese is particularly filling. Minimize salty foods, though; thirsty guests will tend to compensate by drinking more.

5. Reduce the time of the event by about 15 to 20 minutes. This will make a big difference in the amount of food and beverage served, and few guests will mind the early cutoff.

6. Limit "landing space." If there is no place to set a drink, it is less likely to be lost and replaced when half empty. This can significantly reduce beverage costs.

7. Schedule the event on a weeknight. Most guests will consume more beverages on the weekend.

8. Although more common to hotel catered events, a club may suggest the host price the function with the understanding that the first two drinks per person are included in the price, with the attendee expected to pay for additional beverages. In this case, the function host pays for the first two drinks, and all attendees receive two drink tickets. If they want additional beverage, they must purchase additional drink tickets from the function cashier. Under this arrangement, a host agrees to a fixed function price; he or she does not have to worry about inheriting a huge bar bill. (Note: since most private clubs maintain next-to-no cash on premise, cash-handling arrangements will need to be made and cashier fees charged to the host.)

Some price-reduction alternatives can be very risky for the club. For instance, it is not a good idea to allow a host to eliminate courses from a set menu. Removing the salad course to save money for the function host can leave guests with the wrong impression. They may assume that the club is in the habit of cheating its customers. Or they may assume the club is incompetent, in that the staff forgot to serve the salad.

The club also is vulnerable if it allows the host to tinker with the club's standardized buffet and/or beverage service. For instance, to save money, a host may want you to pour inexpensive liquor, open the bars late, delay replenishing some near-empty chafing dishes, and/or close some food stations a little early. These strategies can reduce significantly the guests' price-value perceptions. Furthermore, with a buffet meal and/or host bar, the club is usually committed to providing enough food and beverage for the guaranteed number of guests.

Another risky money-saving proposition is allowing a host to use group members as volunteer labor. For instance, many groups use their own paid staff, or member volunteers, to handle things such as ticket collection, name badge preparation, and record keeping. This is a very common occurrence for business functions or reunions. However, the club must ensure that the process is correct as well as fitting with the club's service standards.

Some hosts want to use their own food and beverage in order to save money. This practice should be prohibited. The club has no quality control over these items, yet it may still be liable for any problems they cause. Furthermore, the use of personal food and beverage may violate local liquor laws or the local health district's sanitation regulations and seriously damage the club's reputation.

Sometimes the catering executive must help hosts juggle their budgets. A client could be asked to permit the club to manipulate his or her budget in order to gain maximum satisfaction and productivity. For example, the club could suggest that the host change a sit-down breakfast to a continental breakfast and redirect the savings to the dinner meal function. For example, if the host budgeted $25.00 for breakfast, you could recommend a $20.00 breakfast and add $5.00 to the dinner, thereby resulting in a more memorable dinner event instead of two mediocre meals. Above all else, a club cannot jeopardize its reputation or sacrifice its standards to meet a host's budget restrictions. It is more appropriate to serve less-expensive menu items and beverages but still serve them in sufficient quantity and give excellent service.

Special Needs

Hosts who have special needs may be more concerned with nonprice issues than with prices. The fact that they have special requests and unique demands may indicate that they are prepared to pay more to ensure satisfaction. However, as with all price negotiations, the need for something special does not mean a client has an unlimited budget.

Some hosts may need the club to carry out a specific theme. For instance, corporate functions normally require the club to work with company officials to ensure that the corporation's logos, trademarks, and other similar trappings are interwoven throughout the event. Business clients are particularly fond of ice carvings that display these messages. This usually means that the club will be forced to work a little longer and a little harder to ensure success.

Similarly, some functions may have special entertainment needs. For instance, organizers of a high school reunion may want to include a beach party as part of their event. This could require an outside decorator, or in some cases the club may have to truck in sand, green plants, and other necessary materials, as well as break them down and take them out when the function ends. Once again, more logistics, more work, more trouble; however, there is more potential profit as well as satisfied guests who are sure to remember fondly the club who handled their requests so graciously and expeditiously.

Another special need clubs must be able to handle is the request for nonsmoking areas. For instance, a banquet room may need to be sectioned in such a way that smokers and nonsmokers will be satisfied. Special equipment, such as technologically superior venting systems, and additional administrative time, such as processing guests' reserved seating requests, will add to the club's cost of doing business. Unfortunately, it would appear that the club cannot expect to charge more for this service because people view it as a given; to remain competitive, the club will need to accommodate this need.

There will also be some special needs that the club may find to be too risky to accommodate. For instance, a member may want the chef to prepare a special meal using the member's personal recipes. This type of request will require the chef to work closely with the member to test the recipes. Unfortunately, if the recipes are not suitable for quantity-cooking procedures, the club will need to confer diplomatically with the member and suggest acceptable alternatives. If the member's personal recipes cannot be prepared properly in large quantities, guests will notice the dilution in quality and may be quick to assign culpability to the club.

Probably the most common type of special need is the host who has one or more diet restrictions. Some guests will have medical restrictions, while others may have religious restrictions or health and lifestyle concerns. The typical medical restrictions are fat-, sugar-, and sodium-restricted diets. Occasionally there will be a guest who is allergic to one or more food groups; for example, many people are allergic to shrimp, peanuts, and/or strawberries. You also might encounter guests who bring their own food; for instance, some dieters are on a programmed dietary regimen where they must consume products made specifically by the dietary firm.

There are several types of religious diet restrictions that the club may be asked to honor. For instance, some clients may request kosher food service. Some may require meatless meals. And some may need a specific type of food and/or beverage as part of a religious ceremony.

Some functions may have one or more health and lifestyle concerns that may tax the club's ability to run a smooth function. For instance, a party may have a few vegetarian guests. There may be some guests who refuse to eat fried foods. Other guests may want to avoid politically unpopular foods, such as veal. Still others may insist on frozen yogurt instead of ice cream.

Club catering departments will usually bend over backwards to honor special requests. But, unless they are processed correctly, they can cause problems. For instance, most chefs are willing to offer a choice of fried, baked, or broiled chicken. However, if the majority of the guests are receiving fried, the banquet staff must not serve the broiled alternative until all the fried products have been delivered to the other guests. If you do not serve the unusual item last, a few other guests will decide they want it. Result: an unhappy kitchen staff and some confused and/or disgruntled guests.

If special requests are made by a host, the club first must determine if it is able to accommodate them. Because most clubs make it a habit to provide members with any request they can possibly serve, club personnel are used to working with special requests. But, while no club representative wants to say no, sometimes it cannot be avoided. Learning to say no by saying yes is a fine artform most club personnel have had to learn.

If the club is able to honor special requests, and if it agrees to do so, the catering executive should document that special needs were handled correctly. For instance, if a host requests that a special type of meat, oil, or condiment be used, the wise catering executive will see to it that suppliers provide special certificates or invoices attesting to the fact that these items were ordered and delivered. Or if a host requests a low-sodium, low-fat meal, pertinent recipes approved by a registered dietitian or obtained through a "healthy" cookbook or software package should be available for inspection.

It is important to point out that, when meat is ground or otherwise processed, for example, its origins cannot be determined easily or with any degree of certainty. Even a laboratory analysis cannot ensure that the origins will be uncovered. Consequently, it is very important to keep appropriate records in case a dispute arises.

Some disputes may result in legal action. For instance, in the book *Convention and Banquet Management*, Falkner notes that a caterer once served a banquet where a client of Indian ancestry specifically requested that the meal be prepared with lamb instead of beef. During the meal, some guests commented that the meat was beef, and so no one ate the meal. The client refused to pay, noting that the contract had not been honored by the hotel. The resulting legal battle was very unpleasant, time consuming, and costly.

But in the end the hotel won its case primarily because adequate records were maintained and credible witnesses presented verbal evidence in court.

Guarantees

The club must have an accurate estimate of the number of guests expected at the function. To ensure as much as possible an accurate estimate, the typical club expects the host to provide a guaranteed number. Setting guarantees, though, is often a treacherous activity. There is a natural reluctance on the part of hosts to commit themselves. Likewise, the sales representative wants to minimize the club's risk.

Depending on the size of the function, some flexibility does usually exist when the guarantee number needs to be made, but the typical club requires a guarantee at least 48 hours prior to the event. Some clubs expect a 72-hour guarantee if a weekend or holiday is included in the time period prior to the event. While this amount of time may seem excessive to the average member, actually it is very short given the amount of work and effort that goes into preparing the average function.

For instance, the club will need to purchase food, beverage, and supplies for the event. The kitchen staff will need to schedule production and labor. The banquet setup crew or housemen must be scheduled. And the banquet captain must go over the A-list and B-list for food servers, cocktail servers, buspersons, bar backs, and bartenders.

A function planner from the corporate market or an experienced meeting planner may try to negotiate a 24-hour guarantee. They also tend to lowball their estimates, especially for breakfast functions. A 24-hour guarantee is generally too short. It places an onerous burden on the kitchen and catering staffs, not to mention the other club departments involved with the event. About the only time you can live with such a short time period is when the host is ordering standard food and beverage items that are offered on the other club menus. Anything more complex or unique must be implemented at least 48 hours in advance.

At times you may need to consider a compromise guarantee. For instance, when negotiating with a client who wants a 24-hour guarantee time period, you may allow the client to guarantee a range of guests. For instance, a meeting planner may estimate 90 to 110 attendees. The club may agree to this if, in return, it enjoys a sufficient guarantee time period.

A similar situation arises when a host is willing to guarantee 100 guests 48 hours in advance, with the understanding that the club will be able to serve, say, 125. The club can usually do this if it is willing to set up open seating.

Open seating essentially means that the housemen will set up two or three extra tables to handle any last-minute needs. These tables should not be set; otherwise guests will spread out and use all available tables, leaving empty spaces throughout the room. Rather, if the guest count suddenly jumps at the last minute, a server or busperson can quickly set a few place settings and serve the extra guests.

However, serving these additional guests the same menu could prove to be impossible in some situations. If the menu is standardized, and the items are used elsewhere in the club, it is not difficult to handle a few extra guests. But if the menu is unique, the additional guests may have to make do with off-menu items. This can harm the club's reputation unless the client sees to it that guests are apprised of the situation in advance. Generally, though, most clients and guests will accept this trade-off.

Quite often the catering sales representative will be working with inexperienced clients who will typically overestimate the guest count. When confronted with this problem, the club will need to educate the client. Club personnel and the host must consider several variables that could impact guest counts. The major variables that can influence the number of guests are:

1. *Attendance records of previous years' events.* You are especially concerned with the historical pattern of preregistration, local ticket sales, number of cancellations, number of no-shows, number of paid attendees, number of other authorized attendees (such as spouses), guarantees, excess over guarantees, and ratio of attendees at a particular meal function to total attendees at the event. According to Gary Budge, past president of the National Association of Catering Executives (NACE), accurate guarantees are based primarily on a thorough, competent analysis of historical as well as current information.

2. *The type of event.* It might be easier to estimate guest count for a wedding than for a customer-appreciation party.

3. *The number and types of speakers and celebrities who will attend.* Again, it is easy to forget to count these guests. Or, conversely, you may inadvertently double count the guests at the head table—once when tallying the registrations and once again when checking the VIP list.

4. *The number and types of competing events.* For instance, other similar functions, major sporting competitions, and political events will tend to reduce guest counts.

5. *Purpose of the event.* If it is a command performance—for example, a retirement party or a civic event involving a lot of members—you can expect all invited guests to attend.

6. *The type of meal.* Breakfast tends to attract fewer guests than does a luncheon or dinner.

7. *Timing of the event.* If an event is just prior to a three-day weekend, for example, attendance at some types of events might be enhanced, while other types of events may be poorly attended.

8. *The host's attendance policies.* A host may require compulsory attendance of all guests. For instance, the corporate host typically expects all attendees to attend each function. Under these conditions, it may be a bit easier to forecast guest counts for each catered event.

9. *Length of the event.* If a guest suspects that the catered function will last four or five hours, he or she may be very reluctant to attend, especially if a long day of work beckons tomorrow. For example, a long dinner meeting with several speakers will tend to discourage attendance.

COMMUNICATIONS WITH THE HOST

The club must maintain an open line of communication with each host. Generally there is a considerable amount of lead time between the point when an event is booked and when it transpires. An astute catering executive usually uses tracer files to schedule the number and types of client contacts.

Preevent (Prefunction) Meetings

During the lead-time period, the club and club personnel should touch base with the host periodically to discuss the event's progress. Some of these meetings will be "romance" meetings, where pleasantries are exchanged and other social discussions take place. While these may be a necessary preliminary, you are more interested in the detail meetings because this is where anticipated changes will be discussed and early, tentative decisions will be firmed up prior to the event. Figure 3.1 shows one of the tools you can use for these meetings.

Typical issues that are discussed during the detail preevent meetings include:

1. *Timetable.* For example, the host may need to alter the scheduled time for a wedding ceremony in order to accommodate the celebrant's schedule.

2. *Guarantees.* If the tentative booking calls for a price-range guarantee, this will need to be solidified and confirmed. A firm guest guar-

---
PARTY PRELIM

Inquiry .... Tentative .... Definite .... Sponsor Only ....   Assigned To: ....

Date Person Telephoned   ....   Date Person Stopped at Club   ....

Contact   ....   Phone Number   ....

Organization Company   ....

Address   ....

....

Party Description   ....

Member Sponsor   .... # ....   Sponsor Phone   ....

Sponsor Address   ....

Party Date	Approx. Number ....

Cocktail Area   ....   Cocktail Time   ....

Food Area   ....   Food Time   ....

Repeat Function   ....   Repeat Date   ....

Comments

....

....

....

....

....

....

....

....

....

....

....

....

....

....

Bride   ....   Church   ....

Groom   ....   Service Starts at   ....

Date Confirmation Sent   ....   Member   ....   Nonmember   ....

Have Told PBX is in Card Room or Lounge   ....   Sponsor Confirmation Date   ....

Manager Initials   ....   Prelim Initiator   ....   Band Rider   ....

Figure 3.1. Preliminary planning sheet for a party (reprinted with permission of the Houston Country Club).

antee must be established at least 48 hours or more prior to the event, depending on the club's needs or policies.

3. *Use of outside service contractors.* If hosts want to use outside independent contractors such as florists, decorators, and/or audiovisual companies, they must hire them personally and inform the club so that the appropriate accommodations can be made.

4. *Space release.* Club members will often request a certain room of the club at the time of booking. You should always honor these requests unless otherwise OK'd by the member.

5. *Recommendations.* The club may want to contact a budget-conscious client if, for example, the club recently was offered exceptionally low purchase prices for some foods. If the cost of frozen shrimp suddenly plummets, the club's representative might suggest a menu change to take advantage of this price reduction.

6. *Uncontrollable acts.* If, for instance, the menu calls for fresh asparagus and the club finds out that none will be available due to inclement weather conditions, you will need to contact the host as soon as possible so that a suitable substitution can be determined. Likewise, if an unforeseen circumstance requires you to move the event to another function room.

7. *Upgrades.* A host may wish to upgrade his or her event after the initial booking has been made. You should schedule a face-to-face meeting to handle the revisions. Sometimes the club has a last-minute cancellation that could benefit a host. For instance, if a bigger function room becomes available, contact the host to see if he or she might be interested in pursuing this change.

8. *Conditions not met.* For example, a charity ball may require a business license. The club must receive notification that the license has been approved. If the notification is not forthcoming by the agreed-upon date, the club will need to contact the host.

9. *Tastings and sample meals.* If hosts have special food and beverage requests, it is advisable to schedule a preevent sample dinner. Production and service problems can be aired, discussed, and rectified. The menu can be finalized.

Postevent (Postfunction) Meetings

The club should contact all hosts after the events so that the completed functions can be evaluated. These meetings give the club an opportunity to rectify any shortcomings. It also allows the club to solicit referral business, repeat business, and testimonial letters.

Postevent meetings can be excellent learning experiences. To maximize the benefits generated by these meetings, it is recommended that hosts be contacted personally. Telephone and questionnaire responses generally do not disclose as much information. For instance, club personnel want to see the host's facial expressions when he or she is commenting on the event. Many people may not disclose their unhappiness over the phone or on a survey response card, but body language can be most revealing in a face-to-face meeting.

Statistics show that, in the United States, the typical business never hears from over 95 percent of its dissatisfied customers. For every complaint registered, roughly 25 go unreported. Furthermore, the guest will relate his or her unhappiness to a number of other persons whether he or she complains to the club.

Statistics also suggest that, in the United States, of all those buying an identical item, about 10 percent will be unhappy with the purchase to some extent. You cannot expect this 10 percent to speak up. Many of them vote with their feet; that is, they say nothing—they just never return. Face-to-face postevent meetings will help ensure that all complaints and compliments are mentioned. Talking about the event has the tendency to comfort members and leave them with positive feelings about the club. The club should construct an event evaluation form that can be used to guide the discussion during a postevent meeting. Typically, you are interested in the client's satisfaction with the following key areas:

1. *Food and beverage.* You should consider taste, textures, temperatures, presentations, and portion sizes.
2. *Service.* Major considerations are speed, accuracy, professionalism, presentation, and server courtesy.
3. *Decor.* Was it appropriate for the event?
4. *Space.* Some potential issues to ponder are function room size, layout and design, and display setups.
5. *Ancillary services.* You should consider guest satisfaction with restrooms, cloakrooms, valet service, and other similar relevant features.
6. *Outside contractors.* The host should be queried about his or her satisfaction with outside service contractors. This is important if you maintain a list of recommended contractors that needs to be revised periodically.

7. *Last-minute requests.* Hosts should be asked if they were pleased with the club's handling of any last-minute requests.

8. *Timing of event.* Would the host do anything differently? Would he or she alter the starting time? Ending time? If so, why?

9. *General satisfaction.* An overall satisfaction rating should be solicited from the host. An excellent way to gauge this feeling is to ask if he or she would recommend the club and its services to a friend.

10. *Attention to details.* Did the club go out of its way to ensure that all specifics of the function were covered? Was the host happy with the club's attention to detail?

11. *Communication.* Was the communication before, during, and after the event satisfactory?

If personal postevent meetings with the host are infeasible, the club should use these points to construct a questionnaire to be sent to the host. The results of these questionnaires could provide valuable information to help the club improve its future services.

Thank You Letters

A formal thank you letter should be sent after the postevent meeting (Figure 3.2). It should include the normal expressions of appreciation and thanks. In addition, it should be personalized and address specific concerns raised at the postevent meeting. Many clubs will send a signature gift to each client. A typical signature gift is a framed picture from the event (the frame can be engraved with the club's logo).

PROBLEM RESOLUTION

Into each life some rain must fall. The catering executive must see to it that the occasional drizzle does not turn into an uncontrollable thunderstorm. While it is not a good idea to harbor negative thoughts, the sad fact remains that you will sometimes encounter problems with an event. There is no way to avoid it because some members will almost guarantee that they, and the club, will get wet.

Some members cannot resist the temptation to tell the club staff what to do. These persons would never consider directing the automobile manufacturer, but, since they are there when the product is produced and served,

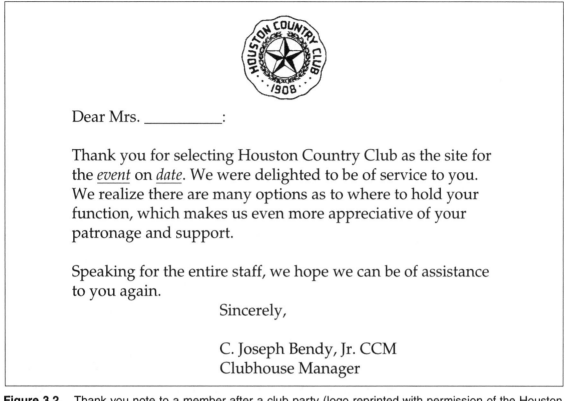

Dear Mrs. _____:

Thank you for selecting Houston Country Club as the site for the *event* on *date*. We were delighted to be of service to you. We realize there are many options as to where to hold your function, which makes us even more appreciative of your patronage and support.

Speaking for the entire staff, we hope we can be of assistance to you again.

Sincerely,

C. Joseph Bendy, Jr. CCM
Clubhouse Manager

Figure 3.2. Thank you note to a member after a club party (logo reprinted with permission of the Houston Country Club).

some of them like to tell you how to do everything. Or worse yet, they want to change things at the last minute.

Excessive Worrying

Experience shows that the major problem encountered by clubs in the area of special events is the worrywart host. Many cannot help second-guessing everything. It is understandable that they would worry because many hosts who are working on major events such as a wedding or large party have never hosted such a major event before. So they worry, fidget, and foresee all sorts of disasters.

The club must try to prevent these hosts from worrying too much. To do this, club personnel must work very hard to gain their confidence. The club must convince hosts that their events will go smoothly and that their guests will be very happy. The best way to gain a host's confidence is to dissipate the typical host's major fear, which is: will the event start and end on schedule and flow smoothly? Many catered functions include nonfood and nonbeverage activities. For instance, a breakfast absolutely must end on time so that attendees can be in meetings on schedule; the dinner must be finished on time or the bride and groom will not make their plane reservations. Some hosts are born to worry. They are a major challenge. However, if the challenge is met, these satisfied clients will most likely become some of the club's most loyal members.

Typical Problems

Inevitably, the club and host will encounter some rough spots along the way. The problems that tend to crop up most often are

- *No-shows.* Hosts want to wait forever if there are any late guests. Keeping a plate warm for late-arriving guests is so common for some types of events that it is no longer appropriate to refer to this as a problem; in many cases, it is standard operating procedure.

- *Unanticipated increase in number of attendees.* Even though you have set guarantees and are prepared to accommodate a few extra guests, every so often you and the host will be overwhelmed with more people than you can handle comfortably. For instance, wedding guests who failed to RSVP may decide at the last minute to show up.

- *Lost and found.* The clubhouse manager generally handles lost-and-found articles. However, the catering executive will certainly hear from the client whose guests have suffered a loss.

- *Tentative hosts.* Some hosts want to put off confirmations and guarantees until the very last moment. This causes a few headaches for the kitchen and service staffs. Sometimes you have to force hosts to make a decision.

- *Underperforming outside contractors.* While it is true that members must make their own arrangements with outside contractors, the club realizes that it may be drawn into any difficulty that arises between them. For instance, if an outside contractor is not paid, the club may be asked to mediate the dispute and play the peacemaker role. In a similar vein, the club may run into difficulty working with outside contractors and coordinating their work. You do not want members to use contractors you know cannot be trusted to do a good job. However, you need to be careful not to give the impression that you are steering members to a few favored contractors.

- *Invoice disputes.* Occasionally billing problems will crop up. The catering executive will need to reconcile any differences of opinion that arise between the member and the club.

- *Fights and other disruptions.* There is always the slim possibility that a medical emergency will occur. A fire could break out, or one or more guests may create a disturbance. If these troubles interfere with the success of the function, the club may need to make some adjustments in the host's final billing.

- *Outside construction.* Some hosts do not like to see signs that say "pardon our dust." More importantly, they do not want to experience construction noise pollution that negatively affects an event's success. If these types of situations arise, the club may need to make some concessions in order to satisfy members and their guests.

- *Interference from other catered events.* At times you might encounter a situation where two catered events overlap to the extent that they bump into one another, causing temporary inconveniences. Likewise, one catered event could generate considerable noise pollution that spills over to another occupied function room. Proper planning and scheduling of events should minimize this problem.

- *Outside demonstrations.* It is possible that a catered function will generate some sort of political discomfort. For instance, a furrier meeting may attract animal rights groups that might organize a mass protest outside of the club. In this case, the club's licensed security department must be briefed so that it can plan its efforts accordingly.

- *Last-minute changes.* At times, the club may encounter a problem at the last minute that precludes it from honoring exactly its contract with a member. For example, a fire at the meat supplier's warehouse may cause a last-minute menu change. Members understandably will not take kindly to these occurrences. These types of problems will test the club's patience, skill, and negotiating abilities.

- *Timing difficulties.* The club manager is not unlike the movie director. He or she must see to it that all event activities take place as scheduled. A successful event must have more than adequate food, beverage, and service. It also must follow a programmed timetable. In some cases, a host actually may overlook some shortcomings in, say, one of the food courses, but he or she will not forgive the breakfast that did not end on time. It is critically important to keep the communications channels open to be able to handle difficulties as they arise.

Handling Customer Complaints

One of the best ways to reduce host and guest dissatisfaction is to anticipate potential difficulties and allow for their occurrence when planning the special events. For instance, many of the typical problems noted above may be reduced or eliminated by setting forth clear, precise instructions in the special events contract. Unhappily though, it is infeasible to wave a contract in front of a dissatisfied person; in some cases, this may backfire and cause additional grief.

According to the results of a recent survey reported in the *Cornell H.R.A. Quarterly*, the ten most frequent customer complaints received by restaurants are:

1. Availability of parking
2. Traffic congestion in establishment
3. Quality of service
4. Prices of drinks, meals, and other services
5. Noise level
6. Helpful attitude of employees
7. Food quality and method of preparation
8. Spaciousness of establishment
9. Hours of operation
10. Quantity of service.

The club will most likely encounter a combination of these types of customer complaints.

Handling customer complaints is a very sensitive undertaking. Ellsworth Statler once suggested that "the customer is always right." Since we are in the service business, we must adopt this attitude. At the very least, while we may not agree that the customer is always right, we must recognize that he or she pays for satisfaction. When dealing with a dissatisfied host, here are some guidelines:

1. *Listen very carefully.* Often the member or host wants most of all to be heard. Listening is also important to enable you to understand fully the nature of the complaint.
2. *Stay calm.* Do not allow the host's anger to incite you.

3. *Be agreeable.* While you must agree with the host that there is a problem and that it needs to be rectified, do not dwell on the negative. Try to move as quickly as possible to outlining mutually agreeable solutions.

4. *Express regret.*

5. *Discuss possible solutions.* Ask the member/guest what suggestions he or she has for a positive resolution of the problem. Agree on a course of action. Be creative during this process. The goal is a happy member/guest.

6. *Don't promise what you can't deliver.*

7. *Thank the member.*

8. *Follow up.* Follow up either in writing or verbally the next day.

9. *Kill them with kindness without appearing to be condescending.* Always be polite—it diffuses anger faster than anything else.

PROTOCOLS

In addition to being polite, club staff members also must be professional at all times. The professional, competent club executive empathizes with members and treats them as he or she would want to be treated. For instance, it is unprofessional to:

Ask an individual's name five times

Shuffle members from one department to another

Make a member repeat what he or she wants to umpteen unseen staff members while being transferred around the club by the telephone operator

Have unknowledgeable employees answering telephone inquiries

Make it difficult for members to contact the staff member responsible for the special functions of a club when they have questions and/or problems that must be handled

Telephone Courtesy

A good deal of special event/catering business is transacted over the phone. Most of the time, a potential host's or member's first impression of the club is the one formed during the initial telephone inquiry. If you have the lowest-paid, least-experienced person answering the phone, a good deal of business and/or goodwill can be lost.

Persons handling telephone inquiries must be trained. They must be able to answer pertinent questions or know immediately who can. The club manager must either train the receptionist or else assign managers to take incoming calls. The phone also must be answered before it rings off the hook. A good rule of thumb is to insist that the phone be answered before the second or third ring.

Do not put members on hold unless it is absolutely necessary. Persons on hold tend to become restless and may hang up. Furthermore, all too often, using the hold button results in a client being cut off and having to call back. In some cases, he or she may decide to call a competitor instead. If you must put members on hold, do it as pleasantly as possible. Ask them if they would please hold, and give them a chance to say something. If you merely say "please hold" and then cut the caller off, he or she may interpret this as a lack of respect and courtesy. If you are transferring callers to another person (not someone they have asked for), tell them to whom you are transferring them and give them the extension number in case they get cut off. That way, when they call back, they can go to that person directly without having to start over with the receptionist.

When you answer the phone, state your name first. For instance, say, "This is John Doe. How may I help you?" You also should thank people up front for calling instead of waiting until the conversation ends.

When a caller asks to speak to another person, usually the receptionist will respond, "May I say who is calling please?" If club staff members are trained to follow this procedure, they must be very careful how they recite this phrase to callers. Sometimes when this is said, a caller may get the impression that he or she is being slighted or that calls are being screened. This can easily occur if the call comes in at the end of a hectic day. While it may be very courteous to avoid screening calls, it may be impossible in a busy office where time is precious and selectivity is needed.

When no one is available to answer the phone, a recorder can be used to take incoming messages. Or a recorded message can relay to members the club's fax number, a staff member's cellular phone number, and/or other methods by which the staff can be contacted. Messages should be returned as soon as possible. Most clubs have a 24-hour callback policy. This ensures that members are attended to as quickly as possible.

When you need to leave a message for a member or host, or if members or hosts need to return your call, make them feel special. For example, give them your direct or private phone number, and inform them that they will not have to go through the operator. Alternatively, you can give them your private cellular line or telephone paging number.

Exceeding Member Expectations

When booking a catered event, many members perceive a degree of risk. For example, a wedding is usually considered the event of a lifetime. There is no margin for error. With business meetings or social meetings, the person put in charge may have little or no experience and wants to look good. Club staff members need to reduce the perceived risk of the client and change negative concerns into positive expectations. Members expect:

Excellent food

High-quality service

Nutrition and health consciousness

Well-prepared and well-presented food

Entertainment (if applicable)

Knowledgeable and experienced staff

Value (quality=price)

Assurance that their needs are understood and will be satisfied

Assurance that the event will be done right

Cultural/religious sensitivity

Choice

Ambience

No waste

Themed events

The following steps can help alleviate client concerns:

1. Providing the confidence and assurance that the club can do the event correctly
2. Offering testimonials from satisfied members
3. Showing videos and photographs depicting successful events
4. Inviting the prospective host to observe a function
5. Developing an open and trusting relationship with the client

To help your members experience exceptional events at your club, it is important that they be knowledgeable about your club's catering program. Make sure that they understand everything from operating procedures to the use of rental items. Act as their special event consultant and problem solver. If applicable, arrange for the chef, banquet manager, and any other key personnel to sit in on meetings. Offer to customize menus and tabletop settings.

Work to be a one-stop-shop special event provider. Have access to flowers, photographers, musicians, wedding cakes, and so on. Either purchase and resell or refer, obtaining a commission from the supplier without increasing the cost to your members. Remember that virtually every desire of your member/host can be met—for a price—and never forget that catering provides an opportunity to serve your members' needs.

4

Working with Other Club Departments and Outside Agencies

T he club catering department does not operate in a vacuum. While it is often the department visible to the member during the event, it depends on many other departments and some outside agencies for its success.

The catering department cannot perform *all* of the necessary tasks; it must have the cooperation of other club departments. Think of the catering department as the orchestra leader—it assembles the players, develops the music, and supervises the performance. A successful catering event, like a pleasing musical performance, comes about when all participants play their roles well.

The purpose of this chapter is to note the other club departments and outside agencies that contribute to the catering department's success and to discuss the major relationships that exist between them and the catering staff.

OTHER CLUB DEPARTMENTS

Kitchen

It is extremely important to have a good working relationship with the chef and his or her staff. These food experts are perhaps the most important players in the catering "orchestra." At times, they will be your salvation.

The chef must know as soon as possible the menu, the number of guests, the timing, and all other relevant aspects of booked functions. He or she must be sure that the proper amount and types of foods are ordered, production is scheduled properly, and an adequate and appropriate workforce is retained for each event. In many clubs, the chef will assist in the planning of the functions.

The chef also must be privy to any and all budgetary constraints. He or she has the last word in costing the menu. If, for example, the catering executive is preparing a competitive bid for a corporate meeting planner, he or she must obtain the chef's food cost estimates.

The chef can work with you in combating budgetary constraints, planning heart-healthy meals, outlining theme parties, and developing other pertinent member-pleasing suggestions. He or she usually knows what will be in season, menu trends, member likes and dislikes, cost trends, quality trends, and product availability. Chefs usually love the opportunity to contribute. Many of them enjoy the opportunity to be creative.

In most clubs, the catering/banquet staff participates with the chef in developing standardized catering menus. Usually the food and beverage director and purchasing agent are also part of the menu-planning team. The menus prepared by this group become one of the major tools for selling banquets, parties, and other catered events within the club.

It is essential to check with the chef before committing to any customized or off-the-menu selections. Many members want something special and disdain the standardized menus. While you may want to accommodate them, you cannot do so without checking with the chef or the sous chef in charge of banquet functions.

Some off-the-menu selections may be infeasible because they cannot be prepared in bulk. For instance, usually it is futile to ask the chef to prepare individual chocolate souffles for 1000 guests, club sandwiches for 750, or whole Maine lobsters for a group of 500. These food items are fairly impossible to produce correctly for large groups. However, most clubs will make every attempt to meet such requests with food items that are similar in taste and presentation, yet can be prepared successfully for large numbers.

Some menu items also may be impossible to produce and serve because the club does not own the necessary equipment. For instance, is there enough broiler and oven space to prepare 500 New York steak dinners? Are there enough slow-cook ovens to cook and hold prime rib for 750 guests? Can the kitchen prepare country-fried potatoes for 1000 guests with the available griddle and steam-table space?

A menu item may not be feasible because the club does not have the appropriate labor to do the work. There may be an insufficient supply of labor, or there may be a lack of labor skills needed to prepare a specific recipe. For instance, is there enough quantity and quality of labor to produce an ice carving, a five-tiered wedding cake, or fancy carved vegetable garnishes?

According to John Steinmetz, to have the best possible working relationship with the chef, you should adhere to the following rules:

1. Consult with the chef *before* promising a special menu or any changes to a standardized menu.
2. Make certain that the chef receives the menus well in advance of the events (at least ten days in advance).
3. Ensure that the chef receives timely updates or guarantee changes, special needs, and other major alterations. Do not wait until the last minute.
4. Do not spring any surprises on the chef.
5. Do not make it difficult, or impossible, for the chef to achieve his or her budget for food, payroll, and other operating costs.

Beverage

Large clubs may employ a beverage manager who reports to the food and beverage director. His or her job description is similar to the chef's in that the manager administers a department that produces finished menu products and serves them to guests.

The beverage manager usually oversees the club's main bars, service bars, special events bars (such as banquet bars), halfway house bars, and beverage service on the golf course.

The catering department typically works with the beverage manager when developing beverage functions, planning beverage menus, and evaluating product and service options. The beverage manager may also help catering managers schedule the appropriate number of bartenders, bar backs, cocktail servers, and buspersons. Bar managers may also need to be involved in locating portable bars and in handling special beverage requests.

Purchasing

Most large clubs employ a full-time purchasing agent. His or her primary responsibilities are to prepare product specifications for all foods, beverages, and supplies; select appropriate suppliers; maintain adequate inventories; obtain the best possible purchase values; and ensure that product quality meets the club's standards.

The purchasing agent normally works very closely with the kitchen and beverage departments. He or she needs to be apprised of all catering events booked by the club in order to purchase the necessary stock.

On a day-to-day basis, the purchasing agent orders sufficient merchandise to satisfy the club's normal business needs. Catering or special events, however, are in addition to these everyday needs and must be handled separately. For instance, if there is a party scheduled requiring 1000 chicken breasts, the purchasing agent must order enough to satisfy the normal needs of the club as well as the additional 1000 needed for the party.

Standard catering menu items are usually readily available from local purveyors. In fact, a menu item may *be* standardized primarily because it is easy to obtain. If a catering sales executive is negotiating for off-the-menu item selections, though, he or she should consult the purchasing agent to see if the products are available, what they cost, and how long it will take to deliver them to the club.

If the catering executive is considering a menu revision, he or she will also need to check with the purchasing agent to see if the planned changes are feasible. Cost and availability trends must be evaluated very carefully in order to avoid menu-planning mistakes.

Receiving and Storeroom

All but the smallest club properties have central storerooms where all food, beverage, and supplies are kept under lock and key. Only authorized personnel are allowed to enter the storage areas and/or obtain products from the storeroom personnel. In a club, these employees are likely to be the purchasing agent and receiving agent. For control purposes, however, it is wise to separate the purchasing function from the receiving function to guarantee that there are no special deals taking place between the purveyor and the purchasing agent.

Receiving agents check in deliveries and storeroom clerks help them move shipments from receiving to the storeroom. The merchandise remains in the storeroom until club department heads requisition them.

In order to obtain these products, usually a department head must fill out a stock requisition form and hand it to a storeroom clerk. These requisitions establish the fact that the department head is now responsible for these items. Once the requisition is processed, the department head can pick up the products.

Most of the products needed to service a catered event are requisitioned by the production and service departments that are handling the special event. For instance, the kitchen will requisition food and the beverage department will requisition beverage. The catering staff will also need to requisition other things such as paper products, decorations, and office supplies.

Housekeeping

The club's housekeeping department's primary responsibilities are to clean function rooms, sleeping rooms (if the club has them), and all other high-traffic areas. Housekeeping also works with maintenance to ensure that the property is kept in good repair. In many clubs, housekeeping/housemen are responsible for the setup of banquets or special events as well.

The housekeeping department, especially the linen room (if a club has one), is the source of table linen, employee uniforms and costumes, laundry and dry cleaning, and valet services. The catering executive within a club must see that the individual in charge of this area has sufficient lead time to ensure that all necessary supplies are available.

In many clubs, housekeeping is responsible for precleaning function rooms and other areas to be used as outlined in the catering department instructions. Housekeeping is also involved with cleaning up after functions. Housekeeping must be apprised of special functions well in advance so that the necessary work can be scheduled and carried out properly.

Function rooms must be cleaned in plenty of time to avoid any embarrassing situations. For example, you do not want last-minute furniture moving going on as guests are arriving.

Function rooms need to be torn down and cleaned immediately after guests depart. If you wait too long to do this, stains have time to set in upholstery or carpets and vermin will be attracted to the debris. Lobbies around function rooms (sometimes referred to as prefunction space if receptions are held there before the main event) require continuous attention from housekeeping. Attendees will leave soiled ash trays, cups, and so forth lying about, and these should be removed as quickly and unobtrusively as possible. Routine dusting, polishing, trash removal, and vacuuming should be done when guests are not present.

Club restrooms need constant attention. Most guests lose respect for management in a hurry if they encounter a dirty restroom. At the very minimum, restrooms must be cleaned thoroughly twice a day. During special events, they must be checked constantly for quick cleanups and restocking of tissues, seat covers, towels, and toiletries. Attendants also need to check periodically for equipment failure and, if found, must report the problem to the maintenance department.

Housekeeping/housemen are also responsible for banquet setup. The banquet setup involves setting up function rooms, tearing them down, and putting away the furniture and equipment. Housemen must work closely with catering to ensure that a function is serviced properly. They must ensure that the furniture and equipment are in place by the correct time. Most important to function room setup is receiving the proper information from club management regarding special events. Housemen must have a good working knowledge of the type, amount, and capabilities of the furniture, equipment, staff, and facilities.

Function room setup begins with information obtained from the client. This information must be complete and conform to the club's physical constraints. Someone has to obtain the proper furniture and equipment, transport it to the correct location, and install it properly. To do this, the house staff must know the needs of the host.

One of the biggest problems housemen deal with in private clubs is proper storage that allows them to store all furniture and equipment as well as transport equipment needed to move these items. Most clubs were not built with the idea of servicing large functions and, therefore, the movement of furniture to accommodate these functions is sometimes difficult and requires forethought. In a perfect world, the storage area should be as close to the function room as possible.

If the club is doing corporate business, the storage area must be able to accommodate meeting equipment such as blackboards, easels, and podiums. It also may need to house audiovisual and lighting equipment. In the case of special theme parties, this storage space must be able to accommodate special decorations and props.

Maintenance

The maintenance department is in charge of all property maintenance and repairs. Its employees perform routine maintenance, such as calibrating oven thermostats, oiling motors, and changing filters. They also are responsible for repairs—fixing broken water pipes, changing burnt-out light bulbs, reconditioning worn equipment, and so on.

Maintenance employees should be made aware of any special events being held in the club so that they can ensure that all equipment is functioning properly. They should also be involved with any setup that requires electricity. Maintenance will also be responsible for determining room temperature needs, taking into account the size of the room, its ceiling height, and the amount of insulation; number of attendees; time of day and outside weather conditions; the type of heating, ventilation, and air conditioning system; the amount of heat given off by appliances, employees, and guests; and the type of function.

Clubhouse Groundskeeper

The club's grounds superintendent is responsible for all outside areas. Normally he or she supervises a moderately large department (10–15 people) that takes care of landscaping, snow removal, pool and spa maintenance, parking lot and sidewalk maintenance, and the primary task of golf course maintenance if the club is a country club.

In most clubs, this is a separate department reporting directly to the general manager. In some small clubs, the clubhouse maintenance staff is responsible for the grounds. For instance, maintenance may handle the pool maintenance and cleaning chores while the grounds crew may take care of the club's other landscaping needs.

Occasionally, a club will book a function to be held on the club grounds (outside). For instance, many weddings are held outside, including the ceremony, reception, dinner, and entertainment. To service these events properly, the catering staff will need to coordinate its efforts with the grounds crew to make sure that any needed tents are erected, sprinkler systems shut off, parking lots roped off, portable heaters or coolers/misters installed, portable lights erected, and so forth.

Steward

The typical large club employs an executive steward whose major responsibilities include supervising kitchen sanitation as well as supervising the china, glass, and silver stockroom. He or she provides one of the key links connecting the kitchen and other food and beverage production areas to the point of guest service. The club's catering staff must work with the executive steward to ensure that sufficient employees are scheduled to clean the dirty dishes, pots, pans, silverware, and utensils generated by catered events. Adequate staff must be scheduled to perform the necessary kitchen, bar, and pantry cleanup after the functions end. If specialized china, glass, and/or silver is needed, the club's catering staff usually must requisition it formally from the executive steward.

Printing Needs

Many clubs have a central copying center to handle their most common printing needs and a contract with an outside printer to handle all unique requirements or jobs that cannot be done in-house. For instance, the club may have computerized desktop publishing capabilities to print standardized menus, but its equipment may be insufficient to produce 4-color, glossy invitations or programs.

The club's catering service uses a lot of printed material. Many catered functions call for printed programs, menus, name place cards, personalized matchbooks, signage, and accounting records. While members can opt to select their own printers, the convenience of an on-site print service is a much appreciated benefit.

When the catering staff has a printing need, it usually must fill out a work requisition form and give it to the person at the club responsible for desktop publishing and printed material. He or she then prioritizes the work and assigns it to the appropriate employee(s) or, if necessary, subcontracts the order to an outside printer.

Room Service

The club room service department usually handles all guest-room food and beverage service. It is responsible for delivering food and beverage menu items and retrieving leftovers, soiled tableware, linen, tables, and equipment.

Generally speaking, catering does not get involved with guest-room functions. However, occasionally the catering staff may need to coordinate with room service to handle special needs of members hosting special events—an example might be, if the bridal party is staying in-house, it may wish to have special food and beverages available during the event.

Human Resources

The human resources department's primary responsibility is recruiting, developing, and maintaining an effective employee staff. It is also responsible for administering many personnel-related matters. For instance, it must process all relevant government paperwork, handle grievances, work with union representatives, and supervise employee compensation packages.

The director of catering for the club will work with human resources whenever there are job openings in the area of special events that must be filled. The typical human resources department's main activities include helping department supervisors develop job specifications and job descriptions and developing and implementing recruiting programs, job application procedures, interviewing procedures, and methods used to process new hires.

When the club needs a new employee for banquets/special events, the manager responsible for this area may need to fill out a job-opening form listing the position, work hours, skills required, and other pertinent job information.

For entry-level banquet jobs, the employment manager conducts pre-screening interviews of job applicants, develops a list of one or more qualified job candidates, and sends it to the manager of the department. The department manager then makes the final hiring decision, usually after personally interviewing qualified applicants.

For supervisory and management banquets/catering/special events positions, the department manager needing the employee often finds a qualified candidate and sends him or her to the human resources department for processing. For instance, a manager may find an appropriate supervisor candidate through his or her membership in the Club Managers Association of America (CMAA) or other professional organizations or through other contacts in the club or foodservice industries.

Once a new employee is hired, he or she is processed by the employment manager. Generally speaking, this process involves employee orientation, uniform fitting (if applicable), ID preparation, and assignment of payroll authorization number, parking place, and employee locker.

The employment manager may also provide a bit of training to new employees. Usually, though, the individual department managers will become involved in the training process at this time.

Golf/Tennis/Pool Professionals

Many catered functions at private clubs involve a recreational activity such as a golf or tennis tournament or pool party; therefore, the professional for the particular area being used needs to be involved in communication regarding the event. In case of a very large function, the club may have to close different recreational areas, and these professionals would need to be involved to ensure that regular members not participating in the event were informed of the changes in club hours of operation.

Controller

The club controller is responsible for securing all club assets. He or she normally supervises all cost-control activities, payroll processing, accounts payable, accounts receivable, and data processing. The banquet department's major relationships with the club controller involve report preparation, auditing, and accounts receivable.

All club departments prepare reports. Many of them are coordinated and printed by the controller's office. For instance, budgets, profit-and-loss statements, and activity reports are usually prepared in final format by the controller's management information system (MIS) based upon information provided by the individual departments.

Some catered events have cash bars. The controller's office may assign cashiers to sell drink tickets to the guests. Guests will then exchange these tickets for beverages. At the end of the function, the cash collection will be compared to the ticket count and the amount of missing beverage inventory. If everything goes according to plan, these three totals will be consistent with each other.

The controller's office prepares final billings and sends invoice statements to the clients. It handles collections and processes payments. If there are any problems, such as invoice disputes, late payments, or bounced checks, the catering department may need to help resolve them.

Security

This is the least-visible club department, but by far not the least important. You know it is doing an effective job when guests do not recognize its presence.

Catered events present unique security challenges for private clubs. Large groups may need someone to control foot traffic. Some groups may have considerable personal property that must be protected, and others may include VIPs who require additional attention. There are groups that have the seeds of potential disruption; for instance, proms and fraternity/sorority parties must have security guards to prevent underage drinking and rowdy behavior.

The catering department must keep security apprised of all special functions because there may be some potential security problems that the security staff can spot that may go unrecognized by the catering staff or the host. If so, security would have an opportunity to reconcile them or head them off beforehand.

Usually the security office receives copies of all banquet event orders in advance. This allows it to schedule the appropriate amount and type of security. It also gives it sufficient lead time to process special needs such as hiring temporary security guards, renting special equipment, and/or setting up perimeter barriers.

Recreation

Most clubs offer several types of recreational activities. Most have swimming pools, health clubs, golf, and tennis. Many catered events will involve recreational activities such as golf or tennis tournaments, swim meets, or card games. The catering department of a club will work in every recreational area of the club at one point or another, and it is important for catering to have a working relationship with the professionals running these areas as well as an understanding of the games so that members and hosts can be accommodated adequately.

OUTSIDE AGENCIES

Government Agencies

While government regulators are not housed in the club, nevertheless they play an important role in achieving the club's business objectives. In some cases, you may need to work closely with one or more of them when planning a special catering event.

For instance, you may need to inform the fire department if you are putting together an outdoor pyrotechnics display for the club's Fourth of July celebration. The fire department may also need to oversee and inspect any portable electrical power setup to ensure it is grounded properly and safe to use in a high-traffic area.

If the event requires some unique live plants or other greenery, the state agriculture department may need to grant approval before you can use them. The local health district's approval also may be required.

Experience shows that the local health district is the government agency that clubs must work with more often than any other regulatory body. Usually any time you need to set up portable, temporary tents, cooking lines, serving lines, and so forth, a sanitarian must approve your plans. He or she must ensure that you do not violate health guidelines.

Subcontractors

The decade of the 1990s is the age of the subcontractor. (Many clubs refer to the use of subcontractors as *outsourcing*.) Many members today want services that the club may be unable to provide itself because it lacks the equipment, labor, and/or expertise to handle the requests properly. Normally it is too expensive to have all resources available if they are used only sparingly.

Nevertheless, you can satisfy these members by cultivating an approved list of outside subcontractors who meet your quality standards and who agree to handle special requests on a per-job basis. For instance, if a member wants a Japanese theme, you may be able to subcontract the sushi bar to a local Japanese restaurant. The same strategy can be used to provide other unique attractions, such as ethnic foods, traditional barbecues, and on-site ice cream production.

In addition to providing member and guest satisfaction, subcontracting can be very profitable for the club. As a general rule, when a club subcontracts, it will add a profit markup of about 20 percent to the subcontractor's charge. Furthermore, since the subcontractor usually provides only one aspect of the catered event, you retain the other profit-making aspects. For instance, you might subcontract only the unique entree and provide the rest of the meal yourself.

Rental Companies

Rental companies, like all suppliers, technically are not part of the club. However, they may be used so much that they become de facto club departments.

Many clubs do not wish to own and store equipment that is used sparingly. It is too expensive and inconvenient to do this. Generally, when specialized equipment, furniture, or decorations are required, it is more economical to rent it. The club should ask the purchasing agent to seek out approved rental companies that can fill these needs.

Clubs do not have to limit their renting to specialized equipment. Conceivably, anything can be rented. However, usually only those items that are needed to help produce a unique and/or unusually large catered function will be rented and the cost passed on to the client; everything else will be owned by the club.

Clubs may rent the following types of equipment.

1. Audiovisual
2. Refrigerated storage
3. Freezer storage
4. Transportation

5. Tableware
6. Service utensils
7. Lighting
8. Off-site production facility
9. Decorations
10. Props for themed events
11. Uniforms and/or costumes
12. Linen

5

Meal Functions

....

Exceptional food and service is a major marketing advantage for any club. While all aspects of a catered function are important, the quality of food and guest services makes perhaps the deepest and most lasting impression on members and their guests.

The club that strives for a competitive advantage would do well to emphasize food that is consistent in quality because this consistency is something some clubs cannot offer. It may be easy for most properties to offer members similar function space, meeting times, and number of sleeping rooms (if available), but this is not the case with food or service.

Other factors may attract potential hosts initially, but food and service are the key variables influencing return patronage. This is especially true if you offer one or more signature menu items from membership dining menus for your special event menus.

Service is just as important as food quality. In most consumer surveys, restaurant patrons usually rank service a close second after food quality. While it may be a bit easier to provide consistent service than it is to ensure consistent food quality, it is by no means a simple accomplishment. Service and food go hand in hand. The successful club will use both to attract and retain profitable special event business.

PURPOSE OF THE MEAL FUNCTION

One of the first things to consider when planning a meal function is the client's reason for scheduling it. Does the host want a meal function primarily to:

Satisfy hunger?

Create an image?

Provide an opportunity for social interaction and networking?

Showcase a person, product, and/or idea?

Present awards?

Honor dignitaries?

Refresh meeting attendees and sharpen their attention?

Provide a receptive audience to program speakers?

Increase attendance at meetings?

The list of reasons is endless. The club's catering executive should query the host about his or her particular reason(s) for having the function so that the appropriate menu and production and service plans can be formulated. For example, many meeting planners plan group meals—especially group luncheons—because they do not feel that there is ample time for attendees to go out for lunch and return on time. Also, a group meal function tends to keep people at the meeting; if they leave the club to eat, they may not return for the other business sessions. If the club's catering executive knows about these considerations and concerns, he or she will tailor the function around the time constraints while simultaneously making it attractive to meeting attendees so that they will not go elsewhere.

FACTORS THAT AFFECT MENU PLANNING

As we've mentioned, the club's catering executive is responsible for developing standardized menus as well as unique menus customized for particular members and/or hosts. He or she also must see to it that the standardized menus are revised periodically in order to keep them current with changing consumer trends. Although most clubs will not change their special event menus as often as they will their member dining menus, they should review them at least twice a year.

You must do all menu planning in cooperation with the chef. It also is a good idea to get input from other department heads, such as the purchasing agent and the food and beverage director. Since people are more concerned with nutritional issues these days, a consulting registered dietitian might be a good addition to the menu-planning team. When planning menus to be used for sporting events at the club, it might be a good idea to include the professional in charge of these areas.

The types of menu items a club can offer its guests depends on several factors. Before adding a menu item to a standardized menu, or before offering to accommodate a host's specific menu needs, the menu planner needs to evaluate all relevant considerations that will affect the club's ability to offer the item and the guest's desire to eat it.

Food Cost

Ideally, the club's catering menus will offer a variety of menu prices to suit the various kinds of functions it is likely to cater. These prices must be consistent with the target markets' expectations. For instance, the budget-conscious market usually will respond positively only if the club offers excellent price/ value options. Consequently, it would be foolhardy to develop menus for budget-conscious groups that contain too many high-cost ingredients. However, clubs, because of the revenue generated from dues, may be in a better position to do this for some civic groups than are other types of caterers.

Many clients appreciate the opportunity to work with several price options when allocating their meal budgets. This is especially true for those who are in charge of planning all meal, beverage, and nonfood functions. These hosts tend to shuffle their budgetary dollars back and forth among these events, which is easier to do if the club cooperates by offering several price variations.

Guest Background

A menu planner should consider the demographics of the group ordering the meal function. Average age, sex, ethnic backgrounds, socioeconomic levels, diet restrictions, employment and fraternal affiliations, and political leanings can indicate the types of menu items that might be most acceptable to the group. Psychographics, such as guests' lifestyles and the ways in which they perceive themselves, are also useful indicators. Age is often an excellent indicator. For example, senior citizens usually do not want exotic or heavy, spicy foods, so you should try to avoid excessive use of garlic, hot spices, and onions. You should also avoid other distress-causing foods, such as herbal teas, monosodium glutamate (MSG), vegetables from the cabbage family, and beans. With this age group, you don't want to overdo it when serving cheese. Most cheeses are high in fat and calories, very filling, and hard to digest.

Guests with special diets will influence the types of foods served. For instance, some persons cannot tolerate MSG (allergic reactions), onions and garlic (digestive problems), spices (allergic reactions), sugar (diabetics), salt (high blood pressure, heart problems), fat (weight problems, triglycerides, high cholesterol), and/or milk products (allergic problems, butterfat, lactose intolerance, or other digestive problems). Some people are allergic to shrimp, strawberries, and peanuts (including peanut oil).

Some guests consume special diets for religious or lifestyle reasons. For example, most Moslems and Jews will not eat pork. Orthodox Jews require kosher-prepared foods. Some people will not eat red meat, but will eat poultry and seafood. Some vegetarians (referred to as "vegans") will not eat anything from any animal source; other vegetarians (referred to as "lacto-ovo" vegetarians) will not eat animal flesh, but will eat eggs and dairy products.

If a group is coming from a previous function where heavy, filling hors d'oeuvres were served, the meal should be lighter. If guests are coming from a liquor-only reception, then the meal should be heavier.

If a group will be going to a business meeting immediately after the meal, you need to serve foods that will keep attendees awake. Protein foods such as seafood, lean beef, and skinless chicken will keep guests alert. Carbohydrates such as rice, bread, and pasta tend to relax guests and put them to sleep. Fats, including butter, whipped cream, and heavy salad dressings, also tend to make guests sluggish and inattentive.

If a group is affiliated with, say, the National Cattlemen's Association, Overeaters Anonymous, or Pickle Packers International, then the menu should reflect these affiliations. In fact, these types of groups will usually insist that the club use a particular ingredient in as many menu items as possible.

Knowing the clientele can play an important role in menu planning. Some groups will not consume certain types of foods. The catering department and the function planner must see to it that politically and healthfully correct foods are made available. For example, serving veal at banquets for animal rights organizations can embarrass the club as well as the clients and their guests, because these groups believe that veal is raised and processed under inhumane conditions.

Politically active groups may insist that the club purchase and serve politically correct products. For instance, you may be prohibited from purchasing beef raised on recently deforested tropical rain-forest land. You may not be allowed to purchase tuna from countries that allow the use of drift nets that trap and kill dolphins indiscriminately. And you may be prohibited from packaging finished food products in environmentally unfriendly disposable containers; you may be asked to use reusable containers and not charge a premium for this service.

Nutrition Concerns

Preparation and service procedures can impact the healthy diet. For instance, many customers will appreciate it very much if the club does some of the following:

1. Serves some low-fat, low-calorie, high-protein meal options.
2. Uses the four Bs when preparing foods (broil, bake, barbecue, and boil).
3. Trims fat from meats.
4. Minimizes (or avoids) frying, grilling, and deep frying.
5. Serves broth-based soups instead of heavy cream-based soups.
6. Serves green salads with vinaigrette dressing instead of with heavy fat-based salad dressings.
7. Avoids serving potato salads and pasta salads that have a high concentration of fat-based mayonnaise.
8. Serves sauces and dressings on the side so that guests can control their own portion sizes.
9. Limits the serving of alcoholic beverages.
10. Provides half-sized portion options.
11. Uses fresh ingredients instead of processed foods to prepare finished menu items. Today's consumers want some fresh choices. They are becoming more adept at recognizing preprepared, processed foods.
12. Provides some menu options that are approved by the American Heart Association (AHA), American Dietetics Association (ADA), and/or the American Cancer Society (ACS).
13. Provides some menu options that are prepared in accordance with the nationally sponsored Project Lean program. This program aims to reduce fat in the diet to the point where 30 percent or less of a person's calories come from fat.

While there is a trend toward healthier, more nutritious foods, recently foodservice operators have noticed a resurgence of comfort foods, or "Haute Grandma" cuisine. For instance, meat loaf, chicken pot pie, hot turkey sandwiches and gravy, strawberry shortcake, and chicken-fried steak appeal to some people because they tend to rekindle warm memories of happier days.

Dessert Choices

Similarly, foodservice managers notice that many guests are loathe to give up their dessert course. In spite of the fact that people are becoming more health conscious, fancy desserts are expected at a club food function. Ironically, when people are "good" they like to reward themselves with a rich dessert. The typical guest feels cheated if the meal ends without a dessert or if the dessert offered is viewed as mediocre.

The dessert creates the last impression of the meal and should be spectacular. A small portion of a rich dessert is sufficient if the presentation is very artistic. For instance, desserts can be made very impressive with platepainting, when served on a large plate, on special tableware (such as ice cream served in chocolate cups), and/or prepared at tableside.

Special dessert presentations can be very effective. For instance, a Baked Alaska parade, where the lights are dimmed and the servers circle the room with the flaming dishes, is a beautiful sight.

Action or performance stations (exhibition cooking) are certain crowd pleasers that are guaranteed to have a favorable impact on guests. Chefs working at these stations can prepare hot crepes with different sauces. Or they can prepare bananas foster, fruit beignets, and/or cherries jubilee to order.

Dessert buffets are also a nice touch, especially when served with champagne, flavored coffees and teas, liqueurs, and/or brandies. This type of service gives the guests an opportunity to stretch—a good idea if you expect the meal function to last more than one and one-half to two hours.

If you provide dessert buffets or dessert action stations, you should prepare bite-sized "taster" dessert items. Guests will appreciate this because many of them will have a hard time choosing. You do not want them to take two or three full desserts because this will increase waste and food costs.

When stocking a dessert buffet, it is a good idea to display full-sized desserts on an upper tier of the table; then, on the lower tier, place duplicate miniature versions of the showcased items. This type of presentation is especially effective if the dessert tasters are placed on mirrored platters. Experience shows that cheesecake, tarts, tortes, cakes, baklava, cannoli, butter cookies, chocolate leaves, and fresh fruit are especially attractive and inviting when presented like this.

Hard-to-Produce Foods

Certain delicate items cannot be produced and served in quantity without sacrificing culinary quality. For example, lobster, souffle, rare roast beef, rack of lamb, and rare roast duckling are almost impossible to prepare and serve satisfactorily for more than a handful of guests.

If a host insists on receiving these types of items, the club may need to implement a creative and costly procedure to accommodate the request. These additional costs would be charged to the host. For instance, most flaming desserts do not lend themselves easily to quantity production. However, a club could install an action station on an elevated platform safely away from tableside. Guests can view the flaming displays without worrying about getting burned, and servers can retrieve the finished desserts when the chefs are finished.

Standardized Menu Offerings

The club's catering executive should encourage a host to order menu items also offered for the club's member dining. Since these items are already purchased and stocked, this will keep food costs under control, and banquet leftovers can be utilized elsewhere.

Usually the club will prepare enough foods to serve more than the guaranteed guest count. This overproduction is necessary to avoid stockouts, that is, running out of food and disappointing guests. Unfortunately, if the menu includes unusual foods that cannot be used in some way for member dining (in soups, appetizers, and so on), a host will need to pay a higher price to defray the extra food costs. With a standardized menu, clients may not have to worry about paying for overproduction.

Seasonality

A club should always try to recommend seasonal foods. The quality of food items is greatly enhanced when they are in season. In-season foods also are more plentiful and less expensive. Lower food costs will increase the club's profitability. Moreover, the lower food costs may allow you to pass on some of the savings to the host in the form of lower price quotations.

Easy-to-Produce Foods

The club's catering executive should resist the temptation of emphasizing only easy-to-prepare foods. Clients may think that these menus lack creativity and flair and may have doubts about the club's capabilities.

Chicken is a very common item served on banquet menus primarily because it is easy to prepare, popular with guests, and versatile. Beef is another very common menu offering for at least three reasons—it is usually a safe choice for hosts, since most people will eat beef at least once in a while; a tremendous variety of cuts are consistently available; it can be prepared and served in many ways.

Seafood has been gaining in popularity, but traditionally it is not a universally accepted food item, so many hosts are reluctant to offer it to their guests. However, you could suggest a surf-and-turf entree that is easy to produce, such as crab legs and broiled chicken breast, which will bridge the gap between the familiar and the unique.

In general, clubs tend to favor poultry, beef, and other similar items that lend themselves to assembly-line production and service. If nothing else, the menu offers meals that are not disastrous surprises, and usually it can be prepared and served very efficiently.

Product Shelf Life

Since catered events do not always run on time, it pays to have foods that will hold up well during service. This is also an important consideration whenever a banquet is scheduled for a large group and you anticipate a few minor logistics problems.

Large pieces of food hold heat or cold longer than small pieces. Solid meats hold temperature better than sliced meats. Lettuce wedges stay fresher and colder than tossed salad. Whole fruit and muffins stay fresher longer than sliced fruit or sliced cake. Whole vegetables hold better than julienne cuts. Generally speaking, cold foods retain the cold temperature longer than hot foods hold heat. Cold foods will stay cold longer if they are served on cold plates, and hot foods will stay hot longer if they are served on warm plates.

Sauces tend to extend a hot food product's holding capacity. They can keep foods from drying out. And they can add color to finished dishes. However, if not used properly, a sauce could run all over the plate, skin over, and/or pick up flavors and odors from other foods or heating fuels.

Examples of hot foods that will stay fresh over an extended period of time are

1. Chicken
2. Oven-browned potatoes
3. Link sausage
4. Green beans
5. Filet mignon
6. Medallions of beef
7. Pork tenderloin in sauce
8. Swiss steak

9. Rice

10. Steamed carrots

11. Sauces

12. Scrambled eggs

Market Availability

Before committing to a specific menu item, the catering executive must ensure that the food is available. It is especially imperative to check the availability of ethnic products before preparing a client proposal.

At times, there are seasonal restrictions, product shortages, and/or distribution shortcomings that interfere with acquiring some products. For instance, while vine-ripened tomatoes may be in season, there may be a temporary shortage and local purveyors may be unable to satisfy your needs.

Menu Balance

The menu planner should try to balance flavors, textures, shapes, colors, temperatures, and so forth. Appetites are stimulated by all of the senses. You should not plan meals that tend to overpower any one of them.

Color is pleasing to the eye. How appetizing would it be if you prepared a plate of sliced white-meat turkey, mashed potatoes, and cauliflower? Guests will be turned off by the lack of color contrast.

Be leery of flavors that clash. For instance, you would not want to serve broccoli, cabbage, cauliflower, and brussels sprouts at the same meal. They are all strong-flavored vegetables and are in the same vegetable family. You need more variety and contrast. You should strive to have something bland, something sweet, something salty, something bitter, and/or something sour on the menu.

Textures also are very important. Ideally, you would have a pleasing combination of crisp, firm, and soft foods.

You should mix product forms, shapes, and sizes, offering as much variety as possible. For instance, a menu could include a combination of flat, round, long, chopped, shredded, heaped, tubular, and square foods.

A temperature contrast will also appeal to most guests. A menu should offer both hot and cold food options.

The type of preparation also offers an opportunity to provide several pleasing contrasts. For instance, an appropriate combination of sauteed, broiled, baked, roasted, steamed, sauced, and pickled foods will be more pleasing to guests than will foods prepared only one or two ways.

The menu planner also should offer several types and varieties of food courses. A client should be able to select an appropriate combination of entree, starch, vegetable, salad, soup, appetizer, dessert, bread, and beverage from the standardized menu offerings. Ideally, the catering sales representative would be able to offer more than one combination within a specific price range.

Equipment Limitations

Certain foods require special equipment to prepare and/or serve properly. For instance, a standing rib-roast dinner for 1000 people usually requires a battery of cook-and-hold ovens. Buffets cannot be set up properly unless sufficient steam-table space and/or chafing dishes are on hand. And a large banquet that requires several hundred deep-fried appetizers cannot be serviced adequately unless you have sufficient deep-fryer capacity.

The size of your food and beverage production and service facilities and their layout and design also impact menu-planning decisions. For instance, while you may have a sufficient number of cook-and-hold ovens, if they are not located correctly, your ability to serve large numbers of guests could be severely limited.

Experience suggests that, if there is any question about equipment capacity, an equipment specialist can usually provide the correct answer. An equipment manufacturer, dealer, designer, sales representative, or leasing company usually is able to help you estimate your facility's capacity and recommend minor, inexpensive changes that can increase it significantly. The chef and club manager may also be able to offer useful suggestions.

Labor

Some menu items are very labor intensive, especially those made from scratch in the club's kitchens. It is not unusual for payroll costs in a private club to be as much as 40 percent or more of a meal function's total price.

Payroll is expensive in the foodservice industry. There are many hidden labor costs that are not readily apparent. For instance, in the typical restaurant, for every dollar paid in salaries and wages, the National Restaurant Association (NRA) estimates that payroll taxes, employee benefits, and personnel-related administrative expenses add another 40¢ to that dollar. As a result, the cook who earns $10 per hour actually costs the house $14 per hour.

To say the least, there is a great deal of pressure in our industry to hold the line on payroll costs. Unfortunately, this may put you in a very awkward position when planning the menu. Many clubs have the advantage of being able to offset these expenses through their member dues and, therefore, they have a competitive edge over outside caterers. But if dues do not offset these expenses, to control payroll, you may need to purchase more convenience foods, reduce menu options, eliminate menu items that require a great deal of expensive expertise to prepare and serve, charge the client more, schedule fewer servers, and/or compromise on other services. The club's catering executive must stay within his or her payroll budget, but it is equally important to avoid alienating members.

Family Recipes

Some club members not only have preconceived menus but also have their own recipes that they want the club to use when producing them. As mentioned earlier, this is a risky, controversial procedure that can generate a bit of difficulty and unhappiness if the final result is unacceptable to guests.

While the typical club does not like to veer from its standardized production and service plans, it will always try to satisfy its members whenever possible. In this situation, the club's staff will need to work with a member or his or her representative to test the recipes. As this requires additional time and effort, an extra charge would be appropriate.

Matching Food and Wine

Generally speaking, delicate, less-flavorful foods should be served with white wines. Red meats, pastas with meat and tomato sauce, and other strong-flavored foods should be served with red wines.

Some wine lists are not based on color. A list could note wines according to their degree of sweetness, lightness, alcoholic strength, or other relevant factors. In fact, it is a good idea to have many wine options available for client selection.

The catering sales representative should be prepared to suggest food and wine combinations to clients. Since many clients are unsure of these selections, it is important to help them make the right choices. Many wine companies provide a service to foodservice professionals whereby a company representative will come to your establishment and help you pair all of your wines and foods. These representatives usually will pair all wines, not just those you purchase from them.

Figure 5.1 includes a list of recommended pairings of food and wine that catering sales representatives and function hosts can use when developing their menus.

Foods	Compatible Wines
Asparagus with hollandaise	Pouilly-Fuisse, Pouilly-Fume, blush wines
Capon	Montrachet, white Burgundy
Cheeses:	
Blue, gorgonzola	Claret, Burgundy, Port, Brandy, Chianti, Champagne
Brick	Rose, white wines, Cream Sherry
Brie	Dry port, Cognac, Calvados, Burgundy, Champagne, Riesling
Camembert	All ports, red wine, pink Champagne, Champagne, Cognac, Riesling
Cheddar	Ports, Sherry, Madeira, Claret, Burgundy, Italian reds, St. Emilion
Colby	Ports, Sherry, Madeira, Claret, Burgundy
Cream	Sparkling wines, Rose, sweet wines
Edam	Tokay, Cold Duck, Claret, Burgundy
Gouda	Tokay, Cold Duck, Rose
Gruyere	Sancerre, Beaujolais
Liederkranz	Dry red wines
Limburger	Dry red wines
Monterey Jack	Rose, white wines, Cream Sherry
Muenster	Rose, white wines, Cream Sherry
Neufchatel	Sparkling wines, Rose, white wines
Port du Salut	Light, dry, fruity wines
Provolone	Dry red wines, dry white wines
Roquefort	Chateauneuf du Pape
Stilton	Fruit wines, Port, Burgundy, Cognac, Sherry
Swiss	Sauternes, Brut Champagne, dry or sweet white wines, Sparkling Burgundy
Chicken, veal	Dry white Bordeaux, very light red Bordeaux, dry whites
Clear soups, consommes	Dry or medium sherries
Cold meats	Dry Alsatian whites
Coq au vin	Volnay, red Graves, light reds
Fish with white sauces	Dry Alsatian wines
Heavy pate	Red Bordeaux
Lamb, beef, roast chicken	Light dry reds
Leg of lamb	Heavy reds, Cabernet Savignon
Light pate	Soave, Alsatian, light reds

Figure 5.1. Example of food and wine pairings.

Lobster	Mersault, Muscadet, dry whites
Nuts	Ports, light red Bordeaux
Oysters	Chablis, dry Riesling, Pouilly-Fuisse
Roast pork	Valpolicella, Beaujolais
Roast veal	Red or white Beaujolais
Salmon	Dry whites
Shrimp	White Burgundies, Muscadet
Steak, beef	Chianti, Bordeaux, Burgundy, Pinot Noir, Merlot
Turbot, trout, bass, sole	White Burgundies, dry whites
Turkey	Light, dry reds or whites, blush wines
Veal scallopini	Beaujolais, fruity reds
Vegetable soups	Soave, dry whites

Figure 5.1.   *(Continued).*

Some clients have personal preferences that could interfere with selecting appropriate wines for the meal. For instance, a client may want to serve red wine with fish. If so, the catering executive should convince him or her to have alternative wines available. If appropriate wines are not at least made available, some guests may think that the club catering department is incompetent. Furthermore, some guests cannot tolerate the histamines and tannins in red wine (they can upset some guests' stomachs); they will appreciate having a choice.

Entertainment Value

Some menu items lend themselves to entertaining displays in the dining room. For instance, action stations are very popular. Seafood bars and other similar food stations are attractive and tend to generate enthusiasm among guests. And flaming dishes, when prepared safely, are always well received by the dining public.

Any form of entertainment is bound to be expensive. For instance, the examples just noted can be very costly. There is considerable setup and tear-down work, labor hours, and labor expertise involved that can strain a client's budget.

On the other hand, special touches may promote attendance. For example, the meeting planner who wants to attract the maximum number of member attendees and their spouses must be willing to provide an extra incentive. Special foods prepared and served in an entertaining, exciting way are sure to enhance attendance. Furthermore, this form of entertainment may be the least expensive way to motivate guests to attend the event.

Menu Trends

It is important to keep up with trends, but it is equally important to be able to differentiate between a trend and a fad or craze. Trends are more permanent. They are like roads, providing direction—a way to go. Fads, on the other hand, are like highway rest stops that come and go along the way.

The move to a healthier diet is a trend. Significant numbers of people want less fat, salt, and sugar in their diets.

Chocolate is a trend. Many people who eat healthy foods all week reward themselves on the weekend with rich, gooey chocolate desserts.

Nouvelle and spa cuisines were fads. Mesquite grilling was another fad. Unlike most fads, though, it was a very expensive endeavor for those properties that adopted it. They went to great expense to remodel the facilities and put in the grilling equipment, only to see the fad die in short order.

How do you tell if a popular type of food is a trend or fad? Take, for example, the resurgence of nostalgic comfort foods such as meat loaf, mashed potatoes, gravy, puddings, and shortcakes. It is often difficult to tell. Complicating matters is the possibility that something can be popular in one part of the country and disdained in others.

Currently clubs have seen a great movement toward champagne, martinis, caviar, and cigar dinners, and wine and beer tastings. Although more popular in some areas of the country than in others, these have been reported trends that most clubs are addressing with revised menus and club special events.

The menu planner can assume a risk by trying to lead the pack. For instance, someone had to get on the cutting edge and introduce goat-cheese pizza with dried tomatoes. On the other extreme, if you are risk averse, you could be classified as a laggard or someone woefully behind the times. It would appear that most properties take the middle ground by staying close behind the leader.

Style of Service

Often the style of service clients want will influence the types and varieties of foods the menu planner can offer. For instance, foods that will be passed on trays by servers during an afternoon reception must be easy to handle and able to hold up well. In this case, sauced items that could drip should not be served but easy-to-eat finger foods would be appropriate.

The service styles that can be used for a catered meal function are

- *Buffet.* Foods are arranged on tables. Guests usually move along the buffet line and serve themselves. When plates are filled, guests take them to a dining table to eat. Servers usually provide beverage service at tableside.

- *Reception.* Light foods are served buffet style or are put on trays in the kitchen and passed by servers. Guests usually stand and serve themselves. They normally do not sit down to eat.

- *Butler.* Foods are presented on trays by servers with utensils available for guests to serve themselves. Typical style of service used for upscale dinners.

- *Action station.* Similar to buffet. Chefs prepare and serve foods at the buffet. Foods that lend themselves well to action-station service include pastas, grilled meats, omelets, crepes, sushi, flaming desserts, and spinning salad bowls.

- *Family style (English).* Guests are seated. Large serving platters and bowls are filled with foods in the kitchen and placed on the dining tables by servers. Guests help themselves and pass the foods to each other. Caterers usually try to avoid this type of service because it has a higher food cost due to excess foods placed on the table. For instance, if there are six guests, you must put more than six pieces of meat on the platter.

- *Plated (American).* Guests are seated. Foods are preportioned in the kitchen, put on plates, and served by servers from the left. The meat is placed in front of the guest. Beverages are served from the right. This is the most functional, common, economical, controllable, and efficient type of service. However, if foods are placed too far in advance, they could run together, discolor, or otherwise lose culinary quality.

- *Plated buffet.* Selection of preplated foods, such as entrees, sandwich plates, and salad plates, set on a buffet table.

- *Preset.* Foods are already on the dining tables when guests are seated. Since preset foods will be on the tables for a few minutes before they are consumed, you must preset only those that will retain sanitary and culinary qualities at room temperature. Water, butter, bread, salad, and cold appetizers are the most common types of preset items.

- *Russian (silver).* Guests are seated. Foods are cooked tableside on a rechaud (portable cooking stove) that is on a gueridon (tableside cart with wheels). Servers put the foods on platters and then pass the platters at tableside. Guests help themselves to the foods and assemble their own plates. Service is from the left.

- *French.* In the most common form of banquet French service, guests are seated. Platters of foods are assembled in the kitchen and servers take the platters to the table. Guests select foods and the server, using two large silver forks in his or her serving hand (or silver salad tongs if the forks cannot be coordinated with one hand), places them on the guests' plates. Each food item is served by the server from platters to individual plates. Service is from the left.

  Cart service is another less commonly used form of French service. It is the type of French service used in fine-dining restaurants or at upscale catered events of no more than 30 to 40 guests. Guests are seated. Foods are prepared tableside. Hot foods are cooked on a rechaud that is on a gueridon. Cold foods are assembled on the gueridon. Servers plate the finished foods and serve them to the guests. Foods and beverages are served to the right. Some foods, such as desserts, are already prepared. They are displayed on a cart, the cart is rolled to tableside, and the guests are served after making their selections.

- *Hand.* Guests are seated. There is one server for every two guests. Servers wear white gloves. Foods are preplated. Each server carries two servings from the kitchen and stands behind the two guests assigned to him or her. At the direction of the captain or maitre d', all servings are set in front of all guests at precisely the same time. This procedure is followed for all courses. This is a very elegant style of service that is sometimes used for small gourmet-meal functions. Cherokee Town and Country Club in Atlanta, Georgia, is well known for this type of service.

- *Wave.* A method of serving where all servers start at one end of the function room and work straight across to the other end. Servers are not assigned workstations. In effect, all servers are on one team and the entire function room is the team's workstation. The wave is typically used in conjunction with plated and preset service styles. Large numbers of guests can be served very quickly. This is an excellent style of service to use if your servers are inexperienced.

If a host is not knowledgeable about service styles, the club's catering executive may wish to explain some of them so that he or she can make informed choices. You should describe only those service styles your staff is equipped and trained to execute properly. Moreover, when pointing out service options, clients must be made aware of any extra labor charges associated with them.

Service styles play an important role in the success of a catered event. Hosts can choose those that may be less expensive (such as preset) or can splurge with French or Russian service. Furthermore, some service styles (such as action station) are very entertaining and can contribute significantly to guest satisfaction.

For variety, you can mix service styles during a single meal function. For instance, you might begin with reception service for appetizers; move into the banquet room where the tables are preset with salads, rolls, and butter; use French service for the soup course; use Russian service for the entree; and end the meal with a dessert buffet.

TRUTH-IN-MENU GUIDELINES

The club must ensure that it does not inadvertently misrepresent menu items. Printed menus, photos, illustrations, signage, verbal descriptions, and other media presentations must not deceive or mislead clients.

The NRA recognized the problem of menu misrepresentation as early as 1923 when it issued a report entitled *Standards of Business Practices*. In 1977, it published the *Accuracy in Menus* report that reaffirmed its position decrying menu misrepresentation.

In some parts of the country, local governments have enacted truth-in-menu legislation. For instance, in Southern California, health district sanitarians are empowered to inspect a restaurant's menu items to determine if customers are receiving the advertised value.

The NRA identifies eleven potential menu misrepresentations. The menu planner must see to it that menu offerings adhere to these guidelines. By doing so, ambiguity will be eliminated and guests will not be unpleasantly surprised.

Misrepresentation of Quantity

If portion sizes are listed on the menu, they must also be noted on the standardized recipes. The sizes noted must be as-served sizes. Alternatively, a size can be noted with a qualifier, such as one-pound steak, weight before cooking.

You may get into trouble if you use terms that are recognized sizes. For instance you cannot use the term *large egg* if in fact you are serving the medium size. According to federal government guidelines, large eggs must weigh 24 ounces (oz), per dozen, while medium eggs must weigh 21 oz per dozen. Anyone using the description *large egg* must serve a 2-oz egg.

Some terminology, such as jumbo shrimp cocktail, can be misleading. There is no established government standard for these types of marketing qualifiers, so you must be careful when using such language.

Some terms have implied meanings. For instance, when a customer notices that you offer a cup of soup and a bowl of soup, he or she is right to assume that the bowl contains the larger portion. Likewise when you list the terms small, medium, and large soft drinks.

Qualifiers, such as *mile high pie, world famous strawberry shortcake,* and *our special, secret sauce,* usually do not mislead consumers because they tend to view these terms as a permissible form of trade puffery. However, the menu planner may want to avoid even the appearance of impropriety and not use any term that cannot be supported.

Misrepresentation of Quality

The federal government, through the U.S. Department of Agriculture (USDA) and the Food and Drug Administration (FDA), has established quality-grading procedures for many foods. For instance, meats, poultry, and fresh produce have standardized quality grades that can be noted on the menu only if you purchase and use products that have received these grade designations from a government inspector. You cannot, for example, note that you serve U.S. Grade AA butter unless you can prove you are purchasing and using this type of item.

Misrepresentation of Price

You will run into problems if you do not disclose all relevant charges. For instance, if there will be an extra charge for each cook at an action station, all-white-meat chicken, no-ice drinks, and so forth, the client must know about it before he or she signs the catering contract.

Misrepresentation of Brand Name

You cannot advertise that you serve a particular brand if in fact you do not offer it. For instance, you cannot say that you offer Sanka coffee if you have another brand of decaffeinated coffee.

Sometimes we are guilty of using brand names as generic terms. For example, we tend to use casually the terms *Coke, Ry-Krisp, Tabasco Sauce,* and *Jell-O,* not realizing they are proprietary brand names. One major foodservice company was sued and eventually had to pay considerable monetary damages because guests were not informed when generic cola was served instead of the Coke product requested.

Misrepresentation of Product Identification

The standard of identity defines what a food product is. The federal government has established standards of identity for approximately 235 foods. For example, maple syrup is not the same as maple-flavored syrup, beef liver differs from calf liver, and ice milk cannot be served if ice cream is noted on the menu.

Misrepresentation of Point of Origin

Some menu items traditionally note specific points of origin, that is, areas of the world where the foods were harvested and/or produced. For instance, some seafood menu items are often preceded by their points of origin—Maine lobster, Alaska crab, and Colorado trout. You cannot make these claims unless you can prove you are purchasing these items from appropriate suppliers and serving them in your dining rooms.

Sometimes a misunderstanding can arise if you use a geographic term that describes a method of preparation. For instance, Manhattan clam chowder indicates that the chowder is tomato based, not milk based or cream based. A naive client could misinterpret this designation; it is up to the menu planner to foresee problems of this type and, if necessary, explain the situation to the client beforehand.

Obviously, french fries do not come from France, Russian dressing does not come from Russia, and Swiss steak does not come from Switzerland. The typical consumer realizes that these terms reflect a method of production and/or service. However, some qualifiers are too close to call and could confuse some guests. For instance, some customers may wonder about the origin of "imported cheddar cheese" while others will not give it a second thought. The astute menu planner should not flirt with these types of potential problems.

Misrepresentation of Merchandising Terms

Sometimes you can get into trouble if you use too much trade puffery when describing menu items. For instance, saying that you serve *only the best meat* implies that you serve the highest government quality grades.

You must avoid using terms such as *fresh daily, home made, center-cut portions,* and so forth unless you can substantiate these claims.

You need to be careful when using any descriptive terminology to market foods. Words such as *silky, crusty,* and *creamy* can place you in an awkward position if the finished menu items do not live up to guests' interpretations of these descriptions.

Misrepresentation of Means of Preservation

The biggest problem in this example is when you say something is fresh when in reality it is fresh frozen, canned, bottled, or dried. The word *fresh* is probably the most overworked and incorrect term on the typical menu. For example, some people react negatively to the words *fresh orange juice* when in fact the product was made from frozen concentrate. Some eyebrows will rise when customers read *fresh shrimp cocktail* on the menu when in reality the shrimp were previously frozen. Even though some guests will ignore strict definitions, you cannot indicate freshness on the menu if the foods you purchase and use to make these menu items were preprepared, processed products. Don't make the mistake of thinking your members/guests won't know the difference.

Misrepresentation of Means of Preparation

Function hosts consider several things when selecting items from a menu, but the way a dish is prepared is probably one of the most important determinants in the selection process.

When a host orders a broiled food, he or she will not be happy with oven-fried, pan-fried, or baked food. Likewise, if the customer orders deep-fried food, roasted, barbecued, or sauteed foods are unacceptable.

Sometimes we encounter difficulty when we book a party for 350 broiled steaks, which usually necessitates browning them on a broiler and then finishing them in a convection oven. Some guests will be able to identify the browned, baked steaks and may be unhappy with the result.

Food preparation terms can also be used indiscriminately. For instance, it is tempting to note on the menu the words *made from scratch.* The prudent menu planner will avoid this description because it may be impossible to obtain raw food ingredients consistently. If a processed substitute must be used once in a while, some guests may notice it and be disappointed.

Misrepresentation of Verbal and Visual Presentations

The club's catering executive must be careful when describing menu offerings to clients. If there is any doubt about the accuracy of the description, he or she should contact the chef. At no time should you promise something that cannot be delivered.

Photos are a major part of the club catering department's selling effort. However, since they always display subjects at their very best, the difference between a picture and the real thing can sometimes be as great as the difference between lightning and a lightning bug.

Even when you try to live up to a pictorial representation, there may be times when it is impossible. For instance, a picture may show seven different vegetables in an oriental dish, but, if one of them is temporarily unavailable, a few members may notice it and cause you an embarrassing moment or two. Always let the host know that the item will be as close to the picture as possible, but in some cases product availability may cause slight variations.

Misrepresentation of Dietary or Nutritional Claims

As of May 2, 1997, the Nutrition Education and Labeling Act (NELA) requires that, if you offer any food item for sale with a nutrition claim, you must be able to prove that claim by *reasonable* means, typically a printout of a standardized recipe showing portion nutritional information. In addition to being deceptive, false claims can be dangerous for function participants. For instance, if you note that an item is *salt free* or *free of preservatives* on the menu, guests on salt-free and/or preservative-free diets can be harmed if they consume an item that in fact is not salt or preservative free.

MENU PRICING

A menu price must cover the cost of food, payroll, and other variable and fixed costs, plus a fair profit for the club, or it must at least meet the club's financial goals for the department. As a general rule, though, the price charged for a particular menu item is based primarily on its food cost.

For example, if the club's food cost for a catered event is estimated to be $9.00 per person, the menu price for this function will range between $18.00 per person (that is, a 50 percent food cost), $36.00 per person (a 25 percent food cost), plus applicable taxes, room-rental charges, etc.

There are other, less-common menu-pricing procedures that you can use. For instance, some clubs like to estimate their total annual expenses (except food costs), add in a fair annual profit, and divide this amount by the estimated number of guests expected during the year. This figure is the average amount of contribution margin (CM) needed from each cover. A menu price for any particular menu item, then, is the food cost for one serving plus the average CM. When using this type of pricing procedure, the menu planner assumes that all costs of doing business, with the exception of food costs, are fixed. Realistically, food is not the only variable cost incurred by the typical foodservice operation. For instance, labor cost is at least a semivariable cost. However, the conservative menu planner realizes that semivariable costs are more fixed than variable. To open the doors, a certain critical mass of labor, utilities, and so forth must be made available, and this critical mass is quite expensive.

A catering sales representative could use this type of pricing procedure when computing competitive price quotations and preparing proposals. Alternatively, he or she could use a variation of it. For instance, a CM could be calculated that does not include food costs or labor costs. The average CM can than be added to the estimate of payroll and food costs needed to serve one guest.

For instance, assume a host wants to book a party for 100 persons and that the catering sales representative knows from experience that the average CM per person must be $5.00. Initially then, we know that the function must earn a total CM of $500 (100 × $5.00). Next, we determine that we will need about 9 servers and food production workers, which is priced out at, say, $700. If the menu desired is precosted at $6.00 per serving, the total food cost is $600 (100 × $6.00). The price quotation, then, will be $18.00 per person [($500 + $700 + $600)/100)] plus applicable consumption taxes, gratuities, and/or service charges.

Another way to price a meal function is to charge one price for the meal, one for labor, one for room rental, one for utilities, and so forth. This type of pricing is more common with off-premises caterers than it is with clubs. As a general rule, clubs do not use this pricing strategy primarily because it is too cumbersome. The typical client does not want to be burdened with an itemized list of charges even though it tends to be less expensive to negotiate for each charge separately. Most hosts prefer a price-per-person bottom line. It is more convenient, and it makes it easier for them to compare price quotations from several caterers.

It is important to note the required amount of applicable consumption taxes, gratuities, and/or service charges when quoting prices to potential clients.

Consumption taxes usually include local and state sales taxes. Some parts of the country also levy an entertainment tax, cabaret tax, and/or luxury tax on commercial foodservice meals. These taxes are usually equal to a set percentage of a catered function's net price. (The net price does not include consumption taxes or gratuities.) Although consumption taxes are usually a set percentage of a function's net price, there are some states and local municipalities that require you to charge taxes on the net price plus the gratuity. Generally, if a gratuity is noted separately on the final bill, and if it is dispensed entirely to employees, you will not have to charge consumption taxes on it. But if you note a service charge on the bill, and if you use this money to pay all employees a flat rate of compensation, then chances are you will need to charge consumption taxes on the function's net price plus the service charge.

The gratuity is divided among various club employees. Usually club politics and traditions dictate who receives a share and what the value of the shares will be. In some clubs, catering managers receive a share, while at others, managerial personnel are excluded. Servers and sometimes setup staff usually are the primary beneficiaries.

In some parts of the United States, state laws govern the distribution of gratuities. For instance, in California, gratuities are "owned" by the service staff. Food and beverage operations can keep service charges, but cannot retain any portion of gratuities. You should check with the local state restaurant association to determine the pertinent regulations in effect in your area.

A host may wish voluntarily to award a tip to one or more club employees because some additional service, or exceptionally good service, was provided. Some hosts may also wish to reward noncatering employees because of their help in making the function an especially memorable one. Some clubs do not encourage extra employee tipping—common practice in noncompetitive food and beverage operations. Staff members are paid straight hourly wages that do not fluctuate due to tips. It is important that the club's policy be clearly stated for both members and staff. If a member feels that the service has been particularly good, in addition to tips, he or she should write a letter to the club general manager praising the employees' special efforts. In most cases, these types of letters can be the most valuable tips employees receive.

Some clubs require tips to be pooled and then distributed to members of the pool, while other properties allow the individual recipient to keep the entire amount. All tips received must be declared by staff members so that management can withhold the appropriate amount of income and social security taxes from the tip earners' paychecks.

Service charges are not gratuities. Nor are they tips. In restaurants, they are added to the customer's guest check in lieu of tips. However, in catering they represent a separate charge for labor and typically are part of an itemized price quotation.

Usually, when a catering sales representative quotes a price, he or she will note a "price, plus, plus." The *price* is the menu price per person, while the *plus, plus* represents the taxes and gratuity. For instance, a price quotation of $20.00++ in Las Vegas tells the host that the total price per person will be $24.80 ($20.00 menu price, plus 7-percent sales tax [$1.40], plus 17 percent service charge [$3.40]).

Many receptions are priced a la carte; that is, clients select the types and amounts of foods they want and pay only for what they choose. For instance, a client may want to order coffee by the gallon, hors d'oeuvres by the piece, deli meats by the platter, and salads by the pound and pay accordingly.

The prices charged for typical food functions usually include all the necessary labor and other overhead charges. About the only time extras are added is when the function is very small (in which case a room charge may be added) or it requires extra-special service (in which case a labor surcharge will be added).

It is rare, but some clubs have "bingo" menus where the client orders, for example, B-5 (breakfast number 5), L-10 (luncheon number 10), or D-15 (dinner number 15), with prices usually listed on a separate sheet. Separate sheets are used so that the expensive standardized menus do not have to be reprinted whenever management decides to revise the menu prices. However, from a guest-satisfaction point of view, it is much better to have the prices next to the respective menu items so that the client does not have to bother flipping back and forth to match menus with prices.

Prices should be reasonable and meet the financial goals of the club. You can charge more, but only if you give more. Clients seek overall value. They are willing to pay more if the quality and/or service justify a higher price. Conversely, they expect to pay less if the quality and/or service are marginal.

MENU DESIGN

The typical club catering department generally designs two types of menus: standardized and customized.

The standardized menu usually is a very lengthy presentation. It covers several pages of suggested appetizers, entrees, desserts, and so forth, along with current prices for each one. It also includes several suggested complete meal packages and their respective prices. Most potential clients pore over these listings when planning their functions.

The standardized menu is one of the catering sales representative's main sales tools. It is a major part of the catering department's brochure. It is perhaps the keystone of the department's marketing plan. Consequently, the club usually spends a great deal of time, money, and effort designing an attractive package. The format, layout, colors, pictures, paper stock, illustrations, graphics, copy, and fonts are normally first rate.

The customized menu is primarily designed for those clients who want something different. For instance, a client may want to assemble a unique set of menu items and print a souvenir or commemorative menu. Some clients request menus printed on souvenir napkins or plates. This is typical with awards dinners, anniversaries, and weddings.

Customizing menus also allows the catering sales representative to work within a client's specific budgetary constraints.

A client may want to develop a specialized menu to include a certain logo, advertising, and/or style. For instance, a local business may want menus printed in the shape of its logo or mascot.

If you are asked to print a customized menu, you should have all menu items listed symetrically in the center of the page, not on one side or the other. You want to avoid a laundry-list type of presentation. If possible, try to distribute the menu items on the page in such a way that they create an attractive visual presentation.

Hosts of business meetings who book several meals may want to communicate the menus to attendees ahead of time. For instance, a professional association convention may last several days. The convention announcements and registration booklets could list each day's menus so that attendees will know in advance what to expect, giving them, if necessary, enough time to make alternate plans.

TYPES OF MEAL FUNCTIONS

Each type of meal presents a unique set of challenges and opportunities. When planning a meal, the catering sales representative must know and understand the meal planner's objectives so that the appropriate menu, room setup, service, and timing can be provided.

Breakfast

Speed and efficiency are extremely important to breakfast meal planners. This is especially true if the attendees will be going to business meetings, seminars, or other events immediately after the meal. The last thing a client wants is to start the day's activities late and throw off the whole day's schedule. Everything must be ready at the appointed time in order to avoid this problem.

Breakfast is a functional meal. Guests need to energize the brain cells. If they skip breakfast, chances are their attention spans will decrease and they will become irritable by 10:00 A.M.

The breakfast menu should contain energizer foods, such as fresh fruits, whole-grain cereals, whole-grain breads, and yogurt. As a general rule, a person should try to start the day with these types of foods because, in addition to providing a bit of energy, they are much easier to digest than fatty foods. This will keep attendees awake and ready to tackle the morning's business needs.

There is a trend away from sweet rolls toward whole-grain, blueberry, and oat-bran muffins and fruit breads, such as banana or date breads. Sugary and fatty sweets such as Danish, doughnuts, and pecan rolls give only a temporary lift.

There must be some variety at breakfast. While many will not eat sugary, fatty foods, they may want to have at least a little taste of one. As much as possible, the menu should accommodate all guest preferences. For instance, you can offer bite-sized portions of several types of foods on a breakfast buffet table.

A buffet is the best type of service to have for breakfast functions because it can accommodate very easily both the early and late risers. And it can be just the thing for guests who are in a hurry because, if there are enough food and beverage stations, a breakfast buffet can easily be over in less than an hour.

The traditional breakfast buffet includes two or three types of breakfast meats, three to six varieties of pastries, two styles of eggs, one potato dish, and several selections of cereals, fresh fruits, cold beverages, hot beverages, and condiments. An English-style breakfast buffet usually includes the traditional offerings along with one or more action stations. For instance, an action station where chefs are preparing Belgian waffles, crepes, and eggs to order is very popular with guests. However, this type of service can significantly increase the food and labor costs, but it can be offered for an extra charge.

For the cost-conscious, the more economical continental breakfast buffet is appropriate. The traditional continental breakfast includes coffee, tea, fruit juice, and some type of bread. A deluxe version offers more varieties of juices, breads, and pastries, as well as fresh fruits, yogurt, and cereals.

If a breakfast buffet is planned, you should separate the food and beverage stations so that those who want their coffee quickly, or who do not want a full meal will not have to stand in line behind those who are deciding which omelet to order. You also should separate flatware and condiments such as cream, sugar, and lemons from the coffee urn areas. Since it usually takes a guest about twice as long to add cream and sugar as it does to draw a cup of coffee, this type of layout will prevent traffic congestion. If separate beverage stations are not feasible, you should have food servers serve beverages to guests at the dining tables.

Conventional sit-down breakfast service usually includes a combination of preset and plated services. This is an appropriate procedure if there is more time available to savor the meal a little longer. Served breakfasts make greater demands on the catering and kitchen staffs, however. More servers are needed, and more food handlers are required to dish up the food in the kitchen. However, unlike buffet service, food costs are more controllable because you, not the guest, control portion sizes.

Many hosts, especially those who wish to socialize, want some added luxury touches such as mimosa cocktails, virgin marys, exotic coffees, puff pastries, and fresh fruit in season.

Many people are not very sociable at breakfast. Also, if the guests trickle in a few at a time, they might spread out in the banquet room so that they can be alone with their thoughts or with their last-minute work. The catering department might want to make newspapers, such as *The Wall Street Journal* and/or *USA Today,* available to those who do not wish to socialize so early in the day.

Refreshment Break

A refreshment break is an energy break. It is intended to refresh and sharpen attention. It also helps alleviate boredom that tends to develop when guests are engaged in tedious business activities during the day.

Refreshment breaks are typically scheduled at midmorning and midafternoon. They are usually located near the meeting rooms. They usually offer various types of "mood" foods, that is, foods that increase guests' enthusiasm to tackle the rest of the day's work schedule.

Ideally, the refreshment break station would include hot and cold beverages, whole fruits, raw vegetables with dip, yogurt, and muffins and other types of breads and pastries that will hold up well and not dry out. Chewy foods such as peanuts, dried fruits, and sunflower seeds should also be available because these types of products are thought to relieve boredom.

The catering manager must ensure that cold beverages are available for each refreshment break, no matter what time of day the break is scheduled. Many guests prefer cold beverages throughout the day, and many of those prefer caffeine-free and diet beverages. In fact, experience shows that over 75 percent of guests selecting cold beverages will choose a sugarless drink such as diet soda, sparkling water, or club soda.

Some refreshment breaks include only beverages. This is especially true with the midmorning coffee break. A beverage-only break does not distract attendees as much as one where several foods are available. Guests get a beverage and are apt to return to business quickly, whereas foods take longer to select and consume, thereby slowing down service and possibly throwing off the rest of the day's schedule.

If speed is a major consideration for refreshment breaks that do offer food, the menu should not offer any foods that will slow down service and cause attendees to arrive late at their next business activity. For instance, when you have a short break, you would not want to offer sliced fruit on a tray. Instead, you should offer fruit kabobs, which can be picked up quickly and easily.

Another major consideration is location—locate the refreshment break station so that it serves the client's needs. Ideally, it should be placed in a separate room or in the prefunction space.

Be sure to provide trash receptacles for waste and trays for dirty tableware. A server should check the refreshment setup periodically and replenish foods and beverages as needed. He or she should remove trash and soiled tableware and not let them stack up. Someone also needs to be responsible for tidying up the break area regularly. Few things are as unappetizing as finding, for example, a half-eaten pastry on a pastry tray next to whole, untouched ones.

Many clients, especially meeting planners, want refreshment breaks available all day. In effect, they want permanent refreshment breaks, generally located at the back of the room.

Meeting planners who are accustomed to conference centers expect permanent refreshment centers. The permanent refreshment center was introduced to our industry by conference centers. If the club wants to compete effectively with these properties, it must offer similar amenities.

Hosts reap many advantages with permanent refreshment centers. For one thing, they feel this will keep attendees around all day. If attendees go off to a restaurant outlet for a cold drink, they may never return for the business activities.

Permanent refreshment centers also provide additional flexibility. For instance, clients do not have to schedule a break at, say, 3:00 P.M. sharp. A break can be taken a little before or a little after 3:00 P.M., that is, whenever there is a natural break in the business activities. Attendees do not have to break at an inconvenient or inappropriate time in order to get a quick snack or drink.

A permanent refreshment center usually stocks coffee, tea, and cold soft drinks all day, with foods being offered only at certain times, say at 10:00 A.M. and 3:00 P.M. (If foods are kept out all day, make sure to serve items that will not dry out—muffins, for example, instead of sliced breads.) All-day nonalcoholic beverage service provides an attractive, comfortable social atmosphere for attendees to congregate and discuss the day's activities.

Some hosts want the traditional refreshment breaks, but they also want them to be preceded by exercise periods. For instance, just before the mid-morning refreshment break, a corporate client may schedule an exercise leader to come in and lead attendees in a few stretching exercises.

Luncheon

Often luncheons are very similar to breakfasts in that they are intended to provide a convenience to attendees and to ensure that they will not roam away and neglect the afternoon's business activities.

If a luncheon is intended solely to provide a refueling stop for attendees, the menu should not include an overabundance of sink-to-the-bottom foods. If attendees eat too much of these foods, they will most likely become drowsy and inattentive later in the day. Sink-to-the-bottom foods are greasy, fatty foods such as cheese omelets and complex carbohydrate foods such as pasta dishes. These products take a long time to digest; for instance, fats can sit in the stomach several hours. Conversely, fruits and vegetables, which are simple carbohydrates, are digested more quickly. Complex carbohydrates are somewhere in between, in that they digest more rapidly than fats, but not as quickly as fruits and vegetables.

Working luncheons usually rely quite a bit on white meats and salad greens. Breads, pastas, heavy sauces, and so forth are usually deemphasized. If served, they usually are served on the side so that guests can take a small taste. Serving these products on the side will tend to discourage guests from consuming too much.

You should have fatty foods on the menu. Some guests will be disappointed if, for example, they cannot have a few french fries or butter pats. The wise director of catering will see to it that options are available to satisfy everyone. For instance, if the main course is chicken, if feasible, you want to offer a choice of fried, baked, or broiled. Another crowd pleaser is the deli buffet. It serves the dieter, the manhandler, and everyone else in between.

Whatever strategy is followed by the working luncheon meal planner, it is important to remember that attendees may be eating several luncheons during their time at the club. In this situation, variety is mandatory.

Most guests are satisfied with the few traditional breakfast selections. But they normally seek greater variety when selecting luncheon menu items. If they do not get it from you, they will go to a restaurant or bar for lunch and be late getting back to the afternoon's business sessions. In some cases, they may get sidetracked and not come back at all.

Many luncheons are nonworking luncheons; for these, refueling and keeping attendees on the property are not major objectives. The nonworking type of luncheon usually involves some sort of ceremony. For instance, many luncheons have speakers, audiovisual displays, fashion shows, awards, announcements, and so forth that may overshadow other objectives.

When you have a ceremonial type of luncheon booked in your club, the logistics are more complicated. For instance, you must ensure that head tables and reserved tables are noted correctly, name badges prepared, audiovisual material installed and ready to go, all lighting synchronized properly, and printed materials, if any, set at each guest's place. You also need to ensure that sufficient labor is scheduled to handle the food and nonfood service demands adequately.

Buffet, preset, and plated services are the typical service styles used for luncheon meals. In most cases, luncheon service is similar to breakfast service. Speed is usually a major concern. Consequently, menus and service styles are usually selected with quickness and efficiency in mind.

Reception

Receptions are often predinner functions designed primarily to encourage people to get to know one another. For instance, most conventions schedule an opening reception, or icebreaker party, to allow attendees to make new friends and renew old acquaintances. If an icebreaker reception is not scheduled, but a dinner is, an attendee usually will meet only the handful of people sitting at his or her dining table.

One thing that most receptions have in common is that they usually include alcoholic beverage service in addition to food. Another common trait is the fact that rarely are they scheduled during business hours; normally a reception begins after 5:00 P.M.

When planning a reception, it is best to locate several food buffet stations around the room, each with a different type of food. This encourages guests to move around and socialize. If possible, you should include one or two action stations. You also should have a server at each station to replenish foods, bus soiled tableware, remove trash, and be a psychological deterrent to curb guests' tendencies to heap their plates and/or return several times.

If beverages are served, the bars and nonalcoholic beverage stations should also be spaced around the room. You should place them a sufficient distance from the food stations so that people have to change locations in order to get a drink. This further increases guest participation and mingling.

If the reception is intended to take the place of dinner, you should offer a complete balance of food type, color, temperature, preparation methods, and so forth to suit every taste. And, since this type of reception normally extends for a longer period of time than the predinner one, and since people will in effect be consuming the equivalent of dinner, sufficient backup food and beverage supplies must be available to prevent stockouts.

The selection of foods offered should have broad appeal. You should be careful when serving exotic foods some guests may not recognize. For instance, if you are serving unusual fish items on a buffet table, you might want to identify them with name cards. Similarly, if unusual foods are passed by servers, the servers should be able to answer any questions posed by guests.

Menu items should be bite sized. This allows guests to sample a wide variety of foods without wasting too much of it. It also ensure that the foods will be easy to consume. Ease of consumption is very important since most guests must balance plates and glassware while moving around.

Menu items must be easy for guests to hold and to eat. For instance, while kabobs are popular items served at receptions, if they are not prepared and assembled properly, guests will have a frustrating experience trying to eat them. If you serve kabobs, you should put the food ingredients only on the bottom half of the skewer. Otherwise, guests will be unable to get all the food off the skewer without making a mess.

Foods also should not be messy or greasy. Nor should they leave stains on clothes or teeth. For instance, you should avoid sauced foods such as barbecued chicken wings that might drip when guests are eating them. Instead, you should offer chicken tenders with a stiff sauce served on the side.

Be certain not to use dinner-sized plates for receptions. These encourage overeating. It also encourages excessive waste because a guest may fill the plate, eat some of the food, set the plate down somewhere, forget it, and then go back for another plate of food. Furthermore, guests with large plates of food will tend to sit down to eat and will not mingle and network very much, if at all.

Seating should be minimized at receptions. You do not want to encourage guests to sit and eat; remember, you want to promote mingling and networking. Seating should not exceed 25 to 30 percent of the guest count. Cabaret-style seating, or park benches, both of which have little or no table space, are suitable.

To encourage mingling, and to control food costs, you should consider having servers pass foods in addition to, or instead of, placing food buffet stations throughout the room. Guests tend to eat less if the foods are passed. Generally, if the foods are displayed on a buffet table where guests can help themselves, they will eat twice as much as they would if all foods were passed butler style by servers. However, you should not have all foods passed. You should have at least one or two food stations and/or action stations to enhance the visual appearance of the function room.

If you offer passed foods, you should only place one type of food on a tray; otherwise guests will take too long to make their selections. If they cannot decide easily what to take, they may take one of each. This will slow down service because the servers will not be able to work the room quickly and efficiently. It also might encourage overconsumption and food waste.

Receptions can be tailored to any budget. Unlike other meal functions, the clients have more flexibility. There are many opportunities to be extravagant or frugal. For example, clients can control the time allocated for the reception; they can offer a seafood bar with a few shrimp and a lot of inexpensive mussels arranged on crushed ice; they can start with expensive hors d'oeuvres and back them up with less expensive cheese and dry snacks. The breakfast, luncheon, and dinner planner generally does not enjoy such a wide array of options.

If the goal is to increase food sales, generally, if you are charging the host according to the amount of foods consumed, you would opt for buffet tables, dinner-sized plates, and self-service. On the other extreme, some passed foods are appropriate if the client is paying a per-person charge for unlimited consumption. Since many clients prefer paying a per-person charge for foods, your service strategies will tend toward passed foods. However, usually you and your clients can find several mutually agreeable positions between these two extremes to satisfy everyone's quality and cost requirements.

Dinner

Dinner is the most typical catered meal. While it shares many similarities with breakfast and luncheon, usually it is a longer, more elaborate affair.

Unlike breakfast or luncheon, a client will be more adventurous when booking a dinner function because he or she usually has more money and time to work with. For example, Russian and French service styles are more likely to be used at dinner than at other meals. Even the buffet, preset, and preplated service styles are enhanced. Furthermore, entertainment is more common at dinner.

Many dinners are part of a theme, ceremony, or other type of major production where foodservice is only one part of the event. Rarely are dinners scheduled merely for refueling purposes.

Dinner guests usually are not on a tight time schedule. They normally do not have to be at a business meeting or any other sort of activity later on in the evening. As a result, some tend to wander in late, while others tend to linger well after the function ends. Catering staff must be aware of these tendencies and plan accordingly.

The catering sales representative should be prepared to work closely with the client in developing the dinner event. Many clients do not have sufficient background or expertise to plan a major function. Nor do they have the creative talents necessary to plan an unforgettable experience.

The catering sales representative must also be aware of the protocols, seating arrangements, and other similar considerations associated with various ceremonies so that the client can be advised correctly.

The catering sales representative should also be prepared to suggest themes that can be used by clients to increase interest in their dinner functions.

Theme parties are in vogue. They add interest and provide a good deal of fun for the guests. Hosts do not need to spend a great deal of money to throw a theme party. Carnival, circus, state fair, drive-ins, fifties, sixties, and Halloween are easy themes to incorporate into the dinner function. For instance, a successful Halloween party needs only a costume contest, harvest buffet, and a few magic props. These are especially popular in private clubs for member functions.

Some clients want to design themes that will enhance the image of the group booking the dinner. For example, a dairy convention may want to hold a party reminiscent of an ice cream social to introduce new frozen dairy products. The catering sales representative will need to work closely with the client to ensure that this party runs smoothly.

A dinner usually is much, much more than a meal. Food and beverage is only one part of it. The catering executive must be able to juggle many attractions when helping clients plan these major events.

Off-Premises Catering

Some clubs go beyond the traditional on-premises meal functions and offer off-premises options. However, there are only a few properties that offer this option. Usually the typical club is unable to perform this service adequately.

Off-premises catering is a very involved business that is much different than on-premise catering. It requires a very different form of management. To do it correctly, you must have a considerable amount of unique, specialized equipment that the typical club does not have.

For example, the off-premises caterer needs on-site preparation and service equipment, as well as transport equipment. The full-service off-premises caterer also needs power generators, freshwater and brown-water wagons, portable furniture, and tents.

Some clubs will not solicit off-premises catering business because they do not want to be put into the unpleasant position of being unable to get maximum use from expensive fixed assets. To perform this service adequately, you need to invest a great deal of money in equipment. In addition to transport equipment, especially trucks and vans, you need expensive portable hot-holding and cold-holding equipment that can be transported off-site. Unless these assets can be rented for a reasonable price, it could be economically disastrous to own them if they are going to be used sparingly. Some clubs will do small dinner parties or receptions in members' homes, provided a high-quality job can be performed.

In addition to investment considerations, the off-premises caterer encounters many problems foreign to the typical club director of catering. For instance, the off-premises caterer must previsit the site and check the layout and design; see what utilities are available; determine what, if any, type of cooking can be performed on-site; have a backup plan in the event of inclement weather; hire qualified drivers; secure communications equipment (such as cellular phones); obtain the appropriate insurance rider; obtain union permission to use on-site employees off-site; and a whole host of additional related details.

The off-premises caterer also encounters many sanitation and safety problems that do not affect the club catering department. For example, the off-premises caterer cannot reuse any leftovers (except sealed condiments), whereas the club may be able to salvage some. Only foods that transport well can be used. The off-premises caterer does not have complete control over the function site, so his or her product liability insurance will be very expensive. The club usually is not set up to remove finished foods safely from the kitchen, to the back door, and onto a waiting vehicle. It may be difficult to secure a potable water source at the site. Garbage and trash removal are more difficult to handle at off-site venues. In addition, equipment used to transport finished foods must be removed from the transport containers and put into serving bowls, trays, and/or pans designed for service.

Other operational problems unique to the off-premises caterer include tying up the club's loading dock and receiving area when stocking the catering vehicle(s); prepreparing products in-house, transporting them, and handling final preparation and service on location; making sure all employees get to the right place at the right time; transporting, setting up, and tearing down all furniture and equipment; controlling shoplifting; setting up and tearing down tents; installing and removing portable heating or cooling equipment; installing and operating electrical power generators; packing items very carefully to eliminate breakage; and qualifying for the relevant business licenses, liquor licenses, and health permits.

Usually the biggest barrier facing the club that wants to get involved with off-premises catering is the lack of adequate vehicles. One way to get around this stumbling block is to borrow another club department's truck or van. Another method used is to rent or purchase old UPS vans, milk trucks, or club laundry trucks; they work well because they back up readily to loading docks and equipment can be rolled in very easily. The only problem with these strategies is that, unless the vehicles meet local health district codes, you cannot use them to transport foods.

If a regular customer or member requests off-premises catering, it is not smart to refuse the request. If the club cannot handle the request, at the very least you should refer the member to a reputable off-premises caterer whose standards and reputation parallel yours. It is a mistake to refer the member to an unknown off-premises caterer who does not share your views.

One form of off-premises catering provided by many clubs is the box-lunch option. For instance, a member may request individual box lunches for a golf outing or lunchtime tournament where he or she doesn't want a full meal served.

Another type of off-premises catering provided by many clubs involves a food or beverage function held outside the banquet areas, but within the club property. For instance, a client may want to book a poolside party, garden wedding, or picnic barbecue.

Most club catering departments are usually able to handle the outdoor function as long as it is on club property. For instance, if there are many requests for picnic barbecues, the club may build a permanent outdoor grill and shelter, complete with hot and cold running water, refrigeration, and storage space.

Another form of off-premises catering that may be thrust upon the catering department is the type that starts out being an on-premises function and eventually ends up being a combination of on-premises and off-premises. For instance, a major banquet may sudddenly require more floor space than the club has available. To accommodate it, a tent and other related equipment can be rented.

In lieu of renting, clubs may wish to purchase one or more tents so that they have them readily available to handle space crunches. Tents are aesthetically pleasing and come in all shapes and sizes. They can be used solely to shelter the foods, or they can house the entire party. Some can be heated, air conditioned, and floored with wood or Astroturf. They also can be used indoors to enhance decor.

It would appear that sooner or later, the director of catering will get involved with some type of off-premises catering function. You must be prepared to handle the occasional request or else risk losing current and future business.

The Internal Revenue Service (IRS) governs unrelated business income for private clubs. For nonresidential private clubs (clubs not located within gated walls of a gated community), off-premise catering is considered to be one of the things defined as unrelated business. Nonprofit clubs can lose their tax-exempt status if the violation is severe or persistent.

6

Beverage Functions

....

Beverage functions almost always include food today. It is very unusual for a beverage function to offer only alcoholic and nonalcoholic drinks. At the very least, function hosts want to include a few
hors d' oeuvres or dry snacks.

In view of increasing host and host-property liability, the wise catering
executive will not book events that offer only alcoholic beverages. For instance, all-evening drinking parties, such as irresponsible fraternity bashes
and bachelor parties, are inappropriate.

This chapter will highlight those catered events where alcoholic beverages are served. Since alcohol is often served at meal functions, make sure
you've read Chapter 5 before continuing with this chapter because much of
that discussion is pertinent to this chapter.

By necessity, Chapters 5 and 6 overlap. Our intent is to highlight the
beverage service aspects of the club catering business. To that end, Chapter
6 should be considered a supplement to Chapter 5, and vice versa.

PURPOSE OF THE BEVERAGE FUNCTION

The purpose of the beverage function will give the catering sales representative an insight into the client's wishes. This information is invaluable when
working with the host to create an exciting, memorable event.

There are many reasons why members schedule beverage functions. However, unlike meal functions, there tends to be at least one common thread running through all of them: these events usually serve as a way for members and their guests to socialize and practice networking.

A beverage function is not a refueling stop. It is not scheduled primarily to give guests the opportunity to recharge their batteries. After all, no one needs to consume alcoholic beverages to survive. Rather, beverage functions offer guests a chance to visit with other guests in a relaxed, leisurely setting. New acquaintances are made and old ones rekindled. Job openings are circulated. Hot tips are exchanged. And the seeds of many successful business dealings are planted.

Another thing most beverage functions share is the time of day they are offered. Usually they are scheduled after 5:00 P.M. Every once in a while you will be asked to offer poured-wine service and/or specialty drinks such as Bloody Marys at a brunch or luncheon meal function. However, it is less common today for a host to request liquor service before the end of the normal business day.

Still another interesting common thread found among beverage functions is that many of them are scheduled before a meal. Premeal cocktail receptions allow strangers the opportunity to get acquainted. For instance, if a guest is invited to a meal function where he or she knows very few of the other guests, it is much easier to meet them while strolling through a reception area than it is sitting at one dining table for the whole evening.

Some receptions are intended to take the place of a meal. For instance, a cocktail reception scheduled from 5:00 P.M. to 8:00 P.M. usually must offer a reasonable variety of foods so that guests can select enough of them to create a meal. Even if these guests expect to go out to dinner later, the host should see to it that sufficient foods are offered to satisfy those guests who will not make alternate dining plans.

A host may schedule a short reception in order to provide some sort of transition period from a long work day to an enjoyable meal function. If a short cocktail reception precedes the dinner, many of the attendees who do not expect to go to dinner may show up for the reception. Once at the reception, some of them may stay for the dinner. This bit of uncertainty could cause difficulty with guarantees and seating arrangements, but proper advance planning should minimize the problem.

Even though there are several commonalities found in each beverage function, the catering sales representative still must query hosts regarding their perceived primary objectives for scheduling them. By knowing as much as possible about hosts' needs, desires, and objectives, the catering executive can suggest the types of functions that will satisfy them.

BEVERAGE MENU PLANNING

It is relatively easy to develop a drink menu. If the host wants a particular type of drink, you should be able to provide it. If you do not have the necessary ingredients in stock, you usually can get them before the date booked for the function. If you have sufficient production and service equipment to handle a standard drink menu, you essentially have enough equipment to prepare and serve just about any type of drink hosts and guests might request.

Most hosts are satisfied with the standard drink menu. This menu usually includes a red, white, and white zinfandel wine; a domestic light beer and domestic regular beer; a few soft drink brands; drink mixers; and at least one brand each of scotch, gin, vodka, bourbon, rum, tequila, and Canadian whisky.

The top-of-the-line drink menu offers a wide selection of liquor brands, both imported and domestic. For instance, a guest who wants a gin and tonic does not have to settle for the one brand offered on the standard drink menu (that is, the club's "well" brand). Chances are he or she can choose from among two or three brands of gin. In other words, guests are offered the choice of several "call" brands.

Some hosts may want to specify each brand of liquor and nonalcoholic beverage offered during the beverage function. However, when shopping for beverage service, most hosts will not want to select all brands. Usually some of them will choose only those few that absolutely must be offered in order to satisfy guests. For instance, some hosts may want to specify the exact brand names of wines served at catered meal functions, but not those liquors served during the premeal receptions.

Instead of specifying each brand name of beverage that must be served at the catered event, most hosts would rather concentrate on the price per drink, price per bottle, labor charges, specific needs (such as a particular style of cocktail service), and/or the price charged for each hour the bar is open. This does not mean, however, that you should ignore the subject of well liquor versus call or premium liquor.

You will need to broach this subject with potential hosts. One way to do this is to develop a drink menu that notes all brand names and the prices charged per container. For instance, you might note that a well brand costs $20.00 per liter, plus, plus, and that a call brand costs $25.00 per liter, plus, plus. If a host desires, he or she can then mix and match well brands and call brands and create a unique drink menu.

Occasionally, you will encounter hosts or guests who have personal drink recipes they want your bartenders to prepare. For example, a guest may prefer a unique type of martini made in a special way. A host may also desire special drinks for the event if it has a special theme. Usually it is no problem for you to honor these requests if you know about them in advance so that you can stock the necessary ingredients. But if guests request off-menu selections at the last minute, you may not be able to accommodate them. While a bartender could run off to one of the club's permanent bar outlets to service a special request, unfortunately this could slow down service drastically and disappoint the other guests.

BEVERAGE MENU PRICING

Beverage functions can be priced several ways. The catering sales representative usually can offer a few alternatives to hosts. However, before discussing pricing procedures with hosts, it is important to determine if the beverage function will be offered as a (1) cash bar; (2) open bar; or (3) combination of cash bar and open bar.

Cash Bar

A cash bar is sometimes referred to as a no-host bar. In order to get drinks at a cash bar, guests will need to pay for them personally. The guests typically must purchase drink tickets from a separate cashier and give them to the bartenders in exchange for drinks. At a small beverage function, the bartenders may take cash and prepare and serve drinks, thereby eliminating the cashier position.

Open Bar

An open bar is sometimes referred to as a host bar. Guests do not pay for their drinks. The client (that is, host) or a sponsor pays for them. Guests can usually drink as much as they want and whatever they want during the beverage function without having to pay. Charges for this type of service are either by the drink count or by the total product consumed.

The catering sales representative must warn the host that some of his or her guests may not take kindly to the open bar that stocks a very limited amount of merchandise. While guests usually will go along with limiting the amount of wine served at a sit-down meal, they may get upset if they must wait in line at a portable bar only to find that their favorite type of beverage is gone. The gin drinker can live with an off brand of gin, but he or she will not be happy if bourbon or rye are the only alternatives left. This also reflects poorly on the club as the guest will perceive this as poor management or planning; therefore, a club manager may refuse to limit quantities but instead might limit the time the bar is open.

Combination Bar

A combination bar includes elements of both a cash bar where the guest pays and an open bar where the host pays. The typical combination bar arrangement involves the host paying for each guest's first two drinks, with the guests then paying for any subsequent ones. For instance, the host may purchase the first two drink tickets and issue them to each guest. After that, guests are on their own. If they want more drinks, they will need to purchase their own drink tickets.

The combination bar is the logical solution for the host who does not want to provide a limited stock of liquor at an open bar, yet cannot afford to allow guests unlimited consumption. Most guests would rather pay for one or two drinks if that is what it takes to get the exact products they want. They will usually ignore the extra costs long before they forget the fact that they were unable to indulge their desires.

Beverage Charges

The way in which liquor charges are set varies somewhat from food menu-pricing procedures. Generally speaking, with food, the menu price offered to potential hosts includes all relevant charges for food, labor, and direct and indirect operating expenses. With beverage, however, potential hosts usually can pick and choose how they want to pay these relevant charges. They can pay one price for everything, or they can opt for an itemized list of charges and pay for each one separately.

1. *Charge per drink.* This is the typical pricing procedure used for cash bars. Normally the price charged per drink is high enough to cover all relevant expenses.

Individual drink prices usually are set to yield a standard beverage cost percentage set by the club. For instance, mixed drink prices are based on a beverage cost percentage ranging from approximately 20 percent to 25 percent; wines and beers are priced to yield a beverage cost percentage of approximately 35 percent. The prices will be lower only if a host pays separately for other relevant charges.

The host sometimes can negotiate away some of these extra charges if a certain level of sales is attained unless he or she requests something special not normally provided by the club.

The price-per-drink method can also be used for open bars. Bartenders can keep track of all drinks prepared and served by ringing up each one on a precheck machine. At the end of the beverage function, a total count will be computed and extended by multiplying the number of drinks consumed by the agreed-upon price per drink. Consumption taxes and gratuities are added, and the final accounting is presented to the host for payment.

Some hosts may want the club to charge a relatively low price per drink at cash bars in order to minimize the financial impact on guests. The catering executive can accommodate these requests by charging hosts separately for the bartenders, cocktail servers, cashiers, security personnel, and/or room rental. Alternatively, he or she could suggest that the client directly subsidize the drink prices by, for example, paying the club $1.00 for each drink served.

When charging by the drink, the catering sales representative may offer a sliding scale of prices depending upon the size of the beverage function. For instance, you might charge $3.50 per drink for the first 500 drinks and then $3.00 per drink for those served thereafter.

2. *Charge per bottle.* This is a common pricing procedure used for open bars. The charge-per-bottle pricing method also is typically used when poured-wine service is offered during a luncheon or dinner meal function.

A physical inventory of all liquor is made at the beginning and end of the beverage function in order to determine liquor usage. Many clubs will charge the host for each opened bottle even though all the liquor is not used. If a host has booked several catering events during a short period of time, the leftover opened liquor could be used at the next function. Before doing this, check any liquor codes that may apply.

A club might charge for partial bottles, although this is an unusual practice. For instance, it could charge the host for each tenth of a container of nonperishable liquor consumed. However, if a container of perishable liquor such as draft beer and some wines is opened, the host is usually charged for the whole container even if some product is left over.

If the host pays for each bottle instead of per drink, he or she may save a bit of money in the long run, although it is usually more difficult to calculate costs and monitor consumption. For instance, if a liter of gin yields 15 drinks at a price of $3.00 each, the expected revenue is $45.00 per liter, plus, plus. Generally, though, a club catering department will not charge this amount if the host purchases the gin on a per-bottle basis. Usually the per-bottle charge in this case will be a little less. However, it cannot be significantly lower unless the host is willing to pay separately for other relevant charges.

3. *Charge per person.* This pricing option usually is available to hosts who want to offer open bars to their guests. Since the open bar reduces the

club's control over liquor consumption, the price per person usually is set fairly high to ensure a fair return.

The amount charged per guest will include a charge for food in addition to beverage. The client's final billing usually is based on the type and amount of foods and liquors desired and the amount of time the bar must remain open. For instance, if a host wants specialized, expensive canapes, quite a few call brands, and/or wants the bar to remain open longer than normal, the catering executive will charge much more per person than if the host settles for standard offerings. This method is often more attractive to hosts because they know the charges up front; there are no surprises.

4. *Charge per hour.* This is similar to the charge-per-person pricing procedure. The major difference is that this pricing method typically includes a sliding scale of charges. For instance, for 150 guests, a host may have to pay $1500 for the first hour of standard bar service and $1000 for the second hour. Since most guest consumption takes place in the first hour, the club can offer a lower price for the second hour and still earn a fair profit.

When using this pricing procedure, the catering executive must consider the number of guests expected. For instance, you might charge $1500 for the first hour if there are 150 guests or less. If you do not consider the number of guests, you have no control over the number of people who can show up at the event. You must have a guaranteed number of maximum guests expected before quoting a specific charge per hour.

To some extent, then, the charge-per-hour pricing strategy must be combined with the charge-per-person pricing strategy. For instance, you might charge $15.00 per person for the first hour, $10.00 per person for the second hour, and so forth. This combination strategy will usually satisfy those hosts who prefer a fixed charge per hour. It also ensures the club will retain control over sales, expenses, and profits.

5. *Flat-rate charge.* This is similar to the price-per-guest pricing procedure. With this pricing method, though, the host pays one bottom-line charge for the beverage function.

The flat-rate charge is usually based on the assumption that guests will consume an average of two drinks apiece during the first hour and one drink apiece per hour thereafter. The charge usually varies according to the number of guests expected and the amount of call liquor requested by hosts.

Some hosts prefer the flat-rate charge to other pricing methods since it is the easiest way to purchase a beverage function. And, no matter how much guests consume, hosts know in advance what the price will be. They do not have to worry about exceeding their budgets. And there is no need for the host to bother with inventorying empty liquor containers or auditing the number of drinks prepared and served.

Labor Charges

Hosts can usually opt to pay for liquor and labor charges separately. Some hosts prefer the convenience of one all-inclusive charge. However, many of them would gladly do some extra work if the potential savings are worthwhile.

When labor charges are segregated from food and beverage product charges, in effect you are giving clients an opportunity to save money. For instance, a host may be able to reduce the meal price if he or she is willing to accept a style of service, such as preset, preplated service, that is not very labor intensive. The same is true with the host who agrees to reduce the number of bartenders. Unfortunately, since these options can sometimes compromise food and beverage quality- and cost-control standards, you should not offer them indiscriminately unless hosts understand the potential trade-offs. Again this may reflect poorly on the club and damage its reputation. It is critically important that the minimum standards of the club are met and not sacrificed.

Sometimes labor charges are waived by the club. For instance, a very large party that generates a great deal of revenue may receive complimentary bartenders and cocktail servers.

Labor charges may also be waived if the beverage function generates a specific level of business. For example, the club may charge for three bartenders to staff a party, but agree to rebate half the charge if 300 or more drinks are served.

Although labor charges are negotiable to some extent, there are some general guidelines, such as the following:

1. *Charge for bartenders.* Customarily, hosts must hire a minimum number of bartenders for a minimum number of hours. For example, a club may have a policy that all beverage functions must have at least one bartender working a four-hour shift. This minimum is particularly common in union properties.

Often the labor charge for bartenders is based on a sliding scale. For instance, if two bartenders are scheduled, the hosts may have to pay $125.00 for the first hour, $75.00 for the second hour, and $50.00 for every hour thereafter.

2. *Charge for bar backs.* Generally speaking, there is no separate charge for bar backs. Their cost is normally included in the charge assessed for bartenders. For instance, if two bartenders are purchased by a client, their cost will normally include the cost of one bar back needed to assist them.

3. *Charge for cocktail servers.* Cocktail servers can cost almost as much as bartenders. For instance, if a host wants a few cocktail servers to

pass trays of filled wine glasses, this little touch of luxury will add significantly to his or her final bill.

Some hosts view cocktail servers as an unnecessary cost. If a beverage function has two or three portable bars set up throughout the room, it may be more convenient to let guests give their orders directly to bartenders instead of to cocktail servers. In fact, in some cases, the additional layer of service imposed by cocktail servers can slow down service as well as add unnecessarily to a host's costs.

4. *Charge for cashiers.* Most hosts will not allow clubs to schedule cash bars unless they agree to employ at least one cashier. They typically will not let bartenders handle cash since this extra work will slow down beverage production and service significantly. It can also be unsanitary if bartenders handle cash and then touch glasses and drink ingredients. Furthermore, bartenders handling cash also creates additional security problems. Separate cashiers are an excellent form of financial checks and balances and must be used if tight control is desired. Sometimes a function will want to use its own cashiers. If this is the case, the bar would function as an open bar with the host paying by the drink.

Hosts may be able to have cash bars without cashiers if state and local liquor codes allow them to purchase drink tickets in advance and resell them to their guests. Unfortunately, this could backfire if guests want to purchase more drink tickets during the function and there is no cashier available to accommodate their needs.

If you allow hosts to purchase drink tickets for resale to guests, you should exert some control over the resale prices. If local laws allow, a host may decide to add a personal profit markup to the prices you charge, thereby leaving the impression with guests that the club's prices are too high when in reality the host is dictating the excessive prices. You should ensure that resale prices are not exorbitant or, if they are, make certain the host informs his or her guests that the club is not responsible for them. As an aside, if a host decides to engage in this repricing strategy, he or she may need a temporary business license.

5. *Charge for security.* It is unusual for a catered function to have extra security assigned to it. However, if a large beverage function has a cash bar and/or there are minors expected at the event, a client may feel more comfortable if the club provides an extra margin of safety.

Since in this situation the club may be at risk, a client may expect the club catering department to absorb the added security costs. However, since the typical club employs a standard, in-house, licensed security service to patrol the entire property, usually the client will need to pay for anything beyond this.

Some hosts may be more than willing to pay a few extra dollars to hire additional security so that they have one less thing to worry about. The catering sales representative should broach this subject with hosts because some of them may be unaware that they can employ additional plainclothes and/or uniformed security and, thereby, gain some peace of mind.

6. *Charge for corkage.* Some hosts may want to purchase liquor from a liquor store, or have it donated, and have it served at their beverage functions. In some cases, the hosts wish to do this because they think they will save money by avoiding the higher prices necessarily charged by the club. In other cases, clients are not concerned about cost, but are motivated strictly by the desire to serve something special that only they are able to obtain.

Some clubs have policies prohibiting guests from bringing in and serving their own food and beverage products. And some state and local government agencies, especially health districts, may prohibit this type of thing. However, if there are no restrictions, and the club is willing to allow hosts to use their own liquor, usually a corkage fee is charged.

The corkage fee charged is typically based on the club's estimated labor cost needed to handle the products. For instance, you may need labor to receive a special delivery, store it, and deliver it to the portable bar. You also may need labor to set up a clean drink area, keep it clean, maintain clean glassware and sufficient ice, and so forth. The more expense involved, the higher the corkage fee must be.

Part of the corkage fee may represent a type of luxury or privilege tax assessed on hosts. For instance, you may want to charge something for the privilege of bringing personal liquor into your licensed establishment. You also want to charge the hosts because you lose the opportunity to serve profitable beverages yourself.

Hosts who want to bring in and serve their own liquor usually will do so only when serving wines. For instance, it is not unusual for a meeting to have a few corporate sponsors, one of which might be a winery. Naturally the winery will want its wines served at one of the catered events. To keep the peace and accommodate a good host, the club usually will make arrangements to honor this request.

A corkage fee is normally quoted on a per-bottle basis with a variation for bottle size. For instance, you might charge $5.00 for each outside wine bottle brought in by the client and served by your staff.

A corkage fee might also be extracted from the host in the form of drink setup charges. For example, if a host brings in a very special, very old brandy that is unavailable locally, you may agree to handle it only if you can charge $2.00 per setup, that is, $2.00 every time you use the liquor to make a finished drink.

Figure 6.1 shows a planning sheet for beverage service.

PRIVATE FUNCTION BAR
REQUIREMENTS

Member: _____   *Day & Date:* _____

Nature of Function: _____   *Room Name:* _____

Number Expected: _____   *Number of Bars:* _____   *Placement:* _____

LIQUOR

☐ *We provide liquor. Charge by the drink*

☐ *They provide liquor. Set-up Charge $3.00 per person*
   We order & pick up   /   Members will bring liquor

WINE

☐ *We provide _____ wine at $____ per bottle*

☐ *They provide wine ($3.00 per bottle corkage fee if no set-up charge incurred)*

☐ *Champagne by the the bottle $_____*   ☐ *Member will bring own champagne*

BEER

☐ *Beer by the bottle*

☐ *Keg Beer: _____Pony Keg   _____Keg   (Brand:_____)*
   ($75)   *($150)*

Special Considerations:

Figure 6.1.   Private party bar plan (reprinted with permission of the Kingston club).

TYPES OF BEVERAGE FUNCTIONS

As with meal functions, each type of beverage function presents unique challenges. In some cases, the number of challenges increases considerably if the beverage function must be arranged around a meal function. For instance, not only must a predinner cocktail reception go off without a hitch, it must also set the stage for the dinner that follows it. Any guest dissatisfaction erupting during the reception may carry over to the banquet service and cause additional unhappiness.

Cocktail Reception

The cocktail reception is one of the most common types of beverage functions. Those held during the work week usually are scheduled during the early evening hours, just after the end of the normal business day. On weekends, there is more flexibility, but, as a general rule, cocktail receptions are ordinarily scheduled after 5:00 P.M.

Cocktail receptions often precede a dinner event. Most are scheduled for only about 45 minutes to an hour. In almost all instances, at least a few foods are served along with the liquor.

Hospitality Suite

In clubs with guest sleeping rooms, members or guests may choose to host a hospitality suite in their room. Sometimes they are set up in two or more guest rooms with connecting doors that can be stripped of their beds and other guest amenities in order to accommodate the reception's production and service equipment, supplies, employees, and guests.

In some cases, a hospitality suite may be set up in a public area. For instance, a small meeting room may be converted to a hospitality suite. This may be less expensive for the host than reserving a sleeping room suite. In addition it may be more convenient for guests to locate.

If a hospitality suite is held in a guest room, usually the club's room service department handles the event. Private hospitality suites are not usually serviced by the catering staff. Generally speaking, catering is involved only when booking the event and/or when the hospitality suite is held in a public area.

Hospitality suites are normally open only in the evening, after the regular business day is over.

Poured-Wine Service

This type of beverage service is part of a meal function. Many dinner events include one or two wines. In some instances, the wines are opened and preset on the dining tables. Guests may serve themselves, or the food servers may be responsible for serving the wine.

At more elaborate meals, cocktail servers, supervised by a sommelier, may be in charge of wine service. This is especially true if guests are offered a choice of wines. It is also more common when a rare and/or expensive wine is served with each course.

Special Events

Alcoholic beverages, especially wines, are often the stalwarts of special functions. For instance, many fund-raising events are centered around wine-and-cheese tastings, meet-the-winemaker dinners, and introductions of new wineries and new wine products.

Unique alcoholic beverage presentations are also used by hosts to generate excitement and enthusiasm at their catered events. For example, you may encounter a host who wants to book a dinner where the first Beaujolais of the season is served. Or there may be some hosts requesting unique selections, such as Bloody Mary breakfasts and champagne parties.

LIQUOR LAWS

Of all the products and services sold by club caterers, none are subject to more governmental control and regulation than liquor sales and service. The club must adhere to liquor laws enacted by federal, state, and local governments. While there is some similarity in liquor laws throughout the nation, usually each state and each local municipality in particular have unique liquor codes.

Illegal Liquor Sales

No matter where the club is located in the United States, there are at least four types of illegal liquor sales that must be avoided by the club catering department.

1. *Sales to minors.* In most parts of the United States, it is illegal to sell alcoholic beverages to anyone under 21 years of age. Usually the law allows you to refuse liquor service to anyone you suspect is under age. This is true even if the person in question shows you what appears to be a legitimate identification card that indicates legal drinking age.

Most parts of the country also prohibit minors from being inside a tavern or liquor store. The catering staff must ensure that minors are not allowed near the portable bar areas.

Admittedly, it is very difficult to police guests' movements during a catered function. While club bars and gift shops are ever vigilant, there is a tendency to relax normal crowd control procedures when serving a private party, especially if there is the feeling that hosts will get upset if you adhere strictly to the letter of the law. However, the catering executive must not surrender to this temptation to relax standards. If you are caught serving minors, you can rest assured that the private party defense will receive a cold reception from the legal authorities. Furthermore, the host will usually be one of the first people to complain that you failed to exercise reasonable care.

2. *Sales to intoxicated persons.* It is illegal to serve alcohol to a person who is legally intoxicated. In fact, in most locales, the law stipulates that you cannot serve alcohol to anyone who even appears to be intoxicated, whether or not they are above the legal limit.

In most states, a person is legally intoxicated if his or her blood alcohol concentration (BAC) is 0.10 percent. In some parts of the country (such as California and Utah), a person is legally intoxicated if his or her BAC is 0.08.

It is impossible for you to accurately predict each guests's BAC. For instance, after consuming one drink, a young person may appear intoxicated. On the other hand, an older guest with considerable drinking experience who has had several drinks may be legally intoxicated, yet he or she may show no outward signs of intoxication.

One way to solve this problem is to keep track of the number of drinks each guest consumes and slow service down whenever a guest has had approximately enough liquor to cause legal intoxication. The average person's liver needs about one hour to eliminate the alcohol in one drink. If he or she has more than one drink per hour, the BAC will increase quickly. For instance, if a person weighing 125 pounds consumes three average drinks (an average drink being one that contains approximately one ounce of alcohol) in one hour, his or her BAC could be 0.10 or above. Unless this person reduces his or her liquor consumption significantly or refrains from drinking during the rest of the catered function, the liver will not have enough time to reduce the BAC to a legal level before the function ends.

Some clubs use other strategies to prevent overconsumption. For instance, instead of dictating the number of drinks a guest can consume, you could offer

- *Minidrinks.* There is a budding trend in the beverage industry of offering smaller drinks at lower prices. For instance, if you normally charge $3.75 for a highball with 1.5 ounces of liquor and 6 ounces of mixer, you might offer one with 0.75 ounces of liquor and 5 ounces of mixer and charge only $2.75. In the long run, guests will probably spend just as much money. Altering the consumption pattern will make the guest more likely to remain sober.

- *Frozen drinks.* Another trend is for bars to offer frozen concoctions that have only a hint of alcoholic beverage. When frozen, the guest is less able to determine the amount of alcohol present. Furthermore, many guests seem to love these types of drinks. Unfortunately, they are much harder to prepare and serve, so you may have to charge more to cover the additional expense. They also take longer to drink, as the typical guest cannot take too much cold too fast.

- *Low-alcohol liquors.* Some states and local municipalities allow the sale of low-alcohol products. For instance, instead of using an 86-proof bourbon, you might be able to purchase a 56-proof product in your area. Even though this product has less alcohol, it is a better choice than merely adding more mixer to the 86-proof product. Excess mixer tends to give the finished drink a washed-out character. The low-alcohol alternative tends to retain the characteristic flavor of the original beverage even though it contains less alcohol.

If there is any doubt about a person's BAC, you must cut that person off. When this is necessary, try to use peer pressure to your advantage. Ask the member, or the host, to help you handle the situation. Be courteous to the guest and minimize the confrontation. Note that you cannot serve any more alcohol, but you can offer food or nonalcoholic beverage alternatives. Or you could see to it that the guest gets a safe ride home. Retain a professional demeanor and do not prolong guest contact any longer than necessary. Cutting off a member or his or her guest is always a difficult challenge. It must be done carefully and in most cases should be handled by a manager.

Some clubs participate in the designated-driver program, where at least one guest in a small group consumes no alcohol so that he or she will be able to drive everyone home safely. Unfortunately, this concept has backfired on some occasions. For instance, if you cut off a guest who is part of a designated-driver group, he or she may become quite agitated. After all, the guest may assume that the designated-driver program allows him or her to get completely intoxicated. The fact that it is illegal to serve visibly intoxicated persons is at odds with the customer who has arranged ahead of time for a safe ride.

Liquor laws are sometimes contradictory, as are some of the solutions we have developed over the years to combat drunk driving. But that does not alter the fact that you cannot serve liquor to an intoxicated guest, even if that person is chained to a table and cannot drive. To do so puts your liquor license, not to mention your career, in jeopardy.

3. *Hours of operation.* Most local municipalities restrict the hours during which liquor can be served in a commercial beverage establishment. For

instance, you may be unable to accommodate a host's request for a champagne brunch because no liquor can be served before noon.

You will need to check the local codes to determine if these restrictions apply to private parties. If they do, you must ensure that catering sales representatives do not book beverage functions during the prohibited hours.

4. *Liquor license.* To serve liquor, you must hold the appropriate liquor license. For instance, a full tavern license, or hard liquor license, is usually needed to serve spirits, wines, and beers for consumption on premises. The typical club usually holds this type of liquor license.

If the club holds only a soft liquor license—that is, a wine-and-beer license, it cannot serve distilled spirits. To say the least, this puts a large crimp in your ability to sell full-service catering functions. It is possible, though, that under these conditions, the hosts may be able to bring in their own spirits, in which case you can earn your revenue by charging corkage fees or drink setup charges.

You may be in an area where the club cannot purchase its own liquor. In this case, you must usually have a private club license or similar license in order to prepare and serve liquor brought in by the host. For instance, in some parts of the country, the guest must buy liquor at a state-operated liquor store and bring it to the club. The guest then pays a drink setup charge for each drink prepared and served. At the end of the function, the guest carries home the leftover product.

Potential Liquor Code Violations

The catering executive must ensure that all local liquor laws are obeyed when booking and serving group functions. While the illegal sales noted in the previous section are common throughout the United States, each local municipality usually has one or two unique regulations that place additional controls on the local liquor licensees. Those that may affect the club catering department are

1. *Food served with beverage.* In some parts of the country, the local Alcohol Beverage Commission (ABC) may prohibit beverage functions that do not offer foods. In these areas, a person applying for a liquor license to sell and serve alcoholic beverages for on-premises consumption must show that he or she intends to serve foods as well.

Alcohol should never be consumed on an empty stomach. Without food to slow down the rate at which alcohol is absorbed into the blood stream, guests run the risk of becoming intoxicated very quickly. If these guests leave the function and drive away in their cars, unfortunate, preventable traffic accidents may occur. By requiring you to serve foods at all beverage functions, the local government authorities are giving society one more weapon to fight these tragic situations.

2. *Bring your own bottle.* Before allowing hosts to bring in their own liquor, you need to check with the local ABC to see if the liquor code permits this. In some parts of the United States, you are not allowed to use liquor purchased from a retail liquor store in a bar operation that serves liquor by the drink for on-premises consumption. You must purchase all liquor from licensed liquor wholesale distributors or, in control states, from the authorized state liquor agency.

3. *Free liquor.* You may be prohibited from giving away any liquor during a catered function. Usually you must sell the beverages for a fair market price.

Similarly, you may be prohibited from offering sliding-scale price ranges to your catering clients. For instance, you may be unable to offer the first 250 drinks for $3.00 apiece and anything over that amount for $2.00 apiece.

In some parts of the country, you are prohibited from offering any other types of sale-price promotions. For instance, happy hours, drink-and-drown nights, two-for-one specials, and so forth are quickly disappearing from our industry.

Free liquor or reduced-price liquor tends to encourage overconsumption. By outlawing these types of pricing practices, the local ABC keeps a tight rein on the irresponsible sale and purchase of alcoholic beverages.

4. *Self-service.* To control further overconsumption of alcohol, some local municipalities may prohibit guests from preparing their own drinks at group functions. If this restriction exists in your area, usually it does not infringe upon the hospitality suite host's ability to allow guests to mix their own beverages.

5. *Alcoholic content of liquor used.* There may be a regulation prohibiting the purchase and use of closed containers of liquors that have exceptionally high alcoholic contents. Some parts of the country prohibit the use of any distilled spirit that exceeds 100 proof.

Some hosts may be unaware of this type of restriction, so it is up to you to inform them. This is especially true for functions that attract attendees from all over the country. You should let these hosts know that some drinks, such as a traditional zombie, cannot be prepared and served.

Similarly, if an out-of-town host wants to bring his or her personal liquor, assuming the liquor code and your club policy permit this, you must ensure that anything brought in does not violate alcoholic content restrictions.

6. *Amount of alcohol per drink.* Some local municipalities may restrict the amount of alcohol you can put into each drink. For instance, doubles, boilermakers, and pitchers of beer may be outlawed because they can cause overconsumption of alcohol. Likewise for drinks that contain more than one type of liquor. For instance, you may not be allowed to prepare and serve drinks such as traditional mud slides, Long Island teas, and scorpions because they contain multiple liquors.

The major problem with a multiple-liquor drink is that one of them can have the same clinical effect on a person's central nervous system as two or three average drinks. The average person's liver can eliminate alcohol from the body only at the rate of about one average drink per hour. The average drink—a typical highball—contains about 0.5 ounce of alcohol. However, a traditional mud slide contains approximately 1.5 ounces of alcohol. If a guest consumes two mud slides in one hour, his or her BAC may exceed 0.10.

7. *Leftover liquor.* The local ABC may prohibit letting hosts or guests take home any leftover liquor. If a host books a beverage function and agrees to pay for each bottle served as well as each bottle opened, you must let him or her know up front that no leftovers can leave the club.

If you face this situation, you could charge hosts the standard price for each full container consumed and a prorated amount for each partial container used. This probably will satisfy all hosts except those who order something special that cannot be reused at one of the club's regular bars for which you can offer no compensation. If these hosts want something special, but are unwilling to leave any of it behind, one way to solve the problem is to ask permission from the host to underorder the product from the liquor wholesaler so that there will be none left over.

Alcohol Awareness Training

Some local municipalities require anyone who sells, serves, distributes, or gives away alcoholic beverages to take an approved server-awareness training course before they are allowed to work in a licensed alcohol beverage establishment. These courses are similar in concept to the sanitation courses that some local health districts require all food handlers to take before they can work in a public foodservice establishment.

The typical server-awareness training involves instruction in:

1. Dealing with minors
2. Recognizing the telltale signs of intoxication
3. Dealing with intoxicated guests

4. Understanding the clinical effects of alcohol on the human body

5. Knowing local liquor codes

Server-awareness training courses offered throughout the United States vary from about 4 hours to 20 hours of instruction. They usually follow the format initially established by the Techniques of Alcohol Management (TAM) course, or the Bar Code course developed by the Educational Foundation of the NRA.

Before hiring a permanent beverage staff member or putting anyone on the A-list or B-list, the catering executive must ensure that the job candidates have the appropriate training. Usually they receive a pocket card after taking the course that they can show to potential employers to prove they have been certified.

THIRD-PARTY LIABILITY

If you serve an intoxicated guest or a minor and he or she goes out and hurts an innocent third party, the club, server, and host may be liable for damages to the injured person.

Some states have passed dram-shop laws that specify exactly your liability in these instances. Under dram-shop legislation, if it is proved that you served a minor or legally intoxicated person who causes damage to a third party, you usually will be held at least partially responsible. For example, if a minor you served gets into a traffic accident and injures someone, the injured party can sue the driver, server, club, and even the host. Chances are the minor does not have the same financial resources as the club. Consequently, the club stands to lose a great deal since it has the deep pockets that a judge or jury can tap for huge financial awards.

In a dram-shop state, usually the club cannot defend itself if it is proved that its employees served a minor or legally intoxicated guest. You cannot, for example, tell the judge that the minor presented what looked like a legitimate ID card. Nor can you plead that "the person appeared to be 30 years old." Such defenses usually are not permitted where absolute liability has been legislated. As a result, if you serve a minor or legally intoxicated person who causes damage to an innocent third party, you can count on being held responsible, period.

It is important for hosts to realize that some states have passed social-host laws. Social-host laws hold function hosts liable for private functions hosted in their homes or at other locations. For instance, if a minor served at a private party held at a club inflicted damage on an innocent third party, the function host and the club could share responsibility for the accident.

Most states do not have dram-shop or social-host laws. However, the club, server, and client still could be held liable under common law. Under common law, an injured third party can sue you for damages. However, it is up to him or her to prove you were negligent in serving the person who caused the accident. For instance, if you can prove that a minor whom you served proved his or her age by showing what appeared to be a legitimate ID, chances are you would be absolved from liability, especially if you can also show that the minor appeared to be older than 21.

Unlike dram-shop or social-host laws, under common law, the burden of proof shifts to the plaintiff. He or she must prove you were negligent and did not exercise reasonable care. As long as you followed generally accepted beverage service principles and practices, usually you can mount an adequate defense. A word of caution: Every jury sees a lawsuit differently. Reasonable care must be a well-established policy within the club.

In addition to the club and the person causing the accident, hosts and servers can also be named parties to a lawsuit under common law. Hosts with deep pockets can rest assured that, one way or another, they will be defendants.

It is imperative that hosts realize the types of risks they incur when booking beverage functions. In some cases, they may need to be reminded of this if they expect you to cater a wild affair such as a stag party. A few minutes spent discussing liability problems faced by our industry should dispel these requests quickly.

7

Function Room Selection and Setup

The catering sales representative must select an appropriate function room to house the event. Along with the host, he or she needs to consider several things when making this selection. The major factors influencing the selection process are a function room's appearance, location, utilities, and amount of floor space.

APPEARANCE

Often the function room's appearance is high on most hosts' priority lists. In fact, frequently a potential host is attracted to the club primarily because of the ambience provided. For instance, a function room in the Chicago Club in Chicago overlooks Lake Michigan. The view is phenomenal. To say the least, many hosts want to book this room regardless of any other advantages or disadvantages it offers.

Room dimensions, ceiling height, columns, exits, entrances, the number and quality of restroom facilities, the colors and types of floor and wall coverings, sound insulation, and lighting are also important, especially for those clubs whose function rooms do not enjoy breathtaking views.

Most room dimensions are acceptable to the host so long as he or she can avoid the bowling-alley effect—hosts will be turned off by a function room that is long and narrow. This type of dimension precludes guest mingling, participation, and networking. It also harms service because many guests will tend to gravitate toward one end of the room; for instance, the bar at one end may be very busy, but the other end may have only a few guests.

Hosts tend to be turned off by columns, especially if they have guest speakers and/or a considerable amount of audiovisual services scheduled (such as films). A few are acceptable, but too many will detract from the catered event unless the catering sales representative can suggest a room setup that will minimize their negative effects. For instance, buffet tables can be arranged between some decorated columns that may enhance the room's appearance. Or the columns can be decorated to enhance a wedding theme.

Usually a function room has a sufficient number of entrances and exits if for no other reason than that the local fire code requires them. Many hosts will take this factor for granted; for instance, they will assume that there will be a sufficient number of crash doors (that is, emergency exit doors equipped with panel bar opening devices that sound an alarm when opened). Other hosts, though, will be very concerned with entrance and exit doors. For instance, some luncheon hosts that have speakers and visual aids scheduled will want to know how easy or difficult it will be to transport their materials to and from the function room.

Doors should not be near a speaker's stand, head table, or display table. You do not want latecomers disrupting the event. For instance, if a movie or slide presentation is part of the event, if possible, have the room set up so that the doors are on the side of the room. By so doing, a latecomer does not have to walk in front of the projector and interrupt the presentation.

As with the number of entrances and exits, many hosts will not evaluate the number and quality of restroom facilities when booking their functions. However, the director of catering will ensure that the facilities are well maintained and easy for guests to locate. Many guests' lasting impressions of the club will be based solely on these factors.

The colors and types of floor and wall coverings are usually the first thing a host sees when viewing a function room. In addition to meeting building code requirements, they should be free from stains and in good repair. They also should be in good taste and executed with style.

If you have any choice in selecting floor and wall coverings before the club is developed, or before it undergoes remodeling, you should choose those that are fire retardant, easy to maintain, and durable. The colors and types of materials used to make these coverings should be consistent with the types of functions booked in the room and the type of lighting used.

Carpeting also needs to be consistent with the club's architectural style. For instance, an old club with traditional architecture, layout, and design would lose some of its atmosphere if a contemporary-design carpet were installed throughout the property.

With carpeting, you are specially concerned with the proper cushioning, installation procedures, traffic rating (that is, medium, heavy, or extra heavy), and maintenance costs. You do not want guests to feel uneven padding, or see ragged seams and/or carpeting that is excessively worn in the traffic areas. Moreover, the carpet selected should be easy to clean and repair.

Unsophisticated hosts may not consider a function room's sound and lighting capabilities when selecting a room. However, if there are any inadequacies, they will be noticed during the event and cause guest dissatisfaction. For instance, if platform speakers are scheduled during the meal function, the room used cannot have any dead space, that is, area(s) in the room where sound is absent or unintelligible.

If the function room is too close to the kitchen, hallways, and service corridors, the setup crew must ensure that sufficient air walls, room dividers, or other types of baffles are installed to prevent unwanted noises from seeping into the function room. Club employees moving about in these behind-the-scenes areas may occasionally cause distractions. For instance, some guests may be unable to hear a platform speaker if employees are overheard shouting, laughing, or talking. Employees should be trained to tread lightly in these areas in order to minimize noise pollution.

A similar type of installation will also be needed if you have to minimize the amount of ambient light, that is, unavoidable light seeping into a darkened room from around doors, draped windows, or production and service areas.

LOCATION

Ideally, the function room should be located next to the production and service areas. This will increase the efficiency of the catering and banquet staffs. It also ensures that foods will be much more attractive and will retain their culinary quality better since there is a shorter road from kitchen to guest.

In some clubs, the kitchen is on one floor level and the function rooms are on other levels. If there are not enough service elevators, it can be a nightmare transporting finished menu items. It can be especially difficult if you need to share the inadequate service elevators with several club departments. For instance, if there is a meal function in the club, housekeeping may be prohibited from using the service elevators during the function period. In this situation, the catering manager will need to coordinate very carefully the use of the service elevators with other club departments. Unfortunately, in our industry, all too often you encounter this type of design flaw. The production and service flow patterns are not always given high priority by architects and designers, especially when they are constrained with a tight property development budget. Even if the construction budget is ample, an architect or designer may not have enough familiarity with the catering department's needs to plan the production, service, and function areas properly.

If the function room is a great distance from the kitchen, the menu planner may be limited to only those foods that hold up well. The banquet staff also will need to use hot- and cold-transport equipment in order to preserve the foods' culinary quality en route. Without this equipment, food items are more vulnerable to quality deterioration when they must be preplated in advance and transported long distances. This could increase food costs if you have to prepare additional items to replace those that cannot be served. The extra effort also could increase labor costs.

UTILITIES

The meeting hosts are concerned about the function room's utility capabilities. Usually the catering sales representative has room schematic drawings that illustrate them. These drawings should be included in any mailed sales solicitation because these hosts will book functions that tend to tax a function room's utilities.

The catering sales representatives must be conversant with each function room's utilities. Clients will be concerned with

1. Types of electricity available in-house
2. Types of electricity that can be brought in
3. Maximum wattage available
4. Maximum lighting available
5. Number of separate lighting controls; for example, if a client will be using rear-screen projection, you will need to darken the area behind the screen while leaving the rest of the room light
6. Heating, ventilation, and air conditioning (HVAC) capacity
7. Closed-circuit TV, radio, and VCR system
8. Closed-circuit audiovisual system

9. Paging system
10. Number, types, and locations of
    a. Electrical outlets
    b. Electrical floor, wall, and ceiling strips
    c. Phone jacks
    d. Dimmer switches
    e. Vents and ducts
    f. Built-in speakers
11. (If the function will be held in an exhibit hall) the number, types, and locations of
    a. Gas hookups
    b. Exhaust fans
    c. Floor sinks (i.e., drains)
    d. Water connections

SPACE REQUIREMENTS

The amount of floor space available is perhaps the function room's critical feature. The catering sales representative must shoulder the responsibility for determining the amount of square footage needed. He or she cannot expect the host to make this calculation.

Several factors influence the amount of space needed, the most critical of which are

1. *Number of guests.* The local fire code will dictate the maximum number of people who can be legally housed in a function room. This maximum usually is an excellent guide when planning a stand-up function, such as a cocktail reception. It can also be a good guide when planning theater or auditorium setups. However, some events, such as banquet or classroom setups, will accommodate fewer persons.

Generally speaking, for most meal and beverage functions, you would be unable to accommodate the maximum number of persons allowed by the local fire code. The room setups required for these types of events will usually reduce significantly the number of guests that can be handled efficiently and comfortably.

2. *Types of dining tables used.* You need to allocate about 10 square feet per guest if seating is at rectangular banquet tables. If round tables are used, you will need about 12.5 square feet per guest. These estimates will

suffice if you are using standard chairs whose chair seats measure 20 inches by 20 inches. You should adjust your estimates if you use smaller chairs (seats measuring 18 inches by 18 inches) or larger armchairs (which usually have a minimum width of 24 inches).

3. *Aisle space.* Space between tables is needed for server access and customer maneuverability. Aisles between tables and around food and beverage stations should be a minimum 36 inches wide and that is tight. It is preferable to have aisles 48 to 54 inches wide. For instance, weddings usually need wider aisles to accommodate the lavish gowns worn by the bride and some guests (see Figure 7.1).

When planning space between tables, remember to leave enough entry and exit room for guests. You should plan to allocate sufficient cross-aisle space, that is, aisles used for guests to collect and funnel in and out of the function areas. A cross-aisle space should be approximately 6 feet wide.

Cross-aisle space is very important when setting large functions. For instance, for a function requiring 100 tables, you cannot set a square layout of 10 tables by 10 tables without allowing some additional space for guests to maneuver comfortably to the middle tables from the outside perimeter. As a general rule of thumb, if you need 100 tables, you should set up four blocks of 25 tables. Within the 25-table block, 36-inch aisle space may be sufficient. However, there should be a 6-foot-wide cross-aisle space surrounding each block of 25 tables.

Before making any final decisions, regarding aisle space, you must check the local fire code for specific requirements.

4. *Dance floor space.* If the function includes dancing, you need about 3 square feet of dance floor per guest. A few clubs use roll-up dance floors. Alternatively, you could use layout squares—a type of portable dance floor that comes in sections of 3 feet by 3 feet (that is, 9 square feet); plan on using one section for every three guests (see Figure 7.2).

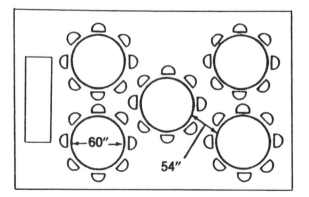

Figure 7.1. Recommended space between tables for weddings and similar functions.

OAK PORTABLE DANCE FLOOR ALSO IN STOCK IN THAI TEAK

Figure 7.2. Typical dance floor installation (courtesy of Sico Incorporated).

As a general rule, if a dance floor is required, the typical setup will measure approximately 24 feet by 24 feet. If using standard 9-square-foot sections, you will need 64 pieces of dance floor, 24 pieces of regular trim, 8 pieces of corner trim, and 256 set screws. The typical total setup covers approximately 600 square feet of floor space.

You usually will need to increase your estimate of dance floor space if you intend to set up two dance floors instead of one. For very large functions, a second dance floor is very convenient. Guests at the back of the room will not have to negotiate the long trail leading to the front where the single dance floor normally is located. On the other hand, this arrangement may divide the group into two subgroups unless you connect two diamond-shaped dance floors. If the function room is big enough, however, you should present this option to the client, along with the pros and cons, and let him or her consider it. Chances are, the client will appreciate the choice.

5. *Bandstand.* You should estimate about 10 square feet per band member. Drum sets usually require about 20 square feet. Large pianos, synthesizers, runways, and so forth also need additional space. Disc jockeys may need considerably more space to hold their equipment and CD collection. You should check the entertainment contract because it may specify the floor space required.

Bandstands and other similar attractions are sometimes elevated on risers. Stage risers come in many shapes and sizes. Their purpose is to elevate speakers, entertainers, or audiovisual equipment so that a large audience can see what is taking place at one end of the function room.

Some risers are nothing more than wooden boxes (4 feet by 8 feet by 6 inches) that can be moved from room to room. The most common ones are the folding risers (4 feet by 4 feet and 4 feet by 8 feet) that can be adjusted to several heights.

Risers may require steps. If so, you should provide steps that have attached handrails and a mechanism that allows them to be connected securely. If a guest falls from an improperly set stage, you might be hit with a lawsuit.

A lawsuit can also occur if someone falls from a riser. To minimize this possibility, risers should always be placed against a wall so that a guest cannot step back and fall off.

6. *Other entertainment.* You may need to allocate additional floor space for speakers, strolling musicians, and other similar entertainment. For instance, if the function includes a speaker or two, you may need space to house a podium, platform, or audiovisual equipment and wider aisles throughout the function room to allow the speaker to interact with the audience. Once again, you should check the entertainers' contracts for exact space requirements.

7. *Head table(s).* Head tables usually need about 25 to 100 percent more floor space than regular dining tables. Furthermore, if the tables will be placed upon risers, you must increase your space estimate accordingly to accommodate the platform area, steps, and the need to spread the table and guest weight properly over the stage. For instance, if using typical platform

sections measuring 4 feet by 4 feet and 4 feet by 8 feet, you would need to connect a 4 by 4 and a 4 by 8 to have enough space to accommodate a dining table measuring 3 feet by 8 feet. In other words, you will need about 48 square feet of platform space to accommodate approximately 24 square feet of dining table space. The 48 square feet will accommodate 4 guests seated at 24-inch intervals. The 12 square feet per person is usually the minimum amount needed for head table guests seated on a platform.

If you have head tables reserved for speakers, dignitaries, and other VIPs who will be addressing the guests after the meal, you may be asked to set up extra dining tables on the floor for these guests, near the head tables, so they can eat without feeling like they are in a fishbowl. Some guests do not want to sit at an elevated table and eat. If there is enough space in the function room, they can eat at regular dining tables, and then move up to the head tables just before the program begins.

Setting up extra dining tables allows you to maximize the number of VIPs who can be accommodated at the head tables. For instance, if you have 10 VIPs and 10 spouses, you can set up 20 place settings (that is, covers) at regular dining tables. And, if the host agrees, instead of setting up a head table for 20, you can set one for only the 10 VIPs. The spouses can remain at the dining tables after the meal.

This table arrangement may reduce your floor space needs and increase the banquet service staff's efficiency. However, you must gain the host's permission to do this because he or she may assume all spouses will be seated at the head table. You do not want to risk alienating guests or placing them in an embarrassing position.

8. *Bank maze.* A bank maze consists of posts (stanchions) and ropes set up to control guest traffic. You may want to use bank mazes to control traffic around cashier and ticket-taker stations. If they are necessary, you will need to allocate more floor space to accommodate them.

9. *Reception needs.* If the function room is used to house a reception and a meal, you will need enough space to handle both phases of the catered event. In most cases, you will be unable to reset the reception area in order to accommodate meal guests. There usually is insufficient time to do this. Furthermore, it is aesthetically unattractive.

To accommodate a reception adequately, you will need about 6 to 10 square feet of floor space per guest.

With 6 square feet, guests will feel a bit claustrophobic; they also will have a bit more trouble getting to the food and beverage stations. Consequently, they may eat and drink less. If a cost-conscious client is paying on a per-person basis where guests can eat and drink as much as they want for one price, you might consider allocating only about 6 square feet per person to keep the price low and your food and beverage costs under control. However, since some guests may perceive this arrangement negatively, you should use it only if other cost-reducing options cannot be pursued.

Seven and one-half square feet is considered to be a comfortably crowded arrangement. It is thought to be the ideal amount of floor space per guest for receptions and other similar functions.

Ten square feet provides more than ample space for guests to mingle and visit the food and beverage stations easily. It is an appropriate amount of floor space for an upscale reception. It is also an appropriate setup if the client is paying according to the amount of food and beverage consumed. You want guests to have enough room to eat and drink as much as they want so that your revenues are maximized.

As a general rule, a director of catering will try to allocate 10 square feet per guest for receptions, after taking into account space needs for equipment, tables, and employees. He or she will allocate more space if it is available. The typical club catering department strives to maintain a reputation for high-quality food, beverage, and service. It will provide as much luxury as it can within its budget, regardless of how the event is sold.

10. *Buffet table.*   All food stations need enough floor space for the tables and aisles. For instance, an 8-foot-long rectangular banquet table needs about 24 square feet for the table and about 60 square feet for aisle space if the table is against the wall or about 100 square feet if the table is accessible from all sides.

When determining the number of buffet tables needed, as well as the number of buffet lines required, you need to consider

   a. Number of guests expected

   b. Length of dining time

   c. Amount of service equipment required

   d. Type of service equipment required

   e. Type of menu

   f. Style of service

   g. Amount of decor desired on the buffet line

   h. Amount of total floor space available in the function room

Generally speaking, you must allocate approximately two running feet of buffet table for each food container needed. For instance, if you have to display 3 hot offerings, 3 cold offerings, and a condiment basket, you should set up a buffet table about 14 to 16 feet long. If you use two standard 8-foot rectangular banquet tables, you will need about 48 square feet of floor space for the buffet table and approximately 150 square feet of standard 3-foot aisle space surrounding the buffet table. The total allocation for this setup, then, is about 200 square feet.

11. *Beverage station.*   For self-service, nonalcoholic beverage stations, the setups are similar to buffet table setups. For instance, a hot-beverage station will need about as much space as a buffet table laden with foods. Bars, on the other hand, will need more space because you need room to store backup stock, ice, and coolers to hold beer and some wines. You also need to allocate enough working space for bartenders, bar backs, and, if applicable, cocktail servers. Generally speaking, the smallest portable bar you can use measures approximately 6 feet by 7 feet, or about 42 square feet. However, when you take into account the aisle and other space needed, you will need to allocate at least 150 square feet for the typical portable banquet bar setup.

If you are setting up portable bars for a large function, you may be able to reduce your space estimates if you can arrange to locate them in pairs. For instance, you may be able to locate two portable bars back-to-back in the middle of the function room so that the bars can share a common area where glassware, ice, wines, beers, and so forth are stored. This will eliminate duplicate storage areas and free up extra floor space.

12. *Side stand and bus cart.*   Similar to buffet table.

13. *Action station.*   Similar to buffet; however, you must allocate a bit more floor space so that guests can congregate and view the chefs' performances. Your floor space estimate also must be increased if the action station is elevated.

14. *Staging area.*   You may need to set up a temporary serving line in the function room. A band or disc jockey may need a place to store shipping containers. A host may need space to store party favors and similar items. You may need to allocate floor space to temporarily store lighting and sound equipment. Or you may need to set up a temporary service corridor on one end of the function room to store hot carts, cold carts, and gueridons. If you anticipate any of these needs, you will need to allocate sufficient space to accommodate them.

If you must allocate floor space for a staging area, you should block it off with pipe and draping so that it does not interfere with the appearance and ambience of the catered event.

15. *Display area.*   Sometimes clients need space to set up their own cashier stations, registration/information tables, kiosks, booths, and so forth. For instance, a host may need a cashier station in order to sell meal tickets to guests who have not prepaid, but who decided at the last minute to attend the event.

If you set up an area to handle all of the client's cashiering and check-in procedures, you must ensure that there is sufficient floor space to accommodate one or more cashiers, desks, tables, chairs, backdrops, service corridors, telephones, waste receptacles, lock boxes (to hold the used tickets and/or receipts to prevent reuse), and so forth. Some hosts may have lists of their display needs along with exact dimensions. If not, you should question them carefully about these requirements so that you do not have to rearrange the function room layouts at the last minute.

16. *Landing space.* This is the area where guests can discard empty plates, glasses, soiled napery, and waste. Generally speaking, the amount of landing space needed can be computed by adopting the space-estimating standards used to forecast buffet table space requirements.

You should set up a few empty tables to accommodate this need. If this is not possible, you can set up folding tray stands with empty trays on them.

Landing space should also be allocated on the buffet tables between and in front of food containers. Guests will need some place to set their drinks while putting food on their plates. They also will need room on the table to set their plates temporarily while deciding what foods to take.

17. *Meeting activity during the meal.* A host may want to have a business meeting and the meal or reception in the same function room. For instance, an association chapter may want the function room divided into two sections—one section housing the reception and the other housing an auditorium-style setup to accommodate the group's program.

The meeting activity can easily be accommodated if the function room is large enough to be divided appropriately. It cannot be accommodated as readily, however, if the meeting and the meal or reception must share the same space.

One way to handle events where space must be shared is to use a conference-room, U-shaped, or hollow-square setup. For instance, with a U-shaped setup, guests can conduct their meeting, and, when it is time to eat, roll-ins can be placed in the hollow section of the setup and foods arrange to allow self-service.

A conference-room setup usually requires no more space than the typical meal function; however, U-shaped or hollow-square setups may need two to three times as much floor space. According to Coleman Finkel, an industry consultant, the U-shaped setup is the least efficient use of floor space. It requires about 42 square feet per person.

18. *Style of service.* This is important if you are planning to use French or Russian service, because these service styles require up to twice as much floor space than the others. Some buffets, especially those where beautiful displays and several tables are used, may also need extra space. For instance, instead of the typical buffet floor space estimate, you may want to increase it by 50 to 100 percent if the function is very elaborate and you want to provide a luxury amount of space for all guests.

19. *Audience separation.* If it is necessary to divide or separate the audience, you may need considerably more floor space. For instance, if you set up smoking and nonsmoking sections, you should set one or two extra tables in each section unless you know exactly how many smokers and nonsmokers to expect. In the worst-case scenario, you will have several half-used tables in each section.

20. *Handicapped seating.* If you expect to have a physically challenged guest, you will need to allocate additional floor space. For instance, a wheelchair-bound guest will need a bit more space at the dining table as well as a wider aisle in which to navigate.

21. *Decor.* Some decorative pieces take up considerable space. You can minimize the amount if the host will agree to use, for example, facades instead of the real items.

PLANNING THE FUNCTION ROOM SETUP

Function room setups must be established well in advance. Table locations, exhibits, displays, locations of food and beverage stations, table sizes, head table, seating mix (that is, the number of each table size needed), table spacings, table settings, and preferred decor usually are planned by the catering sales representative and the host. Though you may occasionally encounter a host who brings in his or her own drawings showing how the room should be set up, most clients do not want to be bothered with these details; they are much more interested in the menu, price, and decor.

Using club floor plans and other schematic drawings that show square footage, dimensions, doors, and other factors that may be important to the host, several visual plans can be developed.

The catering sales representative can obtain templates from Meeting Planners International (www.mpiweb.org) to assist in developing suggested room setups. This professional meeting planners' organization also provides additional function room space/guest count guidelines that can be used to plan the function room arrangement. For instance, it provides a calculus you can use to determine the number of guests that can be seated comfortably, given a particular seating style and the available amount of square footage.

If your club can afford it, you can purchase computer software that will correlate the room's dimensions, location, doorways, service corridors, columns, protrusions, dead space, permanent service installations (such as a permanent bandstand, bar, and/or dance floor), and other limitations with the host's desires and draw out several suggested layouts for consideration (see Figure 7.3). For instance, the typical software program will draw a layout using industry standards for such things as distances between rows of

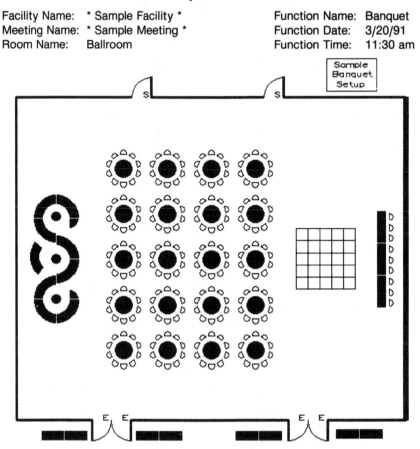

Figure 7.3. Example of computer-generated function room layout (courtesy of SCLM Software, Inc.; MEETINGMATRIX is a trademark of SCLM Software, Inc., and is used with permission).

chairs or tables, aisle space needed, and the optimal angles that should be set to accommodate video presentations. Most of these software packages also will automatically generate standard seating styles. If you are unhappy with a computer-generated layout, you usually can alter the data and ask the computer to draw another layout. You can continue doing this until the host is satisfied with the result.

These exercises provide an opportunity to try out different room set-ups. The host and catering sales representative will then be in a good position to decide what will work best.

These exercises also help the club in many other ways. For instance, the preferred function room setup will indicate the room utility demands that must be accommodated. It also will indicate if the desired menu can be produced and served efficiently.

It is advisable to get the host involved with this room setup planning exercise. Experience shows that the host who is involved from the start is more satisfied with the result, primarily because he or she has a great deal of control over the final outcome. In addition, the involved host tends to be more sensitive to the club's needs and is more willing to consider the club's viewpoints.

Before developing the final plan for the function room setup, it is important to estimate the amount of time needed to accomplish the host's layout and design objectives. When scheduling a function room setup, many things must be considered. Some of these critical factors are

1. *Function room status.* Function rooms used for temporary storage or those being repaired or remodeled cannot be used. If a function room has an existing setup, additional time must be scheduled so that it can be torn down. Furthermore, it is important to know how the room will be used after the catered event ends. Similar functions should be scheduled in the same room. Breaking down one setup only to reset it in another function room is a waste of time, money, and effort. When schedules permit and group sizes are similar, a basic setup can be used several times.

2. *Timing of events.* If the function room will be empty several days before the catered event, its setup can be scheduled during slack time periods. In this case, you have more flexibility. Moreover, usually you can maximize labor productivity.

On the other hand, if there is a meeting scheduled in a function room that ends at 5:00 P.M. and you need to turn over the room for a 7:00 P.M. reception, time becomes your enemy. This type of scheduling demand can increase your payroll costs unless you plan very carefully.

3. *Setup difficulty.* The amount of time needed to perform the final setup depends primarily on the type of setup required. For instance, a theater-style setup requires less time than a schoolroom-meeting setup, and a reception can be set up more quickly than a sit-down dinner.

4. *Function room layout and design.* Usually the catering manager or banquet manager is responsible for preparing the final function room layout and design for all catered events. In some cases, exact locations of food stations, bars, seating, decor, and other requirements must be communicated to the club's catering executive well in advance of the functions' dates. Standardized and frequently used setups, however, do not require complete instructions. Nor do they usually require a significant amount of advance notice. For instance, it is not necessary to draw a diagram of each schoolroom-

meeting setup unless there is something unusual or distinct about the setup. Nor is it necessary to draw a complete layout if you use a system whereby each possible design is assigned a code number that is familiar to all staff members (see Figure 7.4).

5. *Decor.* A theme party or similar function requires additional time to set up properly. Props, plants, flowers, lighting, and so forth must be delivered and located. The amount and type of decorations, where they are stored in the club, or if they must be delivered and set up by outside contractors will determine when the function room can be set and how much of the function room can be set at one time. Larger props should be set first and furniture and equipment set next, with smaller props then set around the furniture and equipment.

6. *Lighting and audiovisual.* Meetings and meal functions sometimes require extensive lighting and/or audiovisual services. Function room setups that include these services usually require an additional setup time, usually referred to as a *rehearsal set.* While complete furniture and equipment setup is not necessary for a rehearsal set, it can be if a band or keynote speaker wants to test the sound system with all other furniture and equipment in place. To say the least, rehearsal sets increase significantly the time and effort needed to set up a function room properly.

Communication is critical for a rehearsal set. When will it take place and how long will it last? Will other setup work continue during the rehearsal set or must it be postponed until after the rehearsal ends? Unplanned rehearsals can seriously interrupt the overall setup schedule. Productivity is compromised if housemen must work in the dark or work while a band is checking sound levels.

7. *Outside service contractors.* If clients are using outside service contractors such as a professional party-planning company, you must ensure that their work dovetails nicely with the club's standard operating procedures. For instance, if an outside service contractor is hired to handle all lighting installations and tear downs, the club must coordinate closely with the crew to maximize productivity and eliminate unnecessary downtime.

Dining Room Layout

When you walk into a banquet room that has been set up, everything should be symmetrical. Round tables should be evenly spaced so that the eye can view attractive, neat rows. All of the table legs should face the same direction. And the points of square tablecloths should form V-shapes over the table legs. When the banquet room is completely set, the host should be

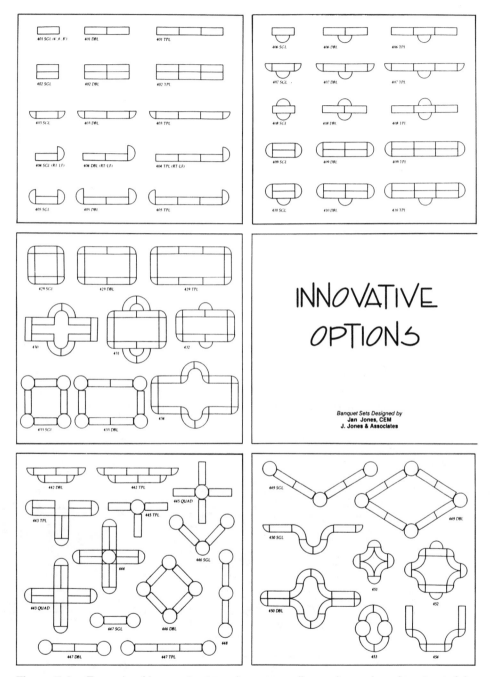

Figure 7.4.   Example of banquet sets and corresponding code numbers (courtesy of Jan Jones, CEM, J. Jones & Associates, Chicago, Illinois).

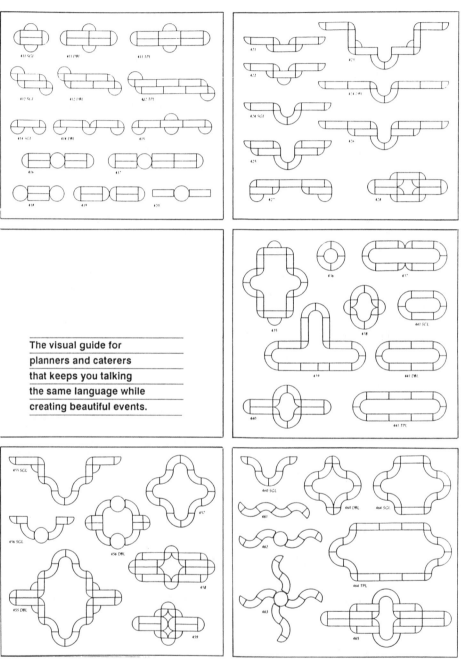

The visual guide for
planners and caterers
that keeps you talking
the same language while
creating beautiful events.

Figure 7.4. *(Continued).*

able to look down a row of tables and see a consistent line of V-shapes surrounding each table leg.

The tables used should meet the height standard of 30 inches. The typical types used in catering are

1. *60-inch round table.* Called a round of 8, or 8-top. It is usually used to seat 6 to 10 guests.

2. *72-inch round table.* Called a round of 10, or 10-top. It is usually used to seat 8 to 12 guests.

3. *66-inch round table.* A compromise table size, it is designed to take the place of the 60- and 72-inch rounds. It can seat 8 to 10 guests. If it uses this table, the club may be able to minimize the different types of tables it carries in stock.

4. *Banquet 6 table.* A rectangular table, measuring approximately 30 inches by 6 feet. These tables are the typical dining tables used in full-service restaurant banquet rooms since many restaurants normally do not own rounds. Clubs usually use rectangular tables only for buffet tables or display tables.

    Some clients may specifically ask for rectangular dining tables because they want picnic-style seating. Generally, though, clubs do not normally use them for dining tables, except where U-shaped, hollow-square, or conference-room setups are required. For instance, a small luncheon with a guest speaker can be more readily accommodated with the U-shaped arrangement. The platform, podium, and supporting props can be set up at the top of the U before the meal is served. The speaker can begin right after dessert. Guests will not have to change seat locations; they can remain in their present seats.

5. *Banquet 8 table.* Similar to the banquet 6. It measures approximately 30 inches by 8 feet.

6. *Schoolroom table.* Similar to the banquet 6 and banquet 8. It is 18 or 24 inches wide and 6 or 8 feet long. It is used for business meetings where classroom presentations are made. Seating is usually on one side only. It can also be used as one-half of a buffet table.

7. *Serpentine table.* A crescent-shaped table. The typical size used is one-fourth of a hollowed-out round table. You also can purchase one that is one-fifth of a hollowed-out round table.

Serpentines are used with banquet 6s and/or banquet 8s to make an oval-shaped buffet line. They also can be used to make a circular-shaped buffet line; for instance, four of them can be assembled to create a hollowed-out circle, where foods can be displayed on the tables and some sort of attraction (such as a floor-mounted fountain) can be displayed in the hollowed-out center.

8. *Half-moon table.* A half-round table. It is typically used to add another dimension to a buffet line. It can also be used by itself to hold, for example, a few dry snacks at a beverage function.

9. *Quarter-moon table.* A quarter-round table. It is generally used as part of a buffet line.

10. *Cocktail table.* A small, round table, usually available in 18-inch, 24-inch, 30-inch, and 36-inch diameters. You can use regular heights (for sit-down service), short heights (for displays), and bar heights (for stand-up bar service).

11. *Oval table.* A table of varying proportions, used primarily as a dining table. The typical one used for catering measures 54 by 78 inches. It can be used to increase room capacity; for instance, you can fit 10 ovals in the space of 8 rounds, thereby accommodating more people with approximately the same amount of space. The oval table also allows a more elegant seating arrangement, in that a host can sit at its head.

Oval tables do present some drawbacks. For instance, their shape makes it more difficult for servers to work around them efficiently. Guests seated on the narrow ends may feel cramped and crowded. There are wheels in the center (so that the tables can be folded up and rolled into storage) that can interfere with some guests' comfort. And, if a few foods are preset in the middle of the table, some guests may be unable to reach them easily.

When taking banquet tables from storage, opening them, and setting them up, be sure that the legs are locked properly. This will prevent unfortunate accidents that can occur if the tables are not set up and adequately secured. If locking bolts are exposed incorrectly, a guest could scratch his or her leg.

You also must ensure that the table legs lock properly when tearing the tables down and putting them away. If the tables are stored on a dolly, they must be secured correctly to prevent accidents and damage.

The seats of the chairs used should measure 17 inches from the floor. The seat-cushion dimension should be 20 inches by 20 inches. The typical stack chair used meets these specifications. Folding chairs usually do not; they are usually too low and, hence, uncomfortable. Folding chairs should be used only for emergency backup or for outdoor picnic-type functions.

When setting up the tables and chairs, think in terms of blocks of no more than 250 seats (five 10-top tables by five 10-top tables). This arrangement, with normal aisle space within the block, and standard cross-aisle space on its perimeter, is an efficient floor design. This type of block layout, or one proportionately smaller, will usually accommodate any type of service.

Ultimately, the seating arrangement used will depend on the purpose of the catered event and the function space booked. For instance, awards banquets, celebrations, theme parties, and so forth will influence the dining room layout as well as the type of tableware, props, napery, floral arrangements, centerpieces, and other decor used.

The purpose of the function also will indicate if a head table is appropriate. These days, fewer groups use head tables, believing that their absence contributes to a more egalitarian arrangement. It is sometimes felt that head tables create an unnecessary barrier between head table guests and the other guests.

If there will be a head table, it is important to specify if it must be on a riser because the platform, just like a dining table, must be set up and dressed appropriately.

The appropriate platform height also must be determined. Platforms, or risers, usually have a minimum height of 6 inches. Using multilevel tiers, you can build them to a height of 36 inches. Generally speaking, the bigger the room, the higher the platform must be so that head table guests can be viewed easily by all guests.

Recall that the typical platform section is 4 feet by 4 feet. Another common dimension is 4 feet by 8 feet. A sufficient number must be assembled, connected properly, carpeted, and decorated or skirted. On the taller setups, lighted steps and hand rails must be installed. Furthermore, utilities usually must be adapted to accommodate a platform's location and other requirements.

Before the banquet setup crew is finished, it must be certain that all ancillary tables, chairs, and equipment are set up. For instance, you may need to deliver and set up podiums, audiovisual equipment, registration/information tables, kiosks, booths, and display attractions.

Finally, the dining room setup is not complete until all outside service contractors, such as decorators, florists, and balloonists, finish their work. You will need to coordinate schedules with these service contractors to ensure that the dining room is ready for service at the scheduled time and that appropriate cleanup is done by them.

Bar Layout

Bar setups are easier to plan than food events. Unlike food, alcoholic beverage service tends to be very standardized. Also, you do not normally set up portable bars with the wide array of equipment needed to prepare and serve a complete line of specialty drinks. Simple mixed drinks, wines, and beers are more commonly served; specialty drinks, such as scorpions, Long Island teas, and frozen daiquiris, are not usually offered.

Bar setups are also a bit easier to plan because the club may have permanent, self-contained banquet bar installations in some function rooms or banquet areas. These bars usually need only one or two bartenders, a bar back, and some inventory, and they are ready to go.

Even in function rooms that use portable bars, some clubs often have designated specific locations for them that are always used. These locations provide the appropriate utilities, space, and accessibility. When planning beverage service, therefore, the catering sales representative and host need only to work around the preallocated space. In effect, you are working with semi-permanent bars that tend to be almost as convenient as permanent ones.

A bar does not pose the same quality-control problems as does food. The product is very standardized. It is a manufactured item, with standardized packaging, quality, and servable yields. And, except for beer and some wines, the inventory has a virtually unlimited shelf life. You can set up bars well in advance of the functions without worrying about spoilage or quality deterioration.

If portable bars are used, and if you need to allocate space for them because there are no designated specific locations, the planning is a bit more challenging. You will need to ensure that they are set up to

1. *Serve all function needs.* For instance, if there is a reception with dinner following, the bars may have to accommodate both events. This implies that there must be enough room to allow guests to approach the bars during the reception and also sufficient service bar area to accommodate guest lines and cocktail servers who may need to handle poured-wine service.

2. *Provide sufficient working space.* Normally you will need at least one bartender and one bar back per bar. If you are catering an upscale function and are using a sommelier, you should allocate some working space so that he or she can handle wine service correctly. Depending on the type of function, you may also need cocktail servers.

3. *Provide sufficient storage space.* A busy bar will need a back bar area in which to store additional in-process inventory. Portable refrigerators, portable ice carts, glassware, and supplier should be available so that service does not lag.

4. *Enhance cost-control procedures.* There must be enough working space to eliminate bottlenecks, which can lead to overpouring and spillage. With cash bars, if there are no cashiers scheduled, the club will need to bring in cash registers for the bartenders to use to ring up sales and hold cash receipts. If drink tickets are sold by a separate cashier, the bar will need a lockbox to store used drink tickets. Furthermore, sufficient standardized portion-control measuring devices, such as Posi-Pour, color-coded bottle pour spouts, and standardized glassware, must be used and appropriate space allocated for them.

5. *Prevent access to minors.* A permanent or semipermanent bar installation is generally positioned to avoid this problem. Portable bars, on the other hand, may not be so closely watched. Nevertheless, local liquor codes usually demand that you provide some type of separation to prevent underage drinking.

6. *Allow adequate space for required cocktail tables and chairs, landing space, cashier(s), and ticket taker(s).*

7. *Accommodate special customer requests.* For example, a host may want you to provide separate stations for draft beer, wine tasting, and spirits and mixed drinks. In this case, you will need to plan your setup very carefully in order to prevent overcrowding.

8. *Allow for a proper accounting of all drinks served.* If the bar service is set up to charge the host for each drink consumed by his or her guests, you will need to allocate space for precheck cash register machines to record the number of drinks served. Alternatively, you could use precounted glassware and calculate total glassware usage at the end of the event.

9. *Enhance security.* Liquor theft is all too common in our industry; tight security will minimize this problem. Usually you will transport all liquor stock in a wheeled, portable, locked cage made of cyclone fencing material. You will want to leave the cage nearby the portable bar so that, if the area must be unattended, the liquor stock can be secured. You also can have the portable bar and locked cage set up well before the catered event is scheduled to begin; when the bartenders and bar backs come on duty, they then can unload the liquor cage and set up the bar.

Buffet Layout

Buffets allow guests to choose their favorite menu items. Guests also have some personal control over the portion sizes. However, since the menu items will be handled by many different people, it is imperative to offer foods that hold up well.

Buffets are generally faster and more efficient than table-service procedures, assuming that there are enough buffet lines to accommodate the guests quickly and efficiently. One of the potential disadvantages of buffets is the possibility that some guests will be finished eating while others are still waiting in line.

If the purpose of the meal function is merely to refuel the guests, slower service may be acceptable. However, if there is a slow service when a program follows the meal, it will be almost impossible to retain everyone's attention and conduct a cohesive event. If you cannot provide enough buffet tables to prevent this problem, you should suggest that the host consider using some type of table service. For example, preset and plated service could be an acceptable alternative. This combination is very efficient primarily because you are able to time the courses.

Some hosts prefer buffets because they are under the impression that buffets are less expensive to implement than table-service styles. However, buffets can be quiet expensive unless you use acceptable techniques designed to reduce their costs.

For instance, low-cost food items, such as some salads and breads, can be placed first on the line so that the guests' plates will be full by the time they reach the entree stations. You can also save a bit of money by using a 9-inch plate instead of a 10-inch one.

Another cost-saving technique is to put small portion sizes on buffets. For instance, instead of serving whole chicken breasts, or even half-breasts, you should cut them into three or four pieces each. Guests who also want to eat another meat on the buffet, but want to sample the chicken, will not have a large piece of chicken, taste part of it, and throw the rest away.

Another cost-control procedure is to have a chef personally supervise the buffet tables. Psychologically, people will avoid loading up their plates if they are being watched. Similarly, the chef could serve the meat course while simultaneously supervising the rest of the line.

While there are many similar types of cost-saving opportunities, the director of catering should not reduce the buffet experience to an institutional chow-line atmosphere. A low-price, low-cost buffet may give some guests the wrong impression of the club's capabilities. It may be foolhardy to court catering clients who do not wish to purchase the quality and value you normally serve.

Regardless of a host's budget, buffets can provide many advantages to both the host and the club. For instance, they provide an acceptable level of customer service. They allow guests to control what and how much they eat. Chefs can use their creative talents to decorate the foods and buffet tables. And labor costs can be trimmed a bit if guests are satisfied with self-service and minimal food offerings.

When laying out the buffet stations, you should try not to put salads, entrees, and desserts on the same table. This will slow up service as the guests will try to take everything at once. Most guests cannot carry two plates, but this does not stop them from trying. The inevitable result: spillage and other food-wasting accidents.

Since guests will form a line anywhere they can, you should avoid setting up the buffet tables near doors or other entryways where they can cause traffic jams.

If the buffet line will be longer than 16 feet, it should be two tables wide, that is, about 4 to 6 feet wide. A long, narrow line is unattractive. A wider line allows you to spread out the foods, create a more aesthetically pleasing depth perception, and enhance the setup with decorations and food displays. If you use long, narrow lines, you should use serpentine tables, which curve and provide more table space per foot.

If the buffet line will include an action station, you will need to allocate enough space to accommodate the in-process inventory of food, preparation and service equipment, the chef, and the guests who will want to congregate and watch the chef create the finished items.

If the action station will be put toward the center of the function room instead of up against a wall, you will need more floor space. An action station in the round usually is set up with several inside and outside tables to allow for maximum chef maneuverability, exposure, and guest accessibility.

It is difficult to determine the number of action stations needed because it depends on the amount of time needed to prepare and serve the foods, as well as the estimated number of guests who will want them in lieu of the other foods displayed on the buffet line. At the very least, you should expect that half of the guests will want something from an action station.

Some buffets incorporate a bit of cafeteria service. If so, there must be enough room allocated so that food servers and chefs can maneuver adequately.

If floor space is at a premium, you should consider using double-sided buffet tables. They can save as much as 20 percent of your available floor space. They also tend to reduce leftovers because, when service slows near the end of the meal, you can close one side of the line and consolidate all foods on the open side.

The buffet should not have an attached self-service beverage station. Whenever possible, beverages, such as wine, hot coffee and tea, and soft drinks, should be served at the table. This provides a bit of personalized table service that guests appreciate. It also makes the overall service much quicker and more efficient. Experience shows that guests take a long time at beverage stations and that bottlenecks are inevitable. Experience also indicates that you should not allow guests to walk across the room balancing two or three cups of hot coffee. Hot drinks should always be served. Guests who have had a few glasses of wine are not prepared to negotiate the pathway to and from the beverage station. You do not want an unfortunate accident to mar the event and, incidentally, make the club liable for employee and guest injuries.

If possible, you should use small containers of food on the buffet line. Try to use containers that hold no more than 25 to 30 servings. In the long run, they will be more attractive than large, elaborately garnished containers. Keep in mind that only the first few guests through the line will see the beautifully garnished large presentations before they are distributed. Furthermore, half- or quarter-full large bowls have a lot of food, but they are unattractive.

Small containers will need more frequent replenishment, so you will incur a bit more payroll expense. However, experience shows that guests will take smaller portions from smaller containers and larger servings from bigger containers. The result: you save more on food cost than you spend for the extra labor. Furthermore, smaller containers usually mean fresher, more attractive presentations.

In lieu of decorating all food containers, it may be more efficient to decorate and embellish the tables and their surroundings. All guests, therefore, will be able to see and appreciate the decor instead of the few lucky ones who get first crack at the food presentations.

Most meal buffets are set with one line for every 100 guests. The maximum amount you can serve efficiently with one line, though, is 120 guests. The break point, therefore, is 120 guests.

The general feeling in the industry is that you are courting disaster and customer dissatisfaction if you cannot maintain these standardized ratios. This is especially true for luncheon meal functions because guests usually arrive all at once. In this case, speed is very critical.

If you set one buffet line for every 50 guests, you can feed the entire group in about 15 minutes. The first guest will take about five minutes to go through the line. After that, there will be about four guests passing through the line every minute. For some luncheons, it might be a good idea to set one line for every 50 guests.

If hors d'oeuvres are served buffet style during a beverage function, some industry experts recommend setting one table for every 50 guests. Fewer, larger tables tend to interfere with bar traffic.

However, if you set one buffet table for every 50 guests, you may need more labor to replenish food supplies. You will have more product distribution problems unless you set up enough service corridors to handle replenishment. And you may have more leftovers with several small buffet tables unless you consolidate some tables toward the end of the event.

For breakfast functions, you may be able to get by with one buffet line for more than 100 guests. Unlike luncheon guests, breakfast guests tend to arrive a few at a time. Even though the typical breakfast buffet will have a great rush during the last 15 minutes of the meal period, usually enough guests will have already been served to prevent any service glitches.

Dinner buffets are usually more elaborate. There are many decorations and more-lavish food displays. If you set this type of buffet, guests will usually take more time to serve themselves. They will want to savor the visual effects and not rush through. Generally speaking, for every hour it takes to serve a luncheon buffet, it will require about one and one-half hours to serve a dinner buffet.

Table Setting

All dining tables and buffet tables must be dressed and outfitted appropriately. The type of meal function, menu, and style of service will influence the quality and type of table decor used.

The table setting is the focus of a function room's decor. It is one thing that guests see throughout the meal. Because it influences the mood in which the patron judges what he or she eats and drinks, you should spend as much time designing the right look as you spend developing the most appropriate menu.

Display tables will often need to be skirted; that is, their sides must be completely covered from the floor to the top of the table. Skirting is draped over the side of the table. It is connected on the table's edges and allowed to fall to just above the floor.

Up until a few years ago, skirting was attached with T-pins, and some clubs still use this method because they think it is more elegant. Skirting today though, is easier to install, remove, and clean. Plastic clips and Velcro fasteners have made installation and removal much easier. Some clips have Velcro on the back. They come in two sizes—standard and angled. Standard fits a tabletop that is three-quarter inch thick, and angled is used for tabletops that are one-half inch thick.

Some skirting has plastic clips attached that clip onto the table. Others have Velcro bands intended to hook onto Velcro-strip tapes that are attached to the table. To avoid sagging, clips are attached at intervals of 2 feet or less.

Table skirting is 29 inches high. Stage (that is, platform) skirting is readily available in lengths ranging from 6 inches to 36 inches. Longer skirting is available, but, if the standard lengths do not meet your needs, you may want use pipe and drape to dress anything higher.

For some skirting, you will need to use a skirting liner. For instance, if you plan to use an elegant lace skirting, you will need to line it so that the uncovered areas do not show through.

Usually all buffet tables, display tables, and platforms are skirted. Some dining tables may also be skirted. For instance, a head table is customarily skirted on three sides. The skirting provides a vanity shield as well as an attractive presentation.

Hot- and cold-food delivery carts should also be skirted. For instance, a roll-in luncheon buffet on a three-tier cart may be used to accommodate a small business meeting. The cart should be skirted from the top to the floor on three sides. The unskirted side, out of guest view, can be opened to remove the foods for service.

You may also want to skirt portable bars and related equipment, such as crushed ice containers and wine and beer coolers. If you have any carts in the room holding backup stock, you may want to skirt them so that they do not detract from the function's overall appeal.

In most cases, you must requisition skirting from the linen room. When calculating the amount needed, you must be very careful to compute the correct total. If, for example, you need enough skirting to cover a banquet-8 table, you will need about 22 running feet (that is, two 8-foot sides plus two approximately 3-foot sides equals about 22 running feet).

Tables should be padded so that table noises are minimized. The typical dining and buffet tables have pad underliners placed underneath the tablecloths. You can purchase tables that have prepadded tops. Generally, prepadded tables are much more expensive than unpadded ones, so the club may wish to pad its own tables. This padding can be permanent—you can buy a roll of padding, cut pieces to fit each table, and staple them to the tabletops—or temporary—the housekeeping department may issue one pad (which is similar to an ironing board pad) with each tablecloth requisitioned.

All tables require napery. Buffet and display tables will need tablecloths, and dining tables will need tablecloths and napkins.

You will also need napery for your beverage stations. For instance, both alcoholic and nonalcoholic beverage stations will need tablecloths. While both types of stations need coasters and napkins, most often you will use disposable paper coasters and cocktail napkins instead of permanent, reusable napery.

Napery adds warmth and color. In the public's eye, cleanliness is its most important attribute. Crisp, clean, stain-free napery helps create a favorable impression.

White is the traditional color of napery. Light colors are used when white does not provide the background desired. Darker colors can be used when a stark contrast is desired or for all-day functions (such as permanent refreshment centers) where the napery, which will get soiled during the day, cannot be changed easily. And darker colors (usually green) are used for schoolroom tables so that meeting attendees can take notes without battling the glare that white napery gives off.

Sometimes you may want to use two or more colors to dress a table such as using white linen with a color overlay to create a different look. For instance, a combination of white and mauve may be appropriate for a buffet table; white and gold may be just right for a table used to display door prizes; white and green is a good combination for landing space around bev-erage napkins (such as fuchsia, gold, or white) provide a startling, crowd-pleasing visual effect. Chair covers that match table linens are also a wonder-ful way to change the look of the room.

Many clubs own their napery and launder it in-house. The alternative is to use an outside laundry or linen supply firm that will deliver clean napery and pick up the soiled articles. In some cases—perhaps for a very large func-tion—you may need to supplement the in-house supply with a temporary rental. There also may be times when you need specialty napery with colors or patterns you do not carry in-house.

Ideally, the manager of the linen room should strive to maintain at least three sets of napery in-house. One set should be clean, on the shelf, and ready to use; the second set should be in the laundry; the third set should be in use in the function rooms. Maintaining this three-par stock ideal is a chal-lenging task because napery has a rather unpredictable useful life.

If you have any choice in selecting the napery, you should choose prod-ucts that are fire retardant, heavyweight, soil resistant, and nonshrinking. You also want no-iron napery that will hold folds readily, cling neatly to the tabletop, and not fade after a few washings.

When selecting napery, the three most important considerations are

1. *Durability.*   How long will it last? What is its expected useful life?

2. *Laundry and maintenance cost.*   How much does it cost to wash? To repair?

3. *Purchase price.*   Most important, the purchase price spread over the expected life of the napery. This long-term purchase price takes into account the cost of washing and repairing the napery. For instance, an expensive product that can be cleaned in cold water and with-stand 300 washings is preferable to a less-expensive item that must be washed in hot water and can be washed only 150 times. Ulti-mately, it is the cost per use that influences napery's overall value.

When ordering linen or requisitioning it from the linen room, you will need to specify the exact measurements needed. Standard tablecloth sizes normally used for banquets are 78-inch and 90-inch round. Regardless of the type and size of table used, the size of the tablecloth should be approximately 18 inches wider than the table diameter so that about 9 inches of cloth will drape over the sides. If the tabletop diameter is 36 inches, you should use a cloth 54 inches square. A table 45 inches in diameter should be fitted with a 64-inch-square cloth; a 54-inch diameter needs a 72-inch-square cloth; and so forth.

If you use rectangular dining tables, the same rule of thumb prevails; that is, the tablecloth should drape about 9 inches over the table's sides.

In general, tablecloths should be large enough to cover the tables and leave some drape, but not so large that the hems lap the chair seats and cause guest discomfort. At most, hems should just barely touch the front edges of the chair seats. Recall that the standard table's height is 30 inches and the standard chair's seat measures 17 inches from the floor. A tablecloth with a 9-inch drape will not touch the chair seats—there will be inches of space between the hem of the tablecloth and the chair.

There are times when you may want to use a round tablecloth whose diameter is double the tabletop diameter. For instance, for an elegant reception, you may want to cover a 60-inch round to the floor with a 120-inch tablecloth instead of with a smaller tablecloth skirting.

Some club properties have one set of napery for catering and another set for the restaurant outlets. In this case, instead of requisitioning tablecloths, you would need to specify *banquet* cloths. This allows you greater control over the use of these items. It also means that you will receive the appropriate sizes and the exact items to serve your purposes adequately.

When placing the tablecloths on the tables, you should be careful to keep the hemmed sides down and the creases up. For instance, on a rectangular table, the main creases should be up, and, as much as possible, they should be centered on the tables. If the tablecloths were pressed incorrectly (that is, where the creases and hemmed sides are both in the same direction), you should keep the hemmed sides down even though the creases will look unattractive or you can iron the cloths on the table to remove unsightly creases. In this case, you must select the lesser of two evils.

The napkins used must be laundered and handled correctly so that they will have enough strength to hold whatever fold you want to use. For instance, you can use the more common napkin folds, such as the pyramid, goblet fan, or Lady Windermere's fan, or you can use something more adventurous and unusual such as the rosebud, bishop's mitre, or candle fold (see Figure 7.5).

How to fold the folds that hold with Visa® napery fabrics.

1. THE CANDLE Fold napkin in half diagonally (1). Fold down base 1/3 way (2). Turn napkin over and roll from bottom to top (3). Tuck corners inside cuff at base of fold and stand (4). Turn one layer of point down and set on base (5).

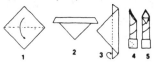

2. BIRD OF PARADISE Fold napkin in half and in half again (1). Then fold in half diagonally with points on the top and facing up (2). Fold left and right sides down along center line, turning their extended points under (3). Fold in half on long dimension with edges facing out (4). Pull up points and arrange on a fabric surface (5).

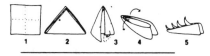

3. THE ROSE Fold all 4 corners of open napkin to center (1). Fold new corners to center (2). Turn napkin over and fold all 4 corners to center (3). Holding center firmly, reach under each corner and pull up flaps to form petals. Reach between petals and pull flaps from underneath (4).

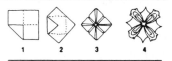

4. THE GOBLET FAN Fold napkin in half (1). Pleat from bottom to top (2). Turn napkin back 1/3 of the way on right (folded) end and place into goblet (3). Spread out pleats at top (4).

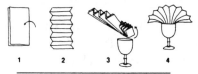

5. ROSEBUD Fold napkin in half diagonally (1). Fold corners to meet at top point (2). Turn napkin over and fold bottom 2/3 way up (3). Turn napkin around and bring corners together, tucking one into the other (4). Turn napkin around and stand on base (5).

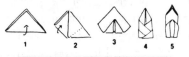

6. LADY WINDERMERE'S FAN Fold napkin in half (1). Starting at bottom, accordion pleat 2/3 way up (2). Fold in half with pleating on the outside (3). Fold upper right corner diagonally down to folded base of pleats and turn under edge (4). Place on table and release pleats to form fan (5).

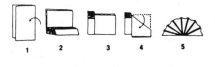

7. CLOWN'S HAT Fold napkin in half bringing bottom to top (1). Holding center of bottom with finger, take lower right corner and loosely roll around center (2), *matching corners*, until cone is formed (3). Turn napkin upside down, then turn up hem all around. Turn and stand on base (4).

8. THE CARDINAL'S HAT Fold napkin in half diagonally (1). Fold corners to meet at top point (2). Turn napkin over with points to the top, fold lower corner 2/3 way up (3). Fold back onto itself (4). Bring corners together tucking one into the other. Open base of fold and stand upright (5).

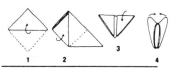

9. PYRAMID Fold napkin in half diagonally (1). Fold corners to meet at top point (2). Turn napkin over and fold in half (3). Pick up at center and stand on base of triangle (4).

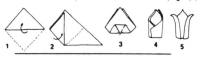

10. THE ARUM LILY Fold napkin bringing bottom up to top (1). Fold corners to top (2). Fold bottom point up to 1" below top (3). Fold point back onto itself (4). Fold each of points at top down and tuck under edge of folded-up bottom and fold down one layer of top point and tuck under base fold (5). Turn napkin over and tuck left and right sides into each other (6). Open base and stand (7).

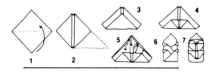

11. THE CROWN Fold napkin in half diagonally (1). Fold corners to meet at top point (2). Fold bottom point 2/3 way to top and fold back onto itself (3). Turn napkin over bringing corners together, tucking one into the other (4). Peel two top corners to make crown. Open base of fold and stand upright (5).

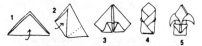

12. BISHOP'S MITRE Fold napkin bringing top to bottom (1). Fold corners to center line (2). Turn napkin over and rotate ¼ turn (3). Fold bottom edge up to top edge and flip point out from under top fold (4). Turn left end into pleat at left forming a point on left side (5). Turn napkin over and turn right end into pleat forming a point on right side (6). Open base and stand upright (7).

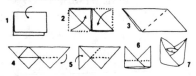

Figure 7.5. Standard napkin folds (courtesy of Milliken & Company, Spartanburg, South Carolina).

For more exotic folds such as those used to decorate serving trays and buffet-line containers, you can use a thin-gauge metal foil insert to give added strength to the napery. For example, you may want to have two gooseneck-shaped napkins adorning each side of a canape tray. The metal foil will give you enough tension to make these folds and ensure that they will hold up throughout the function.

A napkin must be placed at each cover, that is, at each place setting on the dining table. The layout must be symmetrical and pleasing to the eye. If you are using buffet-style service, you may opt to provide the napkins at the beginning or end of the buffet line. For speed and efficiency at casual events, you could roll the flatware inside the napkins.

To complete the dining table setup, you will need to requisition from the executive steward's office an assortment of china, glassware, and flatware. Plates, cups, saucers, flatware, water glasses, wine goblets, roll baskets, condiment containers, wine coolers, carafes, show plates, and other appropriate items must be preset on the dining tables in a symmetrical pattern. However, if you are using buffet-style service, you could let the guests help themselves to some tableware on the buffet line.

There are many other types of tableware needed that traditionally are not preset on the dining tables. For instance, you will need tea pots, pitchers, mugs, serving platters, serving bowls, ramekins, casserolettes, and specialty utensils.

When selecting tableware, most clubs prefer vitrified china or some similar type of product. China retains heat or cold longer than other materials. China is also impervious to salt, alkali, and acid, all of which attack and corrode metal. It can be produced with dishwasher-safe, lead-free glazes and with oven-proof, freezer-proof bodies. In addition, china also resists scratches from knives and other utensils much better than other materials.

Glassware includes stemware, tumblers, goblets, parfaits, decanters, pony glasses, snifters, pilsners, bottles, ashtrays, punch bowls, and cake plates. Clubs usually purchase glassware that has been produced with a heat-treated, rapid-cooled process that ensures durability and long-term attractiveness.

Glassware is one of the most useful decorating tools you can use. It helps set a mood and carry out a theme. Furthermore, clubs can use specialty glassware as a signature; for instance, many clubs have etched crystal.

The standard cover includes plateware set in the center with flatware placed on either side. Forks are placed to the left, knives and spoons to the right. Some dessert flatware may be placed above the center plate.

Flatware is placed in the order in which it will be used by the guest, from the outside in. For instance, the soup spoon would be on the outside, as soup is usually an early course. The knife would be closest to the center plate, with the blade edge facing the rim of the plate. The smaller salad fork would be set farther out than the dinner fork.

The exact place setting depends primarily on the menu and style of service selected by the host. Many catering executives have sample covers set out on credenzas in their offices that can be viewed by hosts wishing to see what they are getting. Hosts can also redesign the sample place settings in order to develop something unique.

Once the desired place setting is developed, pertinent information, such as the number of covers per table (see Figure 7.6), is included in the banquet event order (BEO). Working with these specifications, the banquet captain usually sets a *captain's table,* that is, a sample cover as a guide for the servers to follow when setting the dining tables.

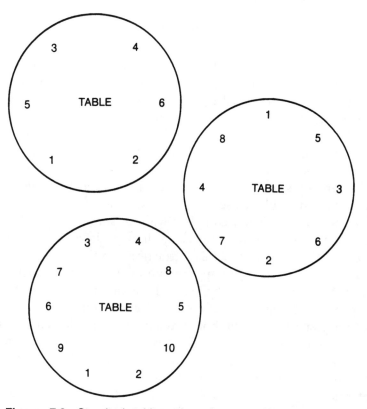

Figure 7.6 Standard table-setting diagrams for even spacing; covers are placed according to numbered patterns.

Some hosts want you to use unique types of tableware in order to complement a theme. For instance, they may want you to display a few antique bowls. If these bowls are used strictly for decorations, you can display them. However, if they will contain food or if they will be placed where they might come into contact with food, you cannot use them unless they are approved by the local health district for use in foodservice operations.

If you own unique decorative items or serving containers, you must be careful to use for foods only those intended to hold foods. For instance, an imported serving bowl could contain lead in its glaze. Care must be taken to ensure that these types of containers are used only to hold and/or display items.

Some dining tables may need nameplates and/or personalized menu cards. For instance, if you are setting a head table, you must see to it that the guests are seated at it correctly. For the head table at a formal event, the first guest of honor should be seated on the host's or hostess's right, with the second guest of honor seated on the left. If a third guest of honor is present, he or she should be seated to the right of the first guest of honor. If there are other dignitaries, they should be balanced back and forth according to rank or prominence.

For the head table at a wedding, the bride and groom should be seated at the center, with the bride sitting on the groom's left. On the bride's left will be the best man, followed by the bridesmaid, groomsman, bridesmaid, groomsman, and so forth. On the groom's right will be the maid of honor, followed by a groomsman, bridesmaid, groomsman, bridesmaid, and so forth. There should be enough room allocated at the head table to accommodate the entire formal wedding party, but, if this is impossible, you should seat the most important members at the head table with the others seated at the dining tables closest to the head table.

Your table setting is not complete without some sort of additional decoration. Most catered events, especially dinners, have centerpieces on the dining tables. They also have similar attractions on the buffet tables. Centerpieces should be attractive and appropriate for the type of function booked. Floral arrangements, candles, lights, and ice carvings are excellent centerpieces appropriate for any type of food or beverage function.

Generally speaking, you should avoid using edible centerpieces. They will be disturbed very early by the first two or three guests who touch them. Once deteriorated, they may detract from the overall beauty of the catered event. Guests may remember little else about the function save the unattractive centerpieces.

In some cases, you may be required to prepare an unusual centerpiece, or to allow the client to prepare it. For instance, many hosts request fun centerpieces, such as piñatas, world globes, or scale models. Many hosts also request centerpieces that highlight their organizations. Often these types of unusual centerpieces are souvenirs in disguise, in that the client expects some guests to take them home.

Centerpieces on dining tables should not interfere with guests' normal sight lines. They should be placed under or over these sight lines. You do not want guests to feel uncomfortable peering under, over, or around them. Or, worse yet, you do not want the guests to place them on the floor where they will hinder traffic or on the next table that is yet to be occupied, thereby ruining that table's setup.

If guests are expected to take centerpieces home after the catered event, you should suggest ways in which the function host can distribute them without playing favorites and offending some guests. For instance, if there is a floral arrangement on a dining table, you could select one cover at the table and code it with a gummed color dot under a preset plate. The function host can announce that the person finding the dot under his or her plate can take home the floral arrangement.

Before setting the tables, the banquet manager must specify the exact setup needed for regular dining tables, head tables, beverage stations, and buffet tables. It is a good idea to diagram in advance the required setup so that the setup crew does not have to scurry around at the last minute for directions. For instance, if special centerpieces must be placed on the head table, the setup crew must know about this before it goes to work.

The banquet setup crew will need to know if some place settings must be set a bit differently than others. For instance, if a guest at the head table needs some props for a speech, his or her place must be identified so that it can be arranged correctly.

All head table guests usually have assigned seating. Occasionally, the host may want to assign specific seats to all guests. Generally speaking, though, guests may be assigned a specific table, but seat assignments are uncommon.

If a few guests will be having off-menu meals, their covers could be identified so that servers do not have to ask everyone who gets what, although most often these guests are told to inform their server that they are having a special meal when they sit down. The banquet captain informs the servers ahead of time about these special requests, so there usually is no need to mark their place settings.

The banquet setup crew will also need to know if there will be a no-smoking section. If the client requests one, it is traditionally set on the left side of the room. The crew will need to set out ashtrays on the tables in the smoking section and signs that say "Thank you for not smoking" on those tables in the no-smoking section. (If you do not put these signs out, guests may think you merely forgot to put out ashtrays; they may just go ahead and light up without thinking.)

Dining room, bar, and buffet layout; required table settings; and other pertinent information will be listed on the BEO. Some BEOs also include a room diagram. However, experience shows that, while the typical BEO details very specifically the dining room, bar, and buffet layouts, it does not always include an exact description of the required table settings. For instance, if the client wants menus, brochures, and handouts placed at each cover, this information must be noted on the BEO. Every detail, no matter how small, is important to the host. You cannot afford to let any details get lost in the shuffle.

EMPLOYEE UNIFORMS

A great deal of a food or beverage function's visual impact can be attributed to the type and style of employee uniforms and costumes used. The typical client does not think about this unless he or she requests a specific theme, in which case special uniforms and costumes will be needed to carry out the theme.

A club may use a standard server uniform for breakfast and luncheon meal functions, with a slightly different server uniform used for evening affairs. Bartenders, cocktail servers, bar backs, and buspersons also wear a standard outfit. These standard uniforms are designed to suit most food and beverage functions adequately.

If the host is a bit more adventurous and has a bit more money to spend, the catering sales representative may wish to broach the subject of alternative employee attire if he or she thinks it would add significantly to the function's success. For instance, you could suggest renting unique garments specifically for the meal function. This little extra touch can be just the thing to make a good event a great event. The staff then become *moving decor* to add to the themed event.

CLEANING AND MAINTAINING THE FUNCTION ROOM

Housekeeping is usually responsible for the cleanliness and routine maintenance of function rooms. Dirty windows, walls, or floors can reduce a function room's quality level and cause guest dissatisfaction.

Function rooms must be vacuumed before each function setup (when the room is empty), with one final sweep or vacuuming just before the catered event is scheduled to begin. Postfunction cleaning is equally vital. Trash and leftover materials must be discarded promptly.

The major cleanliness concern is the loading door of the function room through which dirt can be tracked into the room area. Heavy traffic in this area will hasten carpet deterioration and generate a considerable amount of working dirt. Covering the floor near the loading entrance with old carpets and plastic sheeting can be an effective dirt catcher. Precleaning ramps and loading docks can also reduce the amount of dirt tracked into the room.

Housekeeping also cleans and maintains trash cans and public ashtrays. Constant care during peak periods must be scheduled to ensure an attractive atmosphere.

Burnt-out light bulbs, torn wallpaper, torn carpet, and broken equipment must be replaced or repaired quickly so that the function rooms remain presentable and safe. Quick room turnarounds and constant movement of heavy furniture and equipment will cause damage to doors, floors, ceilings, and walls. Housekeeping must monitor these details consistently.

Frequent inspection and repair can reduce wear and tear of the facilities as well as create a favorable guest environment conducive to memorable, exciting catered events. Housekeeping must handle problems personally or, in many clubs, report the conditions to the club's maintenance department.

COMMUNICATION IN THE FUNCTION ROOM AREAS

Clubs with several function rooms in various locations require coordination and control of banquet staff. It is difficult to monitor employees who are constantly on the move. Managers must select an appropriate method to supervise and communicate quickly with all employees.

One basic, low-cost method of control is the callback method. In this situation, an employee must contact a supervisor when his or her assigned task is completed. The supervisor will know how much time it normally takes to complete the task and can therefore anticipate a pattern of calls from his or her employees. As calls come in, new tasks are assigned on a priority basis. Furthermore, if a last-minute request is received, the supervisor will be able to assign it to the first employee who calls in.

A medium-cost method of control is the beeper method. With this option, beepers are assigned to all employees, or the employees are divided into groups with each group leader holding a beeper. This method allows the supervisor to assign a wide variety of tasks to each employee because the supervisor can quickly call all employees when emergencies arise.

Another advantage of using beepers is the ability to assign one to the host. Instead of trying to track down a host to verify a setup or time, information can be checked quickly.

The major disadvantage with beepers is the time it takes employees to respond when called. When an employee receives a call, he or she must cease working and locate a phone. This stop-and-go action can be time consuming and frustrating, especially if it is continuous. Phone availability is also a consideration; if the only available phone is in a back office, additional time will be lost and labor productivity will plummet.

The most expensive method of communication control is the walkie-talkie method. Walkie-talkies (or cellular phones) eliminate the need to stop what you are doing and locate a phone station. Although some systems can cost thousands of dollars to install, the time and efficiency gained can be well worth the expense.

Lead employees and supervisors can be assigned walkie-talkies and thereby become instantly accessible. Last-minute changes can be communicated immediately. Hosts are very impressed when their requirements change and employees respond to them instantaneously.

With walkie-talkies, supervisors can also monitor the conversation between employees and keep up to date on the movement of furniture, equipment, and labor. For instance, if a request is broadcast to one employee to locate some equipment, another employee monitoring the broadcast can break in with some new pertinent information.

As with beepers, a walkie-talkie can also be issued to a host. Unlike beepers, though, the walkie-talkie ensures instant verification of all details.

EQUIPMENT INVENTORY

The catering department uses a considerable amount of specialized furniture and equipment to set up the function room and serve the catered event. The department should ensure that complete, up-to-date lists of these items are maintained by the steward so that the catering staff knows what is available and what will need to be obtained from a rental company.

These inventory lists should note all chairs, tables, easels, tripods, stanchions, dance floor, audiovisual equipment, gueridons, rechauds, china, glass, flatware, linen, skirting, serving utensils, side stands, trays, bus carts, hot carts, cold carts, permanent centerpieces and other decorations, portable bars, and other furniture items kept in-house. Clubs should invest in computerized systems developed specifically to track this type of inventory.

The equipment lists should be updated monthly. A complete physical inventory should be taken at the end of each quarter so that damaged items can be repaired and missing ones replaced quickly. If there is a good deal of catering business, there might be an above average loss due to damage and/or theft. If so, a physical inventory should be taken more frequently.

8

Production and Service Planning

·····················

Production and service planning must be correlated with host needs to ensure smooth-running functions, satisfied guests, and fair earnings for the club. All factors must be evaluated so that the appropriate plans can be developed. Coordination is vital. Attention to detail is critical. You cannot take anything for granted.

PRODUCTION PLANNING

A production plan lists the types and amounts of finished foods and beverages needed, when they must be ready, and when they should be produced. The chef and banquet manager must have copies of the BEOs so that they can incorporate them into the daily purchasing, production, and work schedules.

Quantity of Food Needed

The chef needs to requisition foods from the club storeroom. If the kitchen staff needs something unusual that the club does not normally carry in stock, he or she will need to prepare a purchase requisition a few days before the meal function and give it to the purchasing department. The purchasing agent will then have enough time to shop around for the product and get the best possible value.

The amount of food that must be requisitioned and produced depends primarily on

1. Number of guests expected
2. Style of service
3. Expected edible yields

You should plan to prepare enough foods to handle the guaranteed guest count plus a set percentage above that amount. Generally speaking, if the guarantee is 100 guests, you should plan for 10 percent more; if the guarantee ranges from 100 to 1000 guests, you should plan for 5 percent more; if the guarantee exceeds 1000 guests, you should plan for 3 percent more.

If the guests are having a sit-down, preplated meal, it is relatively easy to compute the food requisition amounts because you have a great deal of control over the portion sizes. For instance, if the main course is filet mignon, the serving size is 6 oz, and the edible yield percentage for the raw roast beef is 75 percent, you will need to requisition about 55 pounds of raw beef for a party of 100 guests. Fifty-five pounds will be needed to serve 100 guests, plus 10 extra guests. The calculations are

1. Divide serving size by edible yield percentage. This will tell you how much raw product you need per serving.

$$\frac{6 \text{ oz}}{0.75} = 8 \text{ oz}$$

2. Divide 16 oz by the amount of raw product needed per serving. This will tell you the number of edible servings you can get from one raw pound.

$$\frac{16 \text{ oz}}{8 \text{ oz}} = 2 \text{ servings per pound}$$

3. Divide number of guests by the number of edible servings per raw pound. This will give you the amount of raw beef you must requisition.

$$\frac{110 \text{ servings}}{2} = 55 \text{ pounds}$$

If you plan to use reception service and/or buffet service for a meal function, it is not as easy to determine the amount of foods to requisition and to produce. However, there are some rules of thumb that can help you make a reasonable estimate. For instance, in a reception where foods are displayed on buffet tables, guests will consume about seven hors d'oeuvres during the first hour of the reception. Guests generally will eat more during the first hour of a reception.

Another rule of thumb suggests that, if guests need to meet or greet several persons during the function, you would need less food/beverage since there will be less time to eat and drink.

Still another rule of thumb notes that, if you crowd people into a room, they tend to eat and drink less than if they have more space to roam around and visit. A crowded room makes it more difficult for guests to re-visit the buffet tables.

Recall that the way in which you display your foods on a buffet table will encourage or discourage overconsumption. For instance, you gain an extra margin of control by putting the less-expensive items up front and the more expensive items further back and by having a chef serve the meat.

In some cases, you may not be too concerned if you overproduce foods for a buffet. For instance, if you can get the host to agree to eat the same types of menu items that are used in the club's restaurant outlets, overproduction is no problem because you can recycle any leftovers. If the menu items cannot be recycled, either you must have a sharp pencil when making your estimates or you will need to increase your competitive bid price for the catered meal function to take into account the additional food costs.

Unfortunately, it is very difficult to make an accurate determination of the amount of food to requisition and produce when you are dealing with self-service buffets and receptions unless you sell foods by the piece and clients agree to purchase a set amount. For that matter, even per-person pricing can be based on a specific amount and types of food items offered. However, if there are no restrictions placed on the self-service function, you cannot compute reasonably accurate estimates unless there is a good deal of relevant historical data upon which to base them. Even if you do take a lot of time to estimate your needs, you still have limited control over the serving sizes. As a result, you should always add a margin of safety to avoid every caterer's worst nightmare: stockouts.

Quantity of Beverage Needed

It is much easier to determine how much alcoholic beverage you will need than it is to forecast your food requirements. Unlike food, beverage is a standardized, manufactured product. You do not have to worry about spoilage or quality and yield variations. Furthermore, as long as your liquor storeroom is fully stocked with most brands, you should never run out of product. You cannot quickly prepare and serve an extra roast beef dinner if you are out of cooked roast beef, but as long as there is beverage in house, you can make drinks.

Usually the banquet and reception bars are set up with a par stock of beverages, ice, glassware, garnishes, and other necessary supplies about a half hour to an hour before the catered event is scheduled to begin.

The normal par stock used is influenced by

1. Number of guests expected

2. Club's experience with similar catered events

3. Amount of storage space available at the bar

Joseph E. Seagram & Sons Inc. has developed rules that you can use to estimate the approximate amount of liquor needed for an average reception of 100 guests. For instance, if you have 100 guests, you would expect about half of them to consume 3 glasses of wine apiece during the reception. Since each 750-milliliter (ml) bottle of wine contains about 5 drinks, you will need about thirty 750-ml bottles. Consumption trends indicate that you will need about 25 bottles of white or sparkling wine and 5 bottles of red. (Generally speaking, for every 2 bottles of red served, you expect to serve 10 bottles of white or sparkling.)

Joseph E. Seagram & Sons Inc. also suggests that, during the typical reception for 100 guests, 50 percent of them will consume 3 spirit drinks apiece. To accommodate the group adequately, consumption trends indicate that the basic portable bar should be stocked with

Type of Spirit	*Liters*
Blend	1
Canadian	1
Scotch	2
Bourbon	1
Gin	1
Vodka	3
Rum	2
Brandy/Cognac	1

Generally, you should expect liquor consumption to average at least 2.5 drinks per guest during a one-hour reception, particularly if the event attracts a mixed-company crowd. Average consumption tends to drop at very large receptions, and it usually increases at male-only events. However, if you schedule enough help and stock enough inventory to handle 2.5 drinks per person per hour, you should be able to accommodate any type of beverage function adequately.

If the beverage function's drink menu varies significantly from the type you normally serve, bartenders will need to change the types and amounts of beverages usually stocked at the portable bars. For instance, if a drink menu will offer only red and white table wine, gin, bourbon, vodka, scotch, and an assortment of beers and soft drinks, the bartender will need to adjust the typical opening par stock requisitioned from the liquor storeroom.

Usually you do not need to worry about stocking an exact amount of beverage at the banquet or reception bars because you can always depend on the bar back to replenish the supply quickly. Also, experience shows that, if you run out of something temporarily, most guests will wait until the bar back replenishes the supply or they will select another beverage. For instance, if you cannot serve a glass of burgundy because you are waiting a few minutes for more to be retrieved from the liquor storeroom or another club bar, the typical guest will not mind the wait. Or, if you have a substitute red wine, many guests will gladly accept it.

Nevertheless, you should make an effort to forecast your needs as accurately as possible because this will help ensure a smooth-running event. In addition, if beverages need to be iced down, it behooves you to make sure that you have plenty of ice available; you cannot take a room-temperature item and chill it quickly unless you have the specialized equipment needed to do this.

In most instances, it makes no difference if you overstock a banquet or reception bar because the merchandise can be used at other club bars. However, if the club needs to purchase specific beverages for the catered function that are not used in other club bars, you will need to compute as accurately as possible the amount you should order.

For example, a meal function might require a unique dinner wine that must be special ordered by the purchasing agent. If the expected guest count is 100, you will need to order enough wine to serve 110 persons.

Usually you will estimate 2.5 servings of wine per guest for the typical dinner banquet. In our example, then, you will need to order enough wine to serve 275 glasses (110 × 2.5). Since the standard wine glass holds a 5-oz portion (approximately 148 ml), you will need to special order about fifty-five 750-ml bottles of wine. The calculations are

1. Divide the amount of liquor per 750-ml bottle by the serving size. This will tell you how many potential drinks you can obtain per bottle.

$$\frac{750 \text{ ml}}{148 \text{ ml}} = 5.07 \text{ potential drinks per 750-ml bottle}$$

2. Divide the number of servings needed by the number of potential drinks per 750-ml bottle. This will tell you how many 750-ml bottles you will need to special order.

$$\frac{275 \text{ servings}}{5.07} = 54.24 \text{ bottles, rounded to 55 bottles needed}$$

If you take into account overpouring, waste, and the fact that usually you cannot get all of the liquid out of a bottle (some of it will stick to the sides), you will need to increase your special-order size. For instance, if you assume that you will lose 1 oz (approximately 30 ml) per 750-ml bottle, your special-order size will be about fifty-seven 750-ml bottles of wine. The calculations are

$$\frac{720 \text{ ml}}{148 \text{ ml}} = 4.86 \text{ potential drinks per 750-ml bottle}$$

$$\frac{275 \text{ servings}}{4.86} = 56.58 \text{ bottles, rounded to 57 bottles needed}$$

Some suppliers may not allow you to special order anything in less than case-size lots. In our example, then, you may need to special order sixty 750-ml bottles (5 cases, 12 bottles per case) because the liquor distributor may not want to break a case for you. If you are faced with this situation, you may need to add a liquor surcharge to the host's final billing.

Alternatively, you could charge the host for only the amount of wine consumed, keep the leftover product, and run it as a special in one of the club's restaurant outlets. Some unopened leftovers could also find their way into complimentary fruit baskets left for special guests in their hospitality suites.

Opened and unopened wine could be sent to the host's hospitality suite or used for another function. For instance, if the host has booked three meal functions, perhaps the leftover wine can be used for the next event.

The supplier may be willing to exchange unopened leftovers for something you normally use. While the typical supplier may not want to take back in trade one or two bottles, he or she is usually quite willing to take back unopened cases in trade assuming they have not been chilled. If the host agrees, you could charge the host by the case, order extra from the supplier, keep the few leftover loose bottles, return the unopened cases to the supplier, and credit the host for the returns.

Finally, you could charge the client by the bottle or by the case and let him or her take home any leftover wine. Before you do this, though, check the local liquor code to see if it is legal. For instance, the club may need to hold a package-goods liquor license before you can let the host take home unopened liquor. And opened stock may have to be served solely for consumption on premises.

To avoid the leftover problem, you could special order, say, four cases of wine (forty-eight 750-ml bottles), put it all out on the dining tables, and, when it runs out, back it up with another wine. However, make sure that you advise the host before doing this.

Quality of Food Needed

The quality of foods used by the club is dictated by the product specifications and standardized recipes prepared by club executives. For instance, the clubhouse or food and beverage committee may be made up of the clubhouse manager, club general manager, and the chef, as well as individuals from the membership, including board representatives who provide guidance to the club. However, the chef usually has the final responsibility for making these quality determinations.

Before you requisition foods, you must examine the standardized recipes very carefully so that you know exactly what you need. For example, if the recipe calls for Kraft cheese, you must requisition this brand name. You cannot requisition Borden cheese because the recipe is specifically geared for Kraft. Since Borden will be a bit different, the finished product will not be the same if you use Borden instead of Kraft.

Likewise with other product identification factors. You must requisition the correct product quality, size, color, package size, degree of preservation, type of processing, and so forth if you expect to maintain quality control. Actual quality that differs from the standard, expected quality, no matter how slight, is unacceptable.

In addition to quality control, product specifications and standardized recipes help ensure cost control. When you cost out your standardized recipes, you will use purchase prices based on the types of ingredients noted in them. If you use a substitute and do not account for any difference in cost, your final accounting will show an actual food cost that is more or less than what you budgeted. If the actual cost exceeds the budgeted standard cost, the club will suffer a loss. If the actual is less than the standard, hosts will be cheated because they will have received foods that were not consistent with the menu prices quoted.

Quality of Beverage Needed

As with food, the quality of beverage served will depend on the product specifications and standardized recipes used to prepare finished drinks. Unlike food, there usually is one more thing to consider, and that is the host's desires to have certain brand names of liquor served at the catered event.

Some hosts will not specify brand names. Since well brands usually cost less than call brands, some hosts will be satisfied with them. However, consumer preferences indicate that, while people are drinking less today, they are drinking higher-quality products. Premium brands are in vogue, and lately more hosts are asking the club to provide a choice of high-quality wines, spirits, and beers.

Brand names are the primary selection factors used when developing liquor product specifications, standardized recipes, drink menus, and stock requisitions. However, when requisitioning liquor from the liquor storeroom, there are a few additional factors that must be noted.

For instance, you will need to note the container sizes for each product needed. Generally speaking, for spirits, you will use 750-ml or 1-liter bottles if you free pour the drinks and 1.5-liter or 1.75-liter bottles if you use a mechanical dispensing unit to prepare drinks.

When requisitioning beers, more than likely you will want 12-oz bottles or cans. If you have a portable draft-beer dispensing unit, you would requisition the appropriate container size (probably a quarter keg) that fits it.

Wines come in various container sizes. Generally, this flexibility allows the host more cost-saving opportunities. For instance, you can purchase wines in 750-ml and 1.5-liter bottles. Less-expensive products, such as well wines (that is, house wines), can be purchased in larger bottles and in bag-in-the-box containers (that is, a large plastic Cryovac bag of wine inside a cardboard box, usually designed to be used as a self-dispensing package).

As with food, your drink product specifications and standardized recipes help ensure cost and quality control. Without these guidelines, it would be very difficult to forecast accurately the alcoholic beverage costs and the price quotations offered to potential hosts would not be as competitive as they should be.

Food Prepreparation

Food prepreparation, or *preprep*, activities generally are performed a day or more before the meal function. They include all the food production steps that can be performed ahead of time that will not compromise the quality of finished menu items. For instance, if the menu calls for vegetables and dip, a pantry person can prepare these items the day before and refrigerate them. Or, if the menu calls for an egg action station, a cook can preprep some egg mixes, dice the vegetables, and lay out the bacon on sheet pans the night before.

Generally speaking, the larger the function, the more preprep that must be done in advance. For instance, a banquet of 1000 prime rib dinners would require you to start preplating the meals at least one hour in advance and putting them in a hot cart. You would start out plating the rare portions and end up plating the well-done portions.

Some clubs have adopted the *sous vide* form of preprep. This involves the production of finished or semifinished menu items about a week or more before they are needed. After they are produced, the foods are then vacuum packed and stored in the refrigerator until needed. Many clubs are using kosher *sous vide* for their members requiring kosher foods for special events.

Sous-vide production has expanded the number and type of menu items that can be prepreparated. For instance, if you have a party next week and grilled salmon steaks will be on the menu, today you can sear, season, vacuum package, and then cook them in their plastic pouches. When done, the individually packaged steaks must be cooled rapidly and stored in the refrigerator. A few minutes before service, you reheat and plate them.

If you want to prepare foods this way in-house, *sous-vide* technology requires you to invest in some additional kitchen equipment. However, the method offers several culinary advantages. For instance, grilled salmon steaks can be cooked in their own juices and seasonings, and several of them can be served at one time. Under normal cooking procedures, you would be unable to serve grilled salmon steaks to a large group of people while simultaneously maintaining quality control.

Unfortunately, in-house *sous-vide* procedures can contribute to foodborne illness if they are not monitored closely. Sanitation is extremely important when sealing food products in plastic. If harmful bacteria are left in the package, they may grow to the point where some guests consuming the food may become ill.

There are good commercial *sous-vide* products on the market that allow you to provide excellent final results without having to invest in additional equipment. Rethermalization can be done in a steamer or kettle.

The menu planner should try to include as many preprep items as possible. This makes it much easier to plan food production; gives you more control over the labor work schedules; enables you to utilize production labor more efficiently; and ensures that the correct amount of foods will be available when it is time to prepare the finished products.

Bar Prepreparation

Bar preprep is much easier than food preprep. Generally, it includes stocking the portable bars with all nonliquor nonperishables whenever it is convenient to do so. Then, just prior to service, you preprep your nonliquor garnishes, requisition the liquor, load the ice bins, and ice down wine bottles and beer bottles or cans.

If the banquet bars are permanent or semipermanent fixtures, bar backs and/or bartenders can restock them after a catered event according to the specifications noted on the BEO for the next function. For instance, when a party is over, the manager can take an ending inventory and determine the liquor usage for that function. The bar back and/or bartender can then replenish the bar with nonperishables so that the bar production workers the next day need only spend a few minutes prepreping the perishables.

Food Preparation

Food preparation, or prep, activities are performed just prior to the point of service. For example, your preparation schedule for hot foods should dovetail with your guest service schedule. You would not want to produce these products too far in advance, or else they will lose culinary quality. Nor would you want to produce them to customer order, as this will slow down service.

A good food production schedule combines the preprep and prep activities. For instance, if you have a baked chicken item on the menu, you can do some preprep work the night before, such as washing the products, seasoning them, and laying them out on sheet pans. About an hour or so before service, you will prep them, that is, put them in the oven to cook.

Finish Cooking

Finish cooking involves cooking to guest order. For instance, the chef must wait for the guest to order a rare steak; he or she does not prep it in advance.

Finish cooking is the most difficult part of the food production plan. It is also the most labor intensive. You need to schedule a lot of worker hours. And the worker hours must be provided by highly skilled food handlers who can work under the demanding conditions that accompany most finish-cooking activities.

For instance, a chef working at an egg action station must be quick, efficient, and accurate. He or she normally will be producing two or three guest orders at a time and will need to remember them as well as those that are coming in from other guests waiting in line.

Some finish cooking is easier than others. For instance, with a roast beef item, you can preprep the roast the night before, prep it two or three hours before service, and finish cook it—that is, carve and serve it—to customer order. In this case, the finish cooking is a relatively easy task.

Bar Preparation

In most instances, bar prep is synonymous with bar service; that is, the same person who prepares the drink also serves it and, if applicable, collects cash or a drink ticket.

In those instances where a service bar—a bar used only by cocktail servers to obtain drinks for their guests—is used, the prep and service activities are separated. The bartender preps drinks only when the servers order them. For cost-control purposes, a server may open a computerized guest check or give a precheck ticket (or some other record, such as a duplicate guest check) to the bartender before a drink can be prepared. If applicable, the servers are responsible for cash or drink-ticket collection.

Food Workstation Setup

Action stations, serving lines, and buffet tables must be set up prior to service. In some clubs, the kitchen staff has this responsibility, while other properties split the work between the kitchen, banquet setup, and housekeeping staffs. For instance, cooks may be responsible for setting up the serving lines in the kitchen or in the service corridor and setting up the action stations, while the kitchen and banquet setup crews together set up the buffet tables. Generally speaking, the kitchen handles the foods and housekeeping handles the table setups.

Replenishing the Food Workstations

The kitchen is normally responsible for replenishing the food supplies on buffet tables, action stations, and serving lines. Usually a food runner is employed to handle this task. In some cases, though, the service staff might take on this duty. For instance, the kitchen crew may be responsible for stocking backup foods in hot carts and delivering them to a service corridor.

A food server can then be assigned to replenish depleted food workstations with foods taken from these hot carts.

Employees assigned this responsibility typically must do more than merely refill serving containers. They must be able to anticipate customer needs; combine half-empty pans and make the combination appear as attractive as any other container; replace removed food containers with appropriate decor (such as flower displays); and react to the chef's last-minute instructions. They also may need to pitch in and help keep buffet tables and landing space clear of soiled tableware and trash.

Replenishing the Bars

Bar backs are responsible for replenishing liquor, ice, garnishes, glassware, and direct operating supplies, such as coasters, swizzle sticks, and cocktail napkins. Most bartenders will also jump in and help restock merchandise in an emergency, such as when the bar back is helping out at another beverage function that is shorthanded.

Cocktail servers may also help out in a pinch. For instance, if there are one or two special drink requests that cannot be prepared by the bartender because he or she does not have the stock available, a cocktail server may just go to another club bar to fill the order.

Number of Food Production People Needed

Food production differs somewhat from food service in that the food handlers usually have responsibility for food production throughout the club. Handling the catered meal function may not be their only duty. While the banquet service staff concentrates solely on the scheduled meal function to which it is assigned, the typical food handler must juggle many tasks.

It is, therefore, a bit more difficult to determine exactly how much food production labor is needed for a particular meal function. On the one hand, the cooks on duty in a restaurant outlet may be able to handle the entire catered event along with their other responsibilities. At the other end of the spectrum is the catered function that requires a completely separate kitchen crew. For this first type, you may not have any additional variable labor costs, whereas, for the second, the food production payroll will be a significant portion of total expenses.

In general, the number of food-production work hours needed for a catered event will depend on

1. *Number of guests.*
2. *Amount of time scheduled for the catered event.*

3. *Applicable union and club personnel policies.*

4. *Type of service style used.* For instance, action stations require more production labor, whereas the typical buffet that offers only standardized menu items will need less.

5. *Amount of convenience foods used.* Processed foods may be less expensive to prep and serve—you need fewer labor hours to reconstitute them. You also avoid expensive labor expertise because the products require less skill to handle. However, their purchase prices are usually very high because of the built-in labor and energy costs that the manufacturer must recapture.

6. *Amount of scratch production.* This is the opposite of using convenience foods. The closer a food ingredient is to its natural state, the lower its purchase price will be. A significant amount of scratch production results in a low food cost. However, you will end up with a high labor cost since you take on all of the preprep and prep burdens. If the local labor market is tight, the resulting labor cost incurred may be prohibitive.

7. *Amounts of finish cooking needed.* Too much finish cooking wreaks havoc with a food-production labor budget. If the host wants a great deal of this, he or she must be willing to pay a handsome labor surcharge.

8. *Type of menu items offered.* Some products take more time to preprep and prep. For instance, it takes more time to produce meat loaf than roast beef, vegetable soup than onion soup, and gallantine of capon than roast duckling.

9. *Number of last-minute requests.* Flexibility is one of the hallmarks of a successful club catering department. You must be flexible enough to accommodate some unscheduled requests. For instance, you should be ready to produce one or two individual fruit plates or vegetable platters on a moment's notice.

10. *Number of special diets.* It can take almost as long to produce a few special diet meals as it does to take care of 50 standard guest meals. If you know about these needs in advance, you can be ready for them. However, once you start producing a different menu item for each guest, you immediately lose the cost advantage and predictability that catering enjoys over regular restaurant food production and service.

11. *Accuracy of meal-time estimates.* It is not unusual for a meal function to start late and end late. This unfortunately may result in

overtime premium pay for some production staff. It also can cause overtime premium pay in other departments, such as housekeeping, because their work schedules may be thrown out of line.

When catered functions run behind schedule, you must expect to incur a higher labor cost. It is also likely that the foods may lose a good deal of their culinary quality. Ironically, when this scenario occurs, the guests cause you to pay more for the privilege of hearing them complain about the foods' marginal quality.

Some catering managers prepare staffing charts to help them determine the number of food-production work hours needed, how many persons to call in to work the function, and how these people should be scheduled. These charts usually relate the number of work hours needed to the number of expected guests. For instance, if you expect 100 guests, you go down the column headed by 100 on the chart and in each cell there will be a number of suggested work hours needed for each job position. Assume you are allowed 16 food-production hours for 100 guests. If the meal function will last 4 hours, you can divide the 16 work hours into four 4-hour shifts and bring in 4 persons. You also can schedule one 8-hour person and two 4-hour employees. Or you can plan any other acceptable combination.

How you apportion the allowable number of work hours will depend on many of the factors on the previous list. For instance, considerable preprep indicates that maybe you should have an 8-hour person come in the day before. A lot of finish cooking implies an opposite strategy.

Distributing work hours over a work schedule also depends on how many food production persons you want on board before, during, and after the meal function. Usually you will need to stagger the work schedule in such a way that most of your production work hours are scheduled when the bulk of the production must be completed, with the remaining hours to cover the start-up and teardown periods.

Staffing charts work much better in the typical restaurant operation where the menu, production, and service are standardized and there is a consistent pattern of customer arrivals and departures, popularity of menu items, and amount of time it takes to turn the tables. They also work well in service planning because, once you know the timing of the function, menu, number of guests, and style of service needed, you can usually lock into a standardized work schedule.

Kitchen staffing charts must be continually revised unless your catering business settles into some sort of predictable pattern. The director of catering will usually keep a close eye on the staffing chart and change it as needed. He or she also will be forever looking for that elusive pattern that can make it much easier to forecast food production payroll expenses and develop accurate food-production work schedules.

Number of Bar Backs and Bartenders Needed

The number of bar backs needed for a catered function will depend primarily on

1. Number of bars scheduled
2. Capacity of each bar to hold in-process inventories
3. Distance between the bars and the kitchen and storerooms
4. Degree of ease or difficulty associated with retrieving backup stock
5. Number of guests
6. Hours of operation
7. Variety of liquor stock, glassware, garnishes, and direct operating supplies needed at the bars
8. Applicable union and club personnel policies

Unless the catered event is very small, you will need at least one bar back. The typical banquet bar, especially the portable one, does not have a lot of storage capacity. It usually will need periodic replenishment.

If a small beverage function is scheduled, perhaps the bartender can do double duty and take on the bar back's responsibility. However, this could reduce service efficiency and cause guest dissatisfaction if the bartender is in the liquor storeroom and is temporarily unavailable to mix drinks.

The number of bartenders needed for a catered event will depend primarily on

1. Number of bars scheduled
2. Types of drinks that must be prepared
3. Estimated number of drinks to be prepared
4. Number of guests
5. Hours of operation
6. Amount of bar-back work that must be performed
7. Applicable union and club personnel policies

You will need at least 1 bartender for each bar location. For all but very small beverage functions, it is customary to schedule 2 bartenders for each bar plus any wine service personnel needed for the meal. Even for small beverage functions of, say, 50 to 60 guests, you may need 2 bartenders. You may need more than 2 if the event is scheduled for only 45 minutes to an hour. In this case, speed is a high priority—with such a short time frame, guests will normally swamp the bar to make sure they get their desired number of drinks before it closes. Two bartenders may be unable to handle this onslaught.

For large beverage functions, clubs generally will try to get by with one bartender for every 75 guests. The 1 : 75 ratio is usually the minimum necessary if you expect all guests to arrive at the same time. If you do not have enough bartenders when a crowd hits the door, some guests may have to wait up to an hour to get a drink.

If you have over 1000 guests, a bartender-to-guest ratio of 1 : 100 is appropriate. With a large crowd, guests cannot move around as much. With 8 to 10 bartenders, the preparation and service tends to be quicker and more efficient because the bartenders can help each other and keep the lines moving.

The timing of a beverage function can also influence the number of bartenders needed. For instance, if 200 persons are leaving a business meeting and going directly to a cocktail reception, you may want to set a ratio of 1 : 50 so that the guests will be served quickly. If there is a break period between the end of the business meeting and the beginning of the cocktail reception and the club has sleeping rooms where some of the attendees are staying, guests may wish to go back to their sleeping rooms to freshen up, and therefore they will not arrive all at once. They will come in a few at a time. Consequently, you could use fewer bartenders to handle the group.

To alleviate pressure on the bartenders, you could schedule a few cocktail servers to pass glasses of champagne, still wines, bottled waters, and juices. This also adds an extra touch of elegance to the event.

If the catered function calls for cocktail servers and/or a sommelier, perhaps you can reduce the number of bar backs and bartenders you would normally schedule. For instance, one cocktail server could be cross-trained (as a combination bartender and cocktail server, for instance) and scheduled as a floater (that is, fill in as a bartender or server as needed). This flexibility could easily save a few labor hours over the long term.

By the same token, a food server, busperson, captain, or other member of the catering and kitchen staffs could be used to help out the bartenders and bar backs. For instance, it might be more economical to schedule one 6-hour busperson to handle bussing and bar back duties than to schedule one 4-hour bar back and one 4-hour busperson.

If you decide to mix and match job positions and adopt these types of creative scheduling techniques, you will need to check the union joint bargaining agreement, if applicable, and/or the club's personnel policies and procedures manual to see if it is permissible. Furthermore, you must ensure that the relevant staff members have received the proper type and amount of cross-training.

Number of Ticket Takers Needed

If guests must use tickets to enter a function room, or if they need to use them to get into a meal function, you may or may not need to schedule a ticket taker to collect them. In most cases, a host will handle this chore personally; however, on some occasions, you will be asked to provide this service.

Ideally, the host handles the collection of all entry tickets. You should avoid coming between the client and his or her guests in what sometimes could be a confrontational occurrence. You do not want to be put in a position where the club must impose host sanctions on guests. Furthermore, some guests may not appreciate the club assuming this control position.

Drink tickets and meal tickets do not usually cause confrontational problems. Consequently, if guests are required to use them, there generally is no need to schedule separate ticket takers. In these cases, bartenders and chefs can collect them.

Number of Banquet Setup Crew Members Needed

The number of persons needed to set up, tear down, and/or clean the function room will depend primarily on

1. Amount of lead time available
2. Size of the catered event
3. Size of the room
4. Location of the room in the club
5. Amount of time available between functions (For example, how much time do you have to tear down and clean up after a breakfast function and set up for an afternoon reception?)
6. Applicable union and club personnel policies

If you have a lot of time available, and/or if the function planned is for 50 guests or less, usually you can get by with only one crew member. For larger functions, or if time is precious, usually no less than two persons must be scheduled.

Two or more crew members may also be needed if some tasks require the strength and agility of at least two persons to be accomplished. For example, setting up a platform, rolling out and setting up a portable dance floor, or hanging signage or decorations may require two persons working in tandem.

Usually the club wants function rooms set up as soon as possible. All nonperishable items should be set out in advance so that staff members can concentrate on the last-minute details and not have to worry about doing things during prime times (that is, times when guest service is a priority) that could have been done quite comfortably during slack times (that is, down-times when guests are not being served).

SERVICE PLANNING

Unlike production planning, service planning is a much easier task. Once you know the timing of the function, menu, number of guests, and style of service, you usually can forecast an accurate estimate of the number of service work hours needed, the number and types of servers required, and the most efficient work schedule that should be followed.

Types of Servers Needed

Depending on the type of catered event, the banquet manager will need to schedule one or more of the following types of service personnel:

1. Maitre d'
2. Captain
3. Food server
4. Cocktail server
5. Sommelier
6. Busperson

Service Duties

Service personnel are responsible for a wide array of duties. Unlike production staff members, servers are often called upon to jump in at a moment's notice and handle unscheduled requests and/or activities. For instance, while the typical client would not consider asking the chef to change the menu at the last minute, he or she may not be shy about asking the maitre d' to set up an extra dining table, slow down service because the speaker is running a bit late, or push two tables together so that a subgroup of guests can create its own party atmosphere.

Service personnel must be very flexible. All of them should be trained to perform

1. Making napkin folds
2. Doing table settings
3. Placing table pads and tablecloths
4. Presetting foods on dining tables
5. Greeting/seating guests
6. Taking food/beverage orders from guests (if applicable—only if guests have a choice of entrees and/or beverages)
7. Serving food and beverage
8. Submitting food/beverage guest orders to chefs and bartenders (if applicable—also done only if guests have a choice of entrees and/or beverages)
9. Opening wine bottles
10. Pouring wine
11. Providing hot beverage service
12. Providing cold beverage service
13. Crumbing tables
14. Bussing tables
15. Carrying loaded cocktail, oval, and crescent-shaped trays
16. Stacking trays
17. Emptying trays
18. Preparing items tableside
19. Using different service styles
20. Handling last-minute requests for food, beverage, and/or service
21. Handling complaints
22. Directing guests to other facilities in the club
23. Handling disruptions
24. Dealing with intoxicated guests
25. Refusing liquor service to minors
26. Requisitioning tableware from the executive steward

Service Ratios

Service ratios—that is, the number of service personnel needed to handle a given number of guests—are usually established by the catering executive and the club's top management team. These ratios are the heart of the service staffing guide.

The number of service personnel needed depends on many factors. The primary ones are

1. *Number of guests.*
2. *Length of the catered function.*
3. *Style of service used.*
4. *Menu, especially its length and complexity.*
5. *Timing of the event.* For instance, you may need more servers if there will be a considerable amount of time between courses and other activities, such as guests' listening to speakers, dancing, or watching stage shows. Similarly, if the group needs to be fed very quickly, you will need more service personnel; but, since you will not need them very long, you might be able to handle the catered event adequately without exceeding your labor budget. You may be able to staff an entire service time by pulling staff from other club restaurant operations to help for a few minutes in the ballroom.
6. *Room setup.* Is the layout and design conducive to quick, efficient service, or should bottlenecks be expected?
7. *Location of function room.* How much distance is there between the kitchen and the function room? How easily can you go from the kitchen to the function room? Is there enough aisle space? Is the service corridor large enough? Are there enough service elevators?
8. *The probability that overtime must be scheduled.* For instance, experience may suggest that a particular type of catered event and/or a particular type of group will tend to run late. This could result in overtime premium pay for a few service personnel. However, if you can anticipate this problem, you should be able to schedule enough employees to handle the event properly without resorting to overtime.
9. *Number of head table guests.* These guests require much more service attention than do the others.

10. *The amount and type of extraordinary requests.* For instance, a host may want extra labor to seat guests after they go through a buffet line. Some guests may request extra condiments, which will add to the service workload. And some hosts, at the last minute, may want the room rearranged somewhat; usually the service personnel have to handle this type of last-minute request because the setup crew may be unavailable on short notice.

11. *Applicable union and club personnel policies.* Unionized clubs may schedule only the minimum number of service personnel called for in the union contract. Nonunion clubs whose competitors are unionized may also follow these standard ratios.

Experience shows that the minimum number of servers as well as the minimum number of each service job classification that must be scheduled according to union regulations usually are insufficient to provide the level of service required by most club-catered events. You generally will need more servers if, for example, you need to serve a large luncheon very quickly or if you must provide French service for a dinner function.

The joint bargaining agreement's requirements typically provide enough servers to accommodate only the small and/or easy-to-handle groups. However, these service minimums at least give you something to work with when forecasting the number of servers needed.

Many clubs develop strict service ratios and do not vary from them even though a particular situation may call for it. For instance, some properties will budget 1 server for every 16 guests, regardless of the style of service, the type of menu, or whether the servers are responsible for wine service.

If you adhere strictly to this 1:16 ratio, you may risk customer dissatisfaction. Some catered events can be handled adequately under this payroll cost constraint. However, most functions will need more help or else they cannot be serviced efficiently.

Irrespective of the quality of a catered function's food and beverage, room setup, and overall ambience, poor service significantly reduces the members' appreciation and enjoyment of the event. Member surveys consistently show that members rank the quality of service very high on their lists of desired club attributes. They usually place it no lower than second on their lists, ranking it just slightly behind the culinary quality of the food and beverage.

Poor service will overshadow any other favorable aspect of the event. Guests will never be pleased if the service is lacking; they will remember a bad experience much longer than a good one. The club's catering executive who tries to shave service costs to the bone will undoubtedly make a lot of members and guests unhappy. He or she will also jeopardize the reputation of the club.

If the club puts you on a very tight labor budget, at times you will be between a rock and a hard place. You will be asked to maintain the budget, yet provide a level of service that will satisfy guests and encourage hosts to return. You cannot risk coming in over budget. If the catered event's projected revenue will not cover the extra labor costs, the least you should do is ask the host to alter his or her menu or service requirements or agree to pay a modest labor surcharge so that you can schedule adequate staff.

Experience shows that the number of service personnel needed can vary from a low of about 1:8 staff member/guests to a high of approximately 1:40. According to meeting planners, the minimum service ratio is 1:20 for the conventional sit-down meal function with American-style service with some foods preset. If you are using rounds of 10, you should schedule a server for every 2 dining tables. If you are using rounds of 8, 2 servers should be scheduled to handle 5 dining tables.

The minimum busperson-to-server ratio for this sit-down meal is 1:3. If you are using rounds of 10, the busperson-to-table ratio should be 1:6. If you are using rounds of 8, the ratio is 1:8.

Some clubs will schedule a busperson-to-server ratio of 1:2. This is usually done for functions that include several VIPs or where extraordinary service is requested by the host. Generally speaking, though, you can make do with a ratio of 1:3 because servers normally are expected to perform some bussing duties during the catered event.

If the conventional sit-down meal function requires poured-wine service, you normally will need a server-to-guest ratio of at least 1:16. One server is needed for every 2 rounds of 8, and 2 servers are needed for every 3 rounds of 10. One busperson for every 6 rounds of 10 or every 8 rounds of 8 will usually suffice.

If the meal function is served buffet style, usually servers and buspersons can handle significantly more guests. For instance, the minimum service ratio of 1 server for every 20 guests and 1 busperson for every 3 servers could very easily be increased to 1:30 and 1:4.

In some cases, you may want to maintain the ratio of 1 server for every 20 guests for a buffet-style meal function. For instance, if the kitchen schedules a small crew, or if it has to handle several parties, it may be unable to refresh the buffet tables and help serve guests. You could use the balance of your wait staff to focus on these tasks.

If the buffet requires considerable replenishment during the meal, you may need to schedule servers to handle the food-running chores. In this situation, normally you will need a food runner (or other service employee) for every 100 to 125 guests. You will need more runners if they are expected to accommodate several buffet stations spread throughout the function room. Conversely, if there are only a few buffet stations, other food servers who could share the workload, and/or a limited menu, you should be able to schedule fewer runners. Moreover, if the chef employs food runners, you may be able to avoid this responsibility.

If the meal function requires Russian or French service, you can usually serve the guests adequately if you follow the service ratios already noted for the conventional sit-down meal with poured-wine service.

If the meal function includes Russian or French service with poured-wine service, generally you will need at least a ratio of 1:1 for servers and dining tables and of 1:3 for buspersons and dining tables. These ratios are appropriate whether you are using rounds of 8 or rounds of 10.

Head tables should receive the best service. If the catered function has head tables, you should plan to schedule at least 1 server for each head table. If the head table includes more than 8 guests, you should use 2 servers. Ideally, the head table would have its own busperson. If you cannot afford this or do not need a separate busperson, you should assign the head table and 1 or 2 other nearby dining tables to 1 busperson. If possible, you should not have head table servers handling both the serving and bussing chores. The servers should devote their efforts to guest service.

Regardless of the style of service, you will need to schedule at least 1 floor supervisor. This supervisor could be a banquet captain or a maitre d'.

Generally speaking, you should plan to schedule at least 1 banquet captain for each catered event. For very large meal functions, you should plan to schedule 1 banquet captain for every block of 250 guests (that is, for every block of 25 rounds of 10). Alternatively, you could schedule 1 banquet captain for every 10 to 12 servers.

The banquet captain for a small catered event can supervise both the meal service and the reception service. For example, if there are only 100 guests, 1 floor supervisor is sufficient to handle both segments.

If you need to schedule more than 1 banquet captain, you should assign one maitre d' to coordinate their duties. For instance, if you have a meal function for 1000 guests, you typically would assign 1 maitre d' and 4 banquet captains to supervise service. If there is a premeal reception, the maitre d' should supervise both the meal service and the reception.

You should not try to serve a function without a sufficient number of floor supervisors. These men and women play an extremely important role in coordinating service and seeing to it that all guests are served efficiently. For instance, with a sit-down meal function, it is important to have all courses served at approximately the same time. This will not happen by itself. It is a difficult feat to achieve and is almost impossible to accomplish without adequate supervision.

If you need to staff a reception, you must schedule enough servers to supervise the food stations. Generally speaking, you should have one server responsible for every three food stations. If the stations are spread throughout the function room and there is considerable distance between each one, you will need more servers.

The servers responsible for overseeing the food stations can also perform some bussing duties. For instance, they can help replenish the tableware, bus the landing space, and remove waste. Depending on the size and complexity of the reception, you may be able to get by with few or no buspersons.

You will need more servers if you intend to pass food trays during a reception. For a small catered event, 1 or 2 servers would suffice. As the function size increases, you normally need to schedule 1 server to handle a quarter of the function room, an eighth of the function room, and so forth. Generally, you should plan to schedule at least 2 servers for every 75 guests.

You also will need more buspersons if you have servers pass trays during the reception. The servers usually will be unable to pitch in and help with the bussing duties because they will be too busy with guests. You should expect to schedule at least 1 busperson for every 3 to 4 servers.

Even if there is no food served during a reception, you still should schedule at least 1 or 2 buspersons to keep the landing space clear. Perhaps 1 or 2 dining room buspersons could be brought in earlier than the others to cover the reception's bussing needs; then, after the reception, they can help out during the meal function's rush period.

If you are using cocktail servers during a reception to pass trays of premade drinks, you will need at least 1 cocktail server for every 2 to 3 food servers. Usually you need considerably fewer cocktail servers than food servers in this situation because guests tend to approach the food servers more frequently than they do the cocktail servers. For instance, a guest might take a glass of wine from a tray and nurse it all night, whereas he or she will usually take more than one piece of food.

Very few catered events use cocktail servers to take guest drink orders, return to a service bar to fill them, and then go back on the floor to serve them. This type of service is infeasible for large group functions. Generally it is done only for small functions, especially those that cater to VIPs. The typical type of cocktail service used for standard catered events requires the guests to approach the portable bars, get their drinks, disappear into the crowd, and return when they want more drinks. However, if you do use this type of cocktail service to take guest orders, your labor costs will increase significantly. In this situation, at best a server can usually make only 3 or 4 passes per hour through his or her assigned floor area. During each pass, he or she will usually be able to carry, at the most, only 12 to 16 drinks. In the best-case scenario, then, you would need 1 cocktail server to handle 48 to 64 drinks per hour. Furthermore, since this type of service is less efficient and requires more coordination and effort, you will need more bartenders to handle the workload.

Many receptions last only about an hour. Some will last up to 2 hours. If it is a 1-hour period, you normally expect each guest to consume at least 2.5 drinks. For a 2-hour period, you expect each guest to consume at least 3 drinks. If you have a 1-hour cocktail reception for 100 persons and the client wants cocktail servers to take drink orders from guests, you will need about 3 bartenders and 5 to 6 cocktail servers to handle the drink orders efficiently. If you have a 2-hour reception, though, guests will not drink so quickly, and some of them will tend to leave before the reception ends; consequently, you may be able to get by with fewer bartenders and cocktail servers. Unfortunately, in this instance, most guests will do the bulk of their drinking during the first hour, so you may be unable to reduce your service requirements significantly.

When hosts are faced with the exorbitant labor cost associated with having cocktail servers take guest orders, they generally decide against it. But even if a host is willing to pay the extra labor charges, you still might want to discourage such a labor-intensive style of service because there are too many opportunities for the catered event to bog down. For instance, at a predinner reception, if guests need to wait too long for their drinks, the reception, and ultimately the dinner, will probably run much longer than scheduled.

On the other hand, sometimes slower cocktail service can be a virtue. For instance, if there is a host bar at a cocktail reception, guests may be tempted to overindulge, whereas, if they give their orders to a server, their consumption will probably be much less.

Work Scheduling

The banquet manager usually sets aside one day each week to prepare the service work schedules for the following week. Each week, he or she must prepare a fixed work schedule and a variable work schedule.

The fixed schedule represents the minimum number of persons and work hours needed to keep the club catering department open and active, regardless of the volume of business expected. For instance, if there is at least one catered function each day, you will need a handful of permanent full-time and/or permanent part-time persons scheduled to provide the level of service expected by guests.

If a club does a great deal of catering business, these fixed employees can be scheduled solely for catered functions. If the catering business varies, having peaks and valleys, you can still have permanent staff members assigned to catering, although you might have to share them with another club department. For instance, you might have a 40-hour-per-week employee assigned to catering, with the understanding that, if catering business is slow, he or she will work in another area of the food and beverage department.

The more fixed employees you have, the easier it is to prepare your weekly work schedules. It is also more conducive to employee satisfaction. Fixed employees usually have steady, predictable work schedules. They will appreciate the ability to plan their personal lives more accurately.

Variable labor is incremental labor. It will fluctuate with the volume of catering business. The catering department usually must schedule a large number of variable employees each week.

Unlike some of the club's restaurant outlet managers, the banquet manager will need to prepare a variable work schedule each week. Catering business can be predictable, but the uniqueness of each catered function forces you to call A-list and B-list employees every week in order to prepare a proper work schedule.

The work schedules will be based primarily on

1. Types of functions booked that week
2. Expected length of each function
3. Number of guests anticipated
4. Styles of service required
5. Allowable labor costs
6. Employee availability
7. Guest satisfaction needs

Typically, you would use this information, any applicable union regulations, and the staffing guidelines set forth in the club's staffing charts to prepare the appropriate work schedules.

When preparing work schedules, you will need to allocate a sufficient number of work hours to cover the preopening and teardown periods. You should stagger your servers so that some arrive and leave earlier than others. You should aim to have the maximum number of workers available when the catered functions are in high gear and fewer scheduled at function beginnings and endings.

Scheduling the appropriate number of work hours while simultaneously adhering to your labor budget is hard to accomplish in some situations. For instance, if you are working in a union property, the union contract may require you to guarantee each employee you call in a minimum of a four-hour work schedule that day. If you need a few persons one day to cover three-hour shifts, you are free to schedule them for three hours apiece. However, you must pay them for four hours.

We noted earlier in this chapter that the minimum number of servers required in the typical joint bargaining agreement usually does not cause problems for you because this minimum normally is insufficient to handle most types of catered events. However, the minimum number of guaranteed work hours can cause problems if you have several bookings that lend themselves to scheduling several service personnel for less than the minimum.

Even a nonunion club may have a policy of paying a minimum number of work hours. For instance, it may wish to follow these standards in order to compete with unionized hotels for workers. To say the least, this will make it more difficult to schedule some catered functions economically.

Timing of Service

The host and the catering sales representative normally discuss the timing of the service and relay their desires to the service staff. The banquet manager must take these desires and develop a plan that will provide maximum efficiency and a minimum number of bottlenecks.

Service will make or break the catered function. If half the guests are waiting for their entrees while the other half are eating dessert, there is a problem. Also, if the head table, which usually receives the best service, is finished before other guests, the head table guests will have to wait for the others to finish or will have to begin the program while some guests are still being served or are still eating. This is not acceptable.

Timing problems can be minimized or avoided by scheduling extra servers. However, this may be cost prohibitive.

An inexpensive way to minimize timing problems is to preset as much food and beverage on the dining tables as the host will allow and/or that can be done safely. This is especially important if the host is in a hurry. For instance, if the group has only one hour for lunch, many food items such as appetizers, salads, rolls, butter, relishes, and desserts can be preset on the dining tables.

Some clubs offer luncheons that are entirely preset. For instance, salad and/or sandwich luncheons can be preset in such a way that guests can sit down and eat quickly. Servers would need to handle only beverage service and special requests.

To ensure proper timing as well as smooth-running service, the banquet captain will normally call the roll of all service personnel about one hour before the catered function is scheduled to begin. Workstations are assigned. Servers are informed of any special diets, special service requests, and so forth. Also during the roll-call, the captain will describe all menu items so that guest inquiries can be answered without the need for servers to run back to the kitchen and check with the chef.

For most receptions, normally there is a scheduled starting and ending time. Usually a few guests will arrive at the beginning. By the time the reception is half over, all guests will generally be present. Toward the end of the reception, you should begin to see guests leaving, a few at a time.

Some receptions will have all guests there when they open. For instance, a cocktail reception that begins immediately after a group's last business meeting of the day will usually have maximum attendance when the doors open.

About 15 minutes before you want the meal service to start, you should begin calling guests. You can dim the lights in the prefunction area, ring chimes, start music, or make announcements to signal guests that it is time to enter the dining room for dinner. Servers should be standing ready at their stations when guests walk into the room, not against the wall talking with each other.

For most conventional meal functions, the salad course will take about 20 to 30 minutes, and the entree take about 30 to 50 minutes, from serving to removing plates. Dessert can usually be handled in approximately 20 to 30 minutes. Normally, the entire banquet service will be about an hour and 15 minutes for the typical luncheon and 2 hours for the typical dinner event.

More elaborate meal functions may take a bit more time to serve. While the added diversions can enhance the dining experience, long meal functions tend to make guests a little anxious. Even if you are using elaborate service styles or other similar attractions, guests will begin to think something is wrong with the club catering department if the meal lasts much longer than two hours. In addition, recall that some potential guests will be very reluctant to attend a catered event if they suspect it will run on too long.

Teardown Procedures

As the function winds down, servers can begin performing a bit of teardown work. For instance, prior to serving dessert, they can crumb tables and remove nonessentials (such as salt and pepper shakers and extra flatware). While the guests are enjoying their dessert, the servers can refill the condiment containers and put them away.

As guests begin to trickle out, servers can see to it that all utensils and tableware requisitioned from the executive steward are cleaned and returned properly. They can inventory all service equipment. And they can see to it that any necessary paperwork, such as meal-ticket accounting, is completed correctly.

Soon after all guests have left, all dining and buffet tables must be stripped. Soiled and leftover clean napery must be returned to housekeeping. Unless the tables must be set up for the next function, they will need to be broken down and put away by the banquet setup crew.

Housekeeping or maintenance staff members will need to come in and clean the floors, walls, hallways, mirrors, windows, and fixtures. In some clubs, servers help this crew; for instance, at the end of the function, a server may run a vacuum cleaner over the heavy traffic areas.

While housekeeping or maintenance are handling the cleaning chores, an employee or two might be able to help set up for the next scheduled function. For instance, if you are tearing down after a luncheon and there is a dinner scheduled later, the banquet setup crew might want to get a head start by simultaneously tearing down and resetting the room. The crew would most likely appreciate any help service personnel can contribute.

The kitchen staff will also need to recycle a few leftover foods. Sometimes these foods can be used for the next catered function, by the club's restaurant outlets, or in the employee dining room.

If the leftover foods have lost some of their culinary quality, it probably is best to discard them. For instance, foods that have been on a buffet table for an hour or more may be perfectly edible. However, they probably have deteriorated to the point where their appearance, taste, and texture are below your quality standards. You should not risk offending a guest by recycling and serving them again.

If the leftover foods are protein-rich, moist foods, they may have been contaminated during service. These potentially hazardous foods present excellent growing conditions for harmful bacteria. For instance, roast beef, cream-based soups, custards, and protein-rich salads made with mayonnaise or other similar dressings should not be reserved unless you are certain they are safe to eat. If there are any doubts, they should be discarded immediately before they have a chance to come into contact with wholesome foods and contaminate them.

Some hosts may ask you to donate leftover foods they have paid for to a homeless shelter or some other similar charitable organization. This is certainly a socially redeeming activity we can all support. However, if someone contracts a food-borne illness from these foods, the club may be liable for damages.

Some states (such as California) have good samaritan laws that absolve you of liability as long as you used reasonable care when preparing, collecting, and delivering the leftover foods to charitable organizations. If you were not negligent in handling these products, and if you sincerely believe they are safe to eat, you can donate them and not worry about being sued. However, if there is any question about the wholesomeness of the foods, you should discard them. Not only do you risk a lawsuit, you do no one a favor by distributing foods that could make people sick.

CATERING SAFETY AND SANITATION

Food and beverage production and service must be carried out in a safe and wholesome manner. Anyone handling foods and beverages must be trained to practice basic safety and sanitation procedures to ensure that employees and guests do not fall victim to accidents or food-borne illnesses.

All commercial foodservice operations must adhere to the sanitation standards set forth by their local health districts. These agencies periodically inspect food and beverage production and service personnel, equipment, and facilities to ensure that they comply with local rules and regulations.

Catering executives should consider following the sanitation guidelines developed by the Educational Foundation of the National Restaurant Association (NRA) when training employees. In fact, any employee who successfully completes the Educational Foundation's SERVSAFE Applied Foodservice Sanitation course will earn a certification that is viewed favorably by all local health districts.

Production and service equipment and facilities must meet pertinent standards of safety and sanitation. All commercial construction must meet building code guidelines. For instance, in most cities and counties in the United States, all food-contact equipment must display the familiar blue seal of the International NSF. Equipment that does not carry this seal usually cannot be used in commercial food and beverage operations.

Underwriter's Laboratory (UL) and the American Gas Association (AGA) inspect and certify equipment compliance with generally accepted safety standards. For instance, a gas oven displaying the AGA seal is safe to use in commercial production. Most local building codes require all equipment and permanent installations to meet or exceed safety standards promulgated by these types of independent inspectors.

The safe and sanitary food and beverage operation also meets standards set by other local government-inspector-powered agencies. For instance, the fire marshall will periodically inspect for fire hazards such as blocked exits, overcrowding, and discharged fire extinguisher systems.

The Department of Labor is also concerned with safety matters. For example, if you hire a few teenagers to work as buspersons or food runners, they will not be able to perform all types of work. Usually youngsters under 18 years of age cannot operate machinery, such as slicers, food processors, and dough-cutting machines. They also typically cannot fill, refill, or light fuel containers such as Sterno pots.

The local workers compensation agency normally is responsible for enforcing the federal Occupational Safety and Health Act (OSHA). The agency may also insure employees for job-related injuries. Clubs can call upon the agency to help them develop effective employee safety-training guidelines. Furthermore, the agency can visit your property, point out areas of concern, and note what you can do to eliminate these hazards.

There are several safety and sanitation problems that must be controlled by the catering executive. Experience shows that the major ones are

1. *Tableside and action-station cooking.* Exhibition cooking poses many risks, even if it is performed by trained professional chefs who have a great deal of experience with this type of work.

Some parts of the country may prohibit exhibition cooking. You should check the local fire code to see if it is allowed in your area. If it is allowed, check further to see if any restrictions exist.

Action-station cooking does not seem to be nearly as dangerous as tableside cooking. Usually there is sufficient aisle space allocated to minimize the threat of accidents.

Tableside cooking, especially the type involving flaming dishes, poses the most serious risk. For example, to enhance guest and employee safety, ITT Sheraton has a company policy prohibiting this practice.

Rarely does tableside cooking result in a major club fire. The accident would have to be very serious for any resulting fire to combat the modern club's sprinkler system. However, guest injury is another matter.

Flaming dishes are an attractive addition to the catered event. They provide an exciting and entertaining change of pace. Hosts and guests are always pleased with these types of presentations. Unfortunately, the curious guest who gets a little too close to the action is liable to inhale hazardous gas and/or come into contact with a spark or flame. Inhaling gasses tends to be more of a risk than the fire itself. Whenever you flame a dish, you should have an extra server stationed nearby to watch the spectacle and react to any emergency. This minimizes the fire hazard. However, you may not be able to control gasses because you usually cannot see them leaking until some harm occurs.

You must be very careful when using Sterno, butane, propane, or other types of cooking fuels. Propane is especially troublesome and risky. When using propane, it does not matter how much training the chef has had. A leaking tank is not obvious. Furthermore, lighting the burners can provide some anxious moments if too much gas is allowed to enter the burners before they are lit.

Propane is a dangerous fuel. The industry recommends that it be used only outdoors. It is so combustible that—depending upon temperature, humidity, and the amount of air space between the tanks and the grills—there is as much as a 60-percent chance that the equipment will malfunction and cause a serious accident.

Most tableside cooking units use butane fuel—usually the best fuel to use. It is much safer than propane. It also is preferable to Sterno because you can control the temperature and size of the flame much better with butane than you can with Sterno.

Tableside cooking should be limited to a single saute or wok station that is no closer to guests than the diameter of a 60-inch round dining table. The work area must be well ventilated. You should not allow exhibition cooking in a low-ceilinged room or in a room that does not have proper ventilation.

If a host prefers the excitement and attraction of tableside cooking, you can indulge this request safely by providing a flaming display on an elevated platform situated away from the dining areas on one side of the function room. The display can be used to prepare a handful of portions, with the bulk of production performed in the kitchen.

Another compromise is to have a flaming parade around the perimeter of the function room with the lights dimmed. For instance, food servers can carry a few flaming baked Alaska desserts or a few flaming kabobs from the kitchen to a dining room service area. Once there, servers can douse the fires, plate up the foods, and serve a few guests. As with the flaming display, the remaining production and preplating can be done in the kitchen.

2. *Burns.* Even if you do not provide flaming tableside cooking, guests are still subject to accidental burns. For instance, if you have unprotected candle flames on each dining table, napery can be set on fire if the candles tip over. Or guests may accidentally burn themselves or their clothing if they reach over the flame without realizing how hot it is. If you want to put candles on each table, you should use votive-type containers such as chimneys because these setups can prevent accidental burns or fires.

Buffet service also presents several potential hazards that can cause burns. For instance, hot chafing dishes can be very dangerous to the unsuspecting guest. Handles and utensils can get very hot. And the steam created by the typical setup used for chafing dishes can build up and escape, thereby seriously burning someone who happens to be nearby.

Many chafing dishes and coffee urns have little Sterno pots under them. You must make sure that these pots are covered correctly and that there is enough space between the pots and the bottoms of the dishes to prevent the fuel from going wild. If the lid on the Sterno container is left open too wide, vapor can build up under the steam-table pan and ignite, and suddenly you have a flame surrounding the bottom of the pan and possibly even enveloping the whole chafing dish.

If you use Sterno, do not allow anyone to refuel the containers while they are in use. Sometimes you cannot see the slight flame emitted by the fuel. If you try to refuel while the pot is still burning, you may burn yourself very badly. In fact, a young chef in a Las Vegas hotel lost his life when his chef's jacket caught fire while he was trying to refuel Sterno pots on the buffet table. If a pot has burned out, cover it, set it aside, and use another full pot in its place. Later on you can refuel all the pots, long after the flames have been extinguished. If you must refuel Sterno, it should be done in a production area or service corridor, not on the buffet table.

Even though we in the industry tend to refer to Sterno as a generic product, it is in fact a brand name. There are other less-expensive fuels you can use. However, according to Anthony Marshall, Dean of the School of Hospitality Management at Florida International University and a well-known attorney, we should use only the Sterno brand. He warns that, unlike the Sterno brand, other brands are poisonous when eaten. (If in doubt, always look for the telltale skull-and-crossbones decal.) If they are left unlighted on a buffet table, guests may think they are some type of dip, consume some, and possibly die. In fact, Dean Marshall notes a specific incident in which a woman died after consuming an off-brand fuel left sitting on the table where the property was held responsible for her death.

Hot carts positioned throughout the function room pose another burn hazard. Portable steam tables can also be a problem. Similarly, hot-beverage setups can also be dangerous. To prevent accidental burns from these types of setups, you must see to it that any exposed hot surface is clearly marked. For safety purposes, most manufacturers will mark hot surfaces at the factory when the equipment is being manufactured. In fact, some local government agencies may require this type of marking before the equipment can be used in commercial foodservice operations in their locale.

3. *Falls.* Guests are subject to falls. Most of them are unfamiliar with the function room; some of them are not careful when roaming around the room, and they bump into other guests and servers. Furthermore, many of

them may not immediately recognize portable electrical and/or sound drop cords laced throughout the area.

To minimize the possibility of guests falling, never allow any loose item to be placed on the floor. For instance, if a drop cord must be used, make sure it is secured and marked conspicuously.

Similarly, if there is a slope in the floor, mark it clearly. Furthermore, place all tables, carts, tray stands, and other equipment in the correct locations and secure them properly.

4. *Broken glass.* Broken and chipped tableware is another hazard that seems to be more prevalent in catered events than in regular restaurant service. The time pressures associated with most catered functions increase the risk that guests will inadvertently find damaged items.

Usually the staff can spot chipped plateware and remove it from service before it ends up in front of guests. However, the same cannot always be said about broken glassware. Indeed, the possibility of guests finding a piece of broken glass is always present whenever employees are rushing to serve a group of people.

The trend today is to have shorter cocktail receptions. A one-hour reception, or even less, is more common since the shorter time period might reduce guest consumption of alcohol. However, for those groups that still like to drink, the shorter reception means that bartenders will be working very quickly to serve the same number of drinks. The pressure to prepare and serve a lot of drinks quickly tends to increase the risk of broken glassware.

Hurried buspersons and other employees who clear tables and landing space may also increase the number of broken glasses and the possibility of a guest getting a piece of glass in his or her food or beverage. Buspersons should be taught to dump ice out of glasses before placing them in bus trays. Ice in bus trays causes glasses to slip around and bang into each other. The potential for chipped and broken glassware increases, along with the increased possibility that glass chips will get into the food and beverage supply. Likewise, glasses should not be stacked in bus trays; flatware should never be placed into glasses; plates should not be mixed with glasses. All of these actions increase the possibility of broken glass getting into a guest's drink or meal.

Ice or cold water should never be put into hot glasses. The glasses may crack and split. This would not be troublesome if the glass would break completely before it was served to a guest. There is a serious problem, though, if the glass merely sprouts a hairline crack; when the guest sees this, he or she will be leery of all other food and beverage offerings. Worse yet, if a guest actually drinks from this glass, he or she might receive a cut lip.

Glasses should never be used to dip ice out of an ice bin. If the glass breaks, you will need to empty the bin and clean it thoroughly. Use plastic scoops to dip ice and put it into glasses; metal scoops should not be used because they can chip the glasses. The last thing you want is a guest receiving a piece of glass in his or her drink.

5. *Food-borne illness.* One of the club's worst nightmares is to be the cause of an outbreak of food-borne illness. Imagine the agony suffered by a club if members and their guests become ill after attending a special event at your club because, for example, foods were prepared with contaminated fresh shell eggs.

Food-borne illness can be traced to many origins. The products may be contaminated when purchased. They may become contaminated during production and service, or they can become contaminated if stored under improper conditions.

Improper storage conditions for an excessive period of time generally is the biggest problem faced by the typical club catering department. The time/temperature dilemma rears its ugly head whenever potentially hazardous foods must be held for long periods of time on a buffet table.

Potentially hazardous foods must be stored at 40 degrees F or below or 140 degrees F or above. The 40–140 range is the danger zone. If potentially hazardous foods must go through the danger zone (such as when they are cooked), they must go through it as quickly as possible because, at these temperatures, harmful bacteria will thrive.

Foods on a buffet table are especially vulnerable to the time/temperature problem. For instance, if you offer a meat loaf entree, a chafing dish may be unable to maintain the required temperature. If a guest or employee contaminates this cooked food and the food is not served for a while, harmful bacteria can multiply and eventually someone may become ill.

If you are serving cold potentially hazardous foods on a buffet table, they must be kept at or below 40 degrees F. For instance, a cold potato salad made with protein-rich ingredients should never be allowed to sit out unrefrigerated for more than a few minutes. It must be displayed on a cold table.

To prevent these time/temperature problems, you must ensure that the service equipment can hold foods at the proper temperatures, see to it that foods are not kept on the buffet table any longer than necessary, and eliminate possibilities in which guests can contaminate the food by installing sneeze guards in front of the foods.

You could also minimize these types of problems if you are willing to forego the use of some of the more troublesome foods. For instance, if eggs are to be used in a menu item that will not be cooked such as hollandaise sauce, you could use pasteurized, frozen eggs instead of fresh shell eggs. You also could refuse to serve raw meat or seafood.

9

Other Member/ Guest Services

·····························

S ome catered events require much more than food and beverage service than others. In addition to food and drink, some hosts will need unique audio, visual, and/or lighting services. Some will require specialized dining and buffet table presentations. And others may need something extra special to ensure that guests come away from the functions with many happy memories.

Hosts who are planning several meal and beverage functions also may ask for something more than food and beverage service if only to relieve the monotony. They may also want something unusual to recharge guests' batteries so that they have an extra storehouse of energy to draw on when tackling remaining business sessions.

Unique attractions are also used by hosts to highlight celebratory catered events. Awards dinners, weddings, new-product introductions, and the like are made more exclusive and memorable if hosts provide a smorgasbord of food, beverage, and other services specifically designed to maximize their impact on guests.

Clubs can sometimes be in a difficult position when dealing with hosts who want other services. After all, if hosts spend a lot of money for these things, how much will they have left over for food and beverage? You certainly do not want to speak ill of hosts' ideas, but it is your responsibility to point out that they should strike a proper balance between decor and food and beverage. Guests are most impressed with the quality and value of food and beverage received; other services cannot overcome mediocre products. You need to be cautious when discussing these points; at no time should you attempt to feather your nest at the expense of the host's needs and desires.

The catering executive must be prepared to entertain a variety of special requests for other host services. Usually only the small, refueling type of catered meal functions are built solely around food and beverage service.

Most events require some sort of additional service. It can range from the mundane (such as the need for a videotape player, television monitor, overhead projector, and screen) to the spectacular (such as the host who requests a skydiving stunt or one who needs to transport a large ice carving in a service elevator).

The catering executive will need to coordinate many special requests. He or she will need to help plan, organize, and implement a plethora of unusual and unique requirements. He or she may also need to advise hosts of the most effective and economical combination of special services needed to ensure success. Like the bandleader, the catering executive must see to it that all food, beverage, and special services are playing from the same sheet of music.

PROVIDING OTHER GUEST SERVICES

Club caterers specialize in providing food and beverage service. While some are capable of providing additional services, others prefer to leave these to outside experts.

A club cannot be all things to all people. Realistically, it must draw the line somewhere. Cost considerations render it virtually impossible for a club to house all of the specialties that hosts might potentially need.

When dealing with services other than food and beverage, usually the club is faced with four options. It can

1. Provide as many of them as possible itself
2. Steer the host to outside service contractors
3. Expect hosts to find their own outside service contractors
4. Use some combination of these three possibilities

Club Providing Other Host Services

A club usually will provide its own special services only if it is economically feasible to do so or if there are no other outside alternatives that can be trusted to do the work correctly and efficiently.

Some special services can be very profitable, particularly if they are not labor intensive. For instance, providing a few pieces of audiovisual (AV) equipment and one technician to a meeting usually does not involve a lot of variable costs. Consequently, its contribution margin (CM) can add considerably to overall club profits.

Unfortunately, though, some special services are very capital intensive. For instance, most lighting equipment is very expensive. To make matters worse, it tends to become obsolete very quickly, thereby requiring you to replace it periodically with even more expensive items. It is cost prohibitive to let this equipment sit idle. Unless the club uses it often, you may not earn an adequate return on your investment.

Providing a full range of AV services can be another expensive undertaking. AV technology is changing so rapidly that it is difficult to keep pace.

In some instances, a club may be happy to break even with such services as lighting and sound if it means that hosts will spend freely on food and beverage services. In this case, it may be good business to offer the host a loss leader if it helps secure other profitable business for the club.

Outside Service Contractors

Some clubs have a list of approved outside service contractors that they recommend to potential hosts whenever special host services are needed. These contractors are usually the ones the club feels are capable of doing the job properly.

Before a club will add a contractor to the approved list, he or she normally must have adequate references. A club does not want to risk recommending someone whose ineptness will cause host and guest dissatisfaction and ruin the chances of repeat patronage.

Some clubs may not want to recommend any outside service contractor because it represents a possible conflict of interest. They fear someone may accuse them of taking kickbacks. They also run the risk of hosts complaining that they were steered to inadequate, costly outsiders whose lack of ability should have been well known to the catering executives.

Most of the time, the club expects hosts to find their own outside service contractors whenever something extra special is needed. Some clubs do not have the resources to handle these services, nor are some properties eager to assume liability for them.

The catering staff is normally capable of working with any contractor. In fact, the club usually has a written "handbook" of pertinent information that these outside service providers must have in order to plan and implement their work correctly.

Sometimes friction may arise if a host wants to use an outside service contractor that the club would like to avoid. A service contractor may have a good working relationship with the host, but the club may not enjoy the same good fortune. Generally, though, you must be able to work with any outside service contractors selected by hosts.

Many potential hosts have long-standing relationships with several outside service providers. This can be an effective cost-saving measure for the host since a service contractor will normally offer generous hosts volume discounts if they purchase a large amount of services. The club will need to work with these outsiders if it wants to book the catering business.

Combination of In-House and Outside Services

Occasionally, the club may provide some services itself while the host is expected to secure others. For instance, if a meeting needs specialized sound and lighting services, you may be able to provide microphones and speakers, but the client may have to use an outside service contractor to provide the necessary lighting.

Usually the club can provide a handful of the most commonly needed function services. For instance, it is the rare club that cannot provide the basic AV equipment, such as overhead projectors, screens, microphones, speakers, slide projectors, television monitors, videotape players, and film projectors. If nothing else, it can rent a few of these items and relieve the host of this chore.

Occasionally, a club may want to offer a few complimentary host services in order to secure a large catering contract. For example, if a host needs a microphone for the luncheon speaker, a club may provide it free of charge. This type of service is relatively inexpensive to provide because you can usually tap into the club's house sound system (that is, the club's public address system) very easily. But the host will not see it this way. He or she will appreciate the additional consideration and remember it when it is time to plan the next catered function.

AUDIOVISUAL SERVICES

Audiovisual (AV) services are probably the most common type of extra services needed at catering functions. You or another professional must be able to counsel your hosts regarding the best options for them to use. You should be able to help them match their particular needs with the most effective and efficient AV systems.

The catering manager must be careful not to represent the department as being AV experts if, in fact, it is not true. The manager is asking for trouble if he or she gives this impression. If the club decides to provide extensive AV services, to be on the safe side, it should have an AV professional on staff.

The purpose of using AV is to communicate. Presentations are made to sell, train, and inform. The most effective and memorable presentations use AV to show and tell. Without AV support, presentations are apt to lack the punch and power needed to make a lasting impression on guests.

If the message is to be presented only once in an information session such as a sales meeting, a flip chart or overhead projector with transparencies may be sufficient. However, if the objective of the meeting is to teach a group of people or lead them in a brain-storming session, an electronic board would be a better choice.

If complex financial data are being presented to groups, a Power Point presentation may be the best choice, along with backup written copy provided after the meeting. By controlling the timing of the presentation, the moderator will ensure that everyone is looking at the same information at the same time. Telling participants that they will receive a hard copy after the meeting will cut down on their need to read ahead and not pay attention to the data at hand.

If visual presentations need to be altered while they are being displayed, you can use an overhead projector, transparencies, and transparency marking pens. For the more adventurous group, and the one with a little extra money in its budget, you could hook up a personal computer to the appropriate overhead projection machinery. The computer can be a stand-alone computer or it can be on-line, connected to a satellite location in another part of the club or even in another part of the country.

Types of AV Services

Hosts usually can find the AV services they need very easily because there are several types and varieties available (see Figure 9.1). The general types of AV services hosts can order are

1. *Microphone.* There are at least seven types of microphones: lectern, table, floor, lavalier (also called a necklace or lapel microphone), halo (also called a suspended or boom microphone), handheld, and omnidirectional.

(text continues on page 238)

Figure 9.1. Example of typical AV services. (courtesy of John Steinmetz, the Westin Bonaventure, Los Angeles, California).

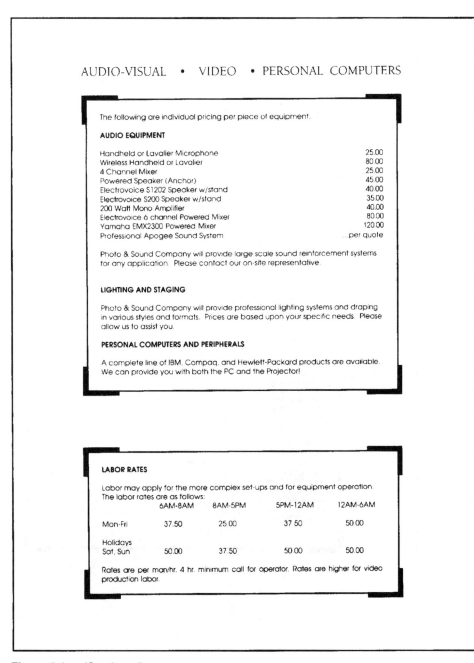

AUDIO-VISUAL • VIDEO • PERSONAL COMPUTERS

The following are individual pricing per piece of equipment.

AUDIO EQUIPMENT

Handheld or Lavalier Microphone	25.00
Wireless Handheld or Lavalier	80.00
4 Channel Mixer	25.00
Powered Speaker (Anchor)	45.00
Electrovoice S1202 Speaker w/stand	40.00
Electrovoice S200 Speaker w/stand	35.00
200 Watt Mono Amplifier	40.00
Electrovoice 6 channel Powered Mixer	80.00
Yamaha EMX2300 Powered Mixer	120.00
Professional Apogee Sound System	...per quote

Photo & Sound Company will provide large scale sound reinforcement systems for any application. Please contact our on-site representative.

LIGHTING AND STAGING

Photo & Sound Company will provide professional lighting systems and draping in various styles and formats. Prices are based upon your specific needs. Please allow us to assist you.

PERSONAL COMPUTERS AND PERIPHERALS

A complete line of IBM, Compaq, and Hewlett-Packard products are available. We can provide you with both the PC and the Projector!

LABOR RATES

Labor may apply for the more complex set-ups and for equipment operation. The labor rates are as follows:

	6AM-8AM	8AM-5PM	5PM-12AM	12AM-6AM
Mon-Fri	37.50	25.00	37.50	50.00
Holidays Sat, Sun	50.00	37.50	50.00	50.00

Rates are per man/hr. 4 hr. minimum call for operator. Rates are higher for video production labor.

Figure 9.1. *(Continued).*

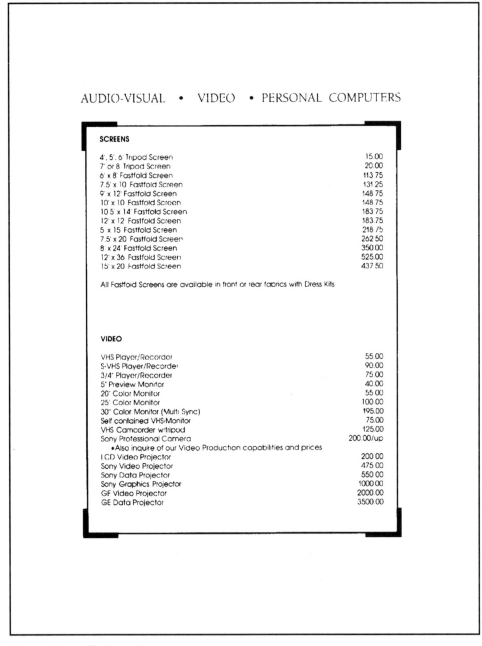

AUDIO-VISUAL • VIDEO • PERSONAL COMPUTERS

SCREENS

4', 5', 6' Tripod Screen	15.00
7' or 8' Tripod Screen	20.00
6' x 8' Fastfold Screen	113.75
7.5' x 10' Fastfold Screen	131.25
9' x 12' Fastfold Screen	148.75
10' x 10' Fastfold Screen	148.75
10.5' x 14' Fastfold Screen	183.75
12' x 12' Fastfold Screen	183.75
5 x 15 Fastfold Screen	218.75
7.5' x 20' Fastfold Screen	262.50
8' x 24' Fastfold Screen	350.00
12' x 36' Fastfold Screen	525.00
15' x 20' Fastfold Screen	437.50

All Fastfold Screens are available in front or rear fabrics with Dress Kits

VIDEO

VHS Player/Recorder	55.00
S-VHS Player/Recorder	90.00
3/4' Player/Recorder	75.00
5' Preview Monitor	40.00
20' Color Monitor	55.00
25' Color Monitor	100.00
30" Color Monitor (Multi Sync)	195.00
Self contained VHS/Monitor	75.00
VHS Camcorder w/tripod	125.00
Sony Professional Camera	200.00/up
•Also inquire of our Video Production capabilities and prices	
LCD Video Projector	200.00
Sony Video Projector	475.00
Sony Data Projector	550.00
Sony Graphics Projector	1000.00
GE Video Projector	2000.00
GE Data Projector	3500.00

Figure 9.1. *(Continued).*

AUDIO-VISUAL   •   VIDEO   •   PERSONAL COMPUTERS

PRESENTATION SUPPORT

Flipchart Easel	15.00
Flipchart Pad*	10.00
Watercolor Marker*	1.50
Electric Arrow Pointer	15.00
Laser Dot Pointer	40.00
Overhead Acetate Roll*	11.00
Overhead Acetate Sheet*	.50
Transparency Pen*	2.00
80 Capacity Slide Tray	5.00
140 Capacity Slide Tray	5.00
T-30 VHS tape*	10.00
T-60 VHS tape*	10.50
T-120 VHS Tape*	12.50
LCD Computer Panel	95.00
Caramate/Audioviewer	35.00
SAFE-LOK Projection Stand	12.50
34" Cart	15.00
54" Cart	17.50

*Note: These items are purchased by end user, and are not "rented". You retain possession at the end of the meeting.

MISCELLANEOUS

Wireless Slide Proj. Remote	20.00
2 Projector Dissolve Unit	40.00
3-Tier Projector Stacker	27.50
2-Tier Sony Video Proj. Stacker	50.00
1000W Followspot	75.00
Xenon Followspot	125.00
3 Light Video Kit	45.00
Lecternette w/Base	50.00
Audio Cassette Recorder	25.00
Audio Cassette with 2 Proj. Dissolve	45.00
Stereo Cassette Deck (Tascam)	40.00
3 Channel Stereo Cassette	60.00
4 Channel Reel-to-reel Deck	70.00
Navitar 6"-9" Lens with Elll bracket	20.00
Keystone Correcting Lens (PC lens)	15.00
Hayes 1200 Baud Modem	35.00
Hayes 2400 Baud Modem	50.00
Walkie-Talkie, 2 channel	25.00

This is a partial listing of our extensive inventory. Please allow us to help you if you cannot easily find the item you require. We look forward to assisting you with a most successful meeting at the Westin Bonaventure! Thank you.

Figure 9.1.   *(Continued).*

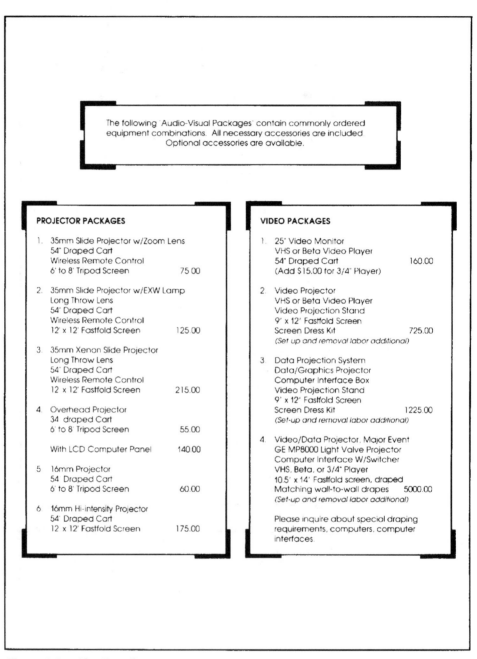

The following 'Audio-Visual Packages' contain commonly ordered equipment combinations. All necessary accessories are included. Optional accessories are available.

PROJECTOR PACKAGES

1. 35mm Slide Projector w/Zoom Lens
   54" Draped Cart
   Wireless Remote Control
   6' to 8' Tripod Screen   75.00

2. 35mm Slide Projector w/EXW Lamp
   Long Throw Lens
   54" Draped Cart
   Wireless Remote Control
   12' x 12' Fastfold Screen   125.00

3. 35mm Xenon Slide Projector
   Long Throw Lens
   54" Draped Cart
   Wireless Remote Control
   12' x 12' Fastfold Screen   215.00

4. Overhead Projector
   34' draped Cart
   6' to 8' Tripod Screen   55.00

   With LCD Computer Panel   140.00

5. 16mm Projector
   54' Draped Cart
   6' to 8' Tripod Screen   60.00

6. 16mm Hi-intensity Projector
   54' Draped Cart
   12' x 12' Fastfold Screen   175.00

VIDEO PACKAGES

1. 25' Video Monitor
   VHS or Beta Video Player
   54' Draped Cart   160.00
   (Add $15.00 for 3/4" Player)

2. Video Projector
   VHS or Beta Video Player
   Video Projection Stand
   9' x 12' Fastfold Screen
   Screen Dress Kit   725.00
   (Set up and removal labor additional)

3. Data Projection System
   Data/Graphics Projector
   Computer Interface Box
   Video Projection Stand
   9' x 12' Fastfold Screen
   Screen Dress Kit   1225.00
   (Set-up and removal labor additional)

4. Video/Data Projector, Major Event
   GE MP8000 Light Valve Projector
   Computer Interface W/Switcher
   VHS, Beta, or 3/4" Player
   10.5' x 14' Fastfold screen, draped
   Matching wall-to-wall drapes   5000.00
   (Set-up and removal labor additional)

   Please inquire about special draping requirements, computers, computer interfaces.

Figure 9.1. *(Continued).*

PHOTO&SOUND

C O M P A N Y

We are Dedicated to Achieving
the Highest Level of Customer Satisfaction
by Providing Superior Service and Technology
for the Presentation and Processing of Information

CORPORATE HEADQUARTERS
116 Natoma Street
San Francisco, CA 94105   (415) 882-7555

CALIFORNIA
Orange County   (714) 540-3348
Fresno   (209) 454-8000
Los Angeles   (818) 575-1924
Sacramento   (916) 920-2421
San Diego   (619) 291-3380
San Jose   (408) 453-6220
San Francisco   (415) 882-7600

ARIZONA
Phoenix   (602) 437-1560

HAWAII
Honolulu   (808) 848-2041

NEVADA
Reno   (702) 331-4765

OREGON
Portland   (503) 224-3456

TEXAS
Houston   (713) 956-9566

WASHINGTON
Seattle   (206) 632-8461

Figure 9.1.   *(Continued).*

2. *Projection screen.* There are two basic types of projection screens: front-screen projection and rear-screen projection. With front-screen projection, the media projector is located within or behind the audience. Images are projected onto one of the following screen surfaces:

a. Matte white—the most common screen surface. It diffuses the available light evenly over a wide area. It is especially useful in large, wide rooms.

b. Glass beaded—the surface contains chemically coated glass beads. This produces superior image brightness (about three times the matte white). However, the optimal viewing angle is much narrower.

c. Lenticular—this type of surface is similar to a lens, in that it controls light and sends it to a predetermined area. It is most often used in stereo projection where viewers must wear 3-D glasses. These screens are normally not very large. The biggest one available measures approximately 6 feet by 6 feet.

With rear-screen projection, the media projector is placed behind the screen and images are projected through the screen surface. The screen surfaces used are made of glass, acrylic, or vinyl.

When compared to front-screen projection, the primary advantages are

a. No chance of interference with projection beam of light

b. No tripping over drop cords or other equipment

c. No need to dim all function room lights, which permits attendees to take notes easily

Its major disadvantages are

a. It takes up a lot of space. Depending on the screen size and type of lens used, you will usually need about 15 to 30 feet behind the screen.

b. The area behind the screen must be completely dark.

c. Since the area in front of the screen must be light, the room must have separate lighting controls.

The type of screen you will need is dependent on audience needs and room dimensions.

If you plan to use slides, the screen should be square in order to accommodate both vertical and horizontal slides. In this case, though, neither type of slide will completely fill the screen. A professionally prepared slide presentation will usually include only horizontal slides so that each image will completely fill a horizontally formatted screen.

The appropriate screen size must be used to ensure comfortable viewing for all audience members. While function room size and layout are important factors, generally speaking, the recommended screen size depends primarily on the audience size. Function planners should use the following screen sizes:

Audience Size	Recommended Screen Size (in Feet)
25–50	4 × 4
50–75	5 × 5
250–500	10 × 10
500–1,000	12 × 12
Over 1,000	14 × 14

Another way to determine screen size involves using the ceiling height to figure screen height. To determine the maximum screen height needed, subtract 4 feet from the minimum ceiling height. If you use the maximum screen height, guests seated in the back row will be able to see the screen unobstructed by heads in the front rows.

3. *Overhead projector.* This equipment bounces an image off of a 45-degree mirror onto a lens placed above the object. Either the object is a transparency, or it could be an acetate sheet that can be written on with a special marking pen by a speaker during his or her presentation. Overhead projectors can be used in a lighted room, though subdued lighting is best.

Overhead projectors come in various sizes. The standard projector accommodates transparencies measuring 8.5 by 11 inches. Smaller sizes are more convenient if clients are using smaller transparencies. For instance, one of the smallest overhead projectors available is the Oxberry PPS-70, which is specifically designed to accommodate minitransparencies measuring approximately 4 by 5 inches.

4. *Sound.* A good presentation depends on the quality of the equipment used to convey it. Without a good sound system, the most carefully planned display will flop.

There are two general types of sound systems: distributed and clustered. The distributed system is preferred when human voices need to be projected. Loudspeakers are placed strategically along the ceiling so that all of the audience is equidistant from the signal (that is, sound) source. The clustered system is used primarily for music. In this case, loudspeakers are usually placed about 15 to 30 feet above and around the stage.

The sound system includes four major components:

a. Signal sources—the most common ones are microphones, audiotape, videotape, and filmstrip with audio track.

b. Audio mixer—this equipment combines several signal sources and sends mono or stereo signals to the amplifier and ultimately to the speakers. The mixing system is usually an audio "box" that accepts hookups from multiple microphones, sound projectors, or tape players and allows these inputs to be mixed through a sound system with the help of an amplifier. Modern mixers automatically adjust for volume, sound level between speakers, feedback, and equalization, thereby minimizing labor costs.

c. Amplifier—this equipment takes the signal from the audio mixer and boosts it to the level required by the speakers.

d. Speakers—there are various types and sizes. They must be arranged in the room in such a way that they can fill it completely with sound.

The sound system can be adapted to include auxiliary equipment. For instance, if a host wants to broadcast a meeting to a satellite location, the appropriate telephone hookups can usually be added very easily to accommodate this need.

Many clubs have a built-in house sound system. These systems are usually adequate for public addresses and background music. However, they ordinarily are not designed to project musical instruments or singing.

5. *AV technician.* For elaborate AV presentations, usually the host will need to hire at least one technician. For instance, if you are using four or more sound sources in a function room, it is recommended that you schedule one AV technician for that room who will coordinate and supervise the production.

In addition to AV technicians, a catered function may need a show coordinator. A coordinator would be necessary for an elaborate, complex event where it is essential to coordinate several productions during a short period of time.

6. *Audio recorder.* The two basic types are reel-to-reel and cassette tape recorders. Several sizes are available.

7. *Video recorder.* Videotape cameras are commonly used to record entire events or parts of events. In fact, it is not unusual for some guests to use their own camcorders to tape the proceedings for their own libraries.

8. *Slide projection equipment*

a. *Carousel slide projector.* This equipment is used to project images from horizontal and vertical slides onto a screen. The slides are placed in front of a single light source one at a time. There are similar slide projectors that do not use a carousel to hold the slides. However, the most commonly used slide projector is still the Kodak carousel.

Some slide projectors have automatic focus, automatic timers for continuous operation, and cordless remote control units. You can also synchronize your presentation with an audiotape player by inserting inaudible pulse tones on the tape that advance the slides automatically.

b. *Messenger slide projector.* This equipment is much smaller than the typical carousel projector. Instead of using a carousel to hold the slides, a magazine is used to stack the slides, which are then gravity fed in front of two light sources. Two light sources allow the images to blend (that is, fade) into each other, thereby eliminating dark spots and ensuring smooth transitions.

This projector is more convenient to use than the carousel slide projector. For instance, the user does not have to insert slides into a carousel; he or she merely needs to stack them in the magazine. Moreover, the user knows exactly which slide is projected on the screen because each slide's number can be displayed on a digital readout attachment.

c. *Xenon slide projector.* This equipment is typically used in large function rooms for large groups. In a large room, the projected images must be big enough for everyone to see. The images projected by the typical carousel slide projector begin to lose clarity and focus if they are enlarged too much. However, the Xenon slide projector uses a very bright bulb and, thus, projects a much sharper, crisper, large picture that can be seen easily from afar.

This projector is a more complicated device in that it usually must be adjusted to accommodate each slide's unique features. Consequently, it cannot be operated by an amateur. Usually an AV technician must be employed to run it.

d. *Dissolve unit.* This equipment allows two or three carousel slide projectors focused on the same screen to create a smooth transition from one slide to another. As the slides advance, they will fade into each other.

9. *TV monitor.* A TV monitor is similar to a regular TV; the major difference is that the monitor produces a much higher picture quality. If a client needs to show a video, he or she can

a. Use a regular TV set wired to accept video.

b. Use a TV monitor wired to accept video.

c. Use a video projection system (usually referred to as a big-screen TV) wired to accept video. This system uses a video projector, a special projection screen (that can be up to 30 feet wide), a video playback unit, and a patch into the club's in-house sound system.

As a general rule of thumb, when viewing videotapes, you should

a. Use a 19-inch TV monitor for 10 people or less.

b. Use a 25-inch TV monitor for 11 to 25 people.

c. Use a 35- to 46-inch TV monitor for 26 to 50 people.

d. Use a big-screen TV for groups of over 50 people.

You could also use a combination of these four options. For instance, in a room with 20 to 40 people, you can use two TV monitors with a common, portable sound speaker.

10. *Video tape player.* Sometimes referred to as video cassette player (VCP). It is designed specifically to play prerecorded video tapes to be shown on a TV monitor. A video cassette recorder (VCR) can also be used to show prerecorded video tapes.

11. *Audiotape player.* This equipment is designed to play prerecorded audiotapes. Some types of equipment used to record audio presentations can also be used to play prerecorded tapes.

12. *Camera.* There are two basic types: film cameras and video cameras. Generally speaking, if a camera is needed, the client will use a videotape camera.

13. *Film projector.* This equipment is used to project prerecorded motion picture film images onto a projection screen. Generally there are four types available: 35 millimeter (mm), 16 mm, Super-8, and 8 mm. Most projectors have built-in sound speakers that are adequate for small groups. To accommodate large audiences, most projectors can be patched into the club's in-house sound system.

14. *Opaque projector.* This equipment is similar to an overhead projector, the major difference being that its light is reflected from above instead of from underneath. It can be used to project from solid materials such as book pages, photographs, or small three-dimensional objects. Unlike the overhead projector, though, when using this equipment, the room must be dark in order to see the images projected onto the screen.

15. *Slide/sound synchronizer.* This is a combination slide and audio-tape presentation. For instance, a carousel slide projector can be advanced automatically by inaudible pulses on one stereo channel, while the other channel can present audio messages, such as music or voice-over narration.

16. *Simultaneous translation.* With this service, translators sit in a booth and listen to a speaker. As the speaker talks, they immediately translate

his or her remarks and deliver the translation into a microphone that feeds into headsets worn by audience members.

There are two basic types of simultaneous-translation systems: cabled and wireless. The wireless is more expensive, but it is more convenient to use. It allows maximum mobility.

Some systems allow audience members maximum control over the headset volume. Although these are more expensive than those without this option, again, they are more convenient to use. They also are preferred by audience members who wish to listen selectively to a speaker's remarks.

Most systems allow audience members to interact with the speaker and each other. For instance, an attendee might want to ask the speaker a question. The question can be easily translated back to the speaker and his or her translated responses can be communicated to the audience just as quickly. You can use several translators to accommodate a number of languages.

If you receive requests for this type of service and you wish to provide it yourself, you should check with local embassies, consulates, colleges, or universities for bilingual persons. Be certain, though, that anyone hired to do this type of work has had formal simultaneous-translation training and/or work experience.

17. *Closed-circuit TV (CCTV).* Usually only the major clubs have this type of capability. The video camera and TV monitors are used by groups mostly to set up interactive training sessions. However, the systems can also be used for other purposes, such as providing security for exhibition areas, VIPs, and cash bars.

18. *LCD panel.* This is an electronic device that sits on top of an overhead projector in lieu of a standard transparency. It is sometimes referred to as an electronic transparency. It is designed to project computer-generated data on the screen. Some models have built-in electronic storage and random-access retrieval capability, which enable the presenter to use some data while storing the rest of it for a later discussion.

19. *Projection table.* Standard projection tables vary in height, weight, and size and are designed to hold projection equipment. They usually have detachable, adjustable legs that can be manipulated for height and storage. They usually have locking casters, heavy-duty cords, and several plug outlets.

Some projection tables are more elaborate. They are designed to interact with other projection equipment. For instance, some have electronic pointers that can be used to enhance a slide presentation.

20. *Slide.* Most slides used today are 35 mm, color film, and 2 inches square (including the mounting). To ensure consistent focus, you should use only glass-mounted slides.

21. *Motion picture film.* Most educational and industrial films today

are either 16 mm or Super-8. Occasionally you will find an 8-mm film. The soundtrack is usually dubbed onto the film during the printing or processing stage. For best results, the soundtrack should be patched into the club's in-house sound system.

22. *Videotape.* The most common videotape formats used today are

    a. VHS (a ½-inch format)

    b. U-matic (a ¾-inch format)

    c. Betacam (a broadcast-quality, ½-inch format)

    d. One-inch (a broadcast-quality format)

If a client will be using two different formats, he or she will need two separate videotape players. None of these videotape formats are compatible with the others' equipment.

23. *Multimedia system.* This is a complete sight/sound environment. It combines audio, visual, and special-effects equipment (such as lasers, computers, and smoke-making machines).

Off-the-shelf multimedia shows can be purchased or rented. For instance, you can rent a standard slide show and insert a few of your own slides to personalize the production. This is much cheaper than commissioning a major production that may be used only once.

24. *Transparency.* The typical transparency is a multi- or single-colored display printed on a thin sheet of transparent plastic or acetate. It is placed on an overhead projector and projected onto a screen.

25. *Electronic board.* This equipment resembles the traditional white-board, but anything written on it can be reduced and printed on paper by an attached printer for immediate distribution to attendees.

26. *Easel.* A three-legged stand designed to hold signs, chalkboards, posters, flip charts, and other types of illustrative material.

27. *Flip chart.* This is a large pad of paper (usually measuring 20 by 24 inches) designed to be used by a speaker to illustrate topics. It is placed on its own stand or on a separate easel. Usually it is set up to include several different-colored marking pens and some masking tape that can be used to tape completed pages on the wall for later reference by the group.

28. *Chalkboard.*

29. *Pad and pencil.*

30. *Compact disc player.*

Recording

Sometimes a host may wish to record a catered event. For instance, it is common to audio record business meetings to have a record of the meeting, distribute tapes to persons unable to attend, and/or have a record for written transcription later on.

When audio recording an event, generally the best results are obtained by patching into the club's in-house sound system. This results in much better sound quality than if you use tape recorders placed strategically at the podium or throughout the function room.

If a host wishes to audio record an event for presentation later on to people who cannot attend the meeting, you should suggest using a reel-to-reel format. This produces the highest-quality tape that can be edited easily. Unfortunately, this format is bulky, expensive, and time consuming, and it does not allow you to duplicate tapes easily.

Cassette recording is much less expensive. It is easy to use and the tapes can be duplicated very easily. Unfortunately, it produces a poorer sound quality, and the tapes are very difficult to edit. However, this format is usually adequate if, for example, the objective is to have a verbal record that will be transcribed by a stenographer after the meeting ends.

If the host wants to use the cassette format, you should suggest that he or she use the Marantz PMD system, or a comparable system. The Marantz PMD is commonly used when a master recording device is needed. It is compact and easy to use, and you can monitor what is being recorded.

Some hosts will want a visual record of the events. If so, they are best advised to use videotape instead of motion picture film. It is less costly, more versatile, and more durable than film.

When video recording, the technician will usually want to place one or more monitors around the room to check for accuracy as well as to broadcast the event to guests who are not close enough to see the action first hand. This way, the technician can show action as it happens, including the speaker's face, audience reactions, and audience members asking questions. If an instant replay is desired, it can easily be presented.

When designing the function room layout with video recording in mind, make sure the cameras are located so that they can "see" everything you want to record. They also should be located outside the traffic lanes. Another important factor is lighting. To ensure a clear, sharp picture, all subjects must be well lit.

Another important part of any recording is the recording microphone. Microphones and microphone placements are very critical. If the audience asks questions, you will need microphones placed strategically throughout the room. Otherwise there will be blank spots on the tape. Furthermore, the speaker may need to repeat the questions.

A speaker using an overhead projector or other similar equipment may want to use a lavalier microphone so that his or her hands are free to manipulate the equipment. This type of microphone will also ensure that the sound will not fade while the presenter is moving about the stage.

Omnidirectional microphones should be used when it is critical to record all sounds. Usually the best one you can use is the PZM type or its equivalent. This is a condenser microphone that resembles a flat metal plate with a bubble on top of it. It has a very wide sound pickup range, which makes it very useful for recording any events or meetings that take place around a large conference table. In addition, it is an unobtrusive piece of equipment that is virtually unnoticed by guests.

When taping any event, make sure that all master tapes are prelabeled. The host should give the AV technician preprinted labels that the technician can use to mark the tapes after they are used. You do not want a mislabeled or unlabeled tape to ruin an otherwise sterling event.

Someone should test the recording system before the host and guests enter the room. Start by going to each microphone and naming its type and location. The AV technician should then play the tape back to ensure that a proper recording is being made.

If a recording is critical, you might suggest that the host use two separate systems. This way you are ensured of a backup system in case the first one fails to record. If both systems are recording, you then have an overlap that can be used to ensure that nothing is lost during tape changes.

Selecting an AV Service Contractor

When a host needs to use an outside AV service, you may be asked to recommend one. If so, you should investigate those available in your local area and develop a list of approved suppliers.

Before adding a firm to your approved supplier list, you must be sure that it will be able to perform adequately. Barbara Williams of Encore Productions suggests you evaluate the following characteristics before deciding if a service contractor can handle clients' needs.

1. You should seek AV professionals with a proven reputation. Ask for references. Call the references and ask:
   a. How capable technically were the AV representatives?
   b. Did the firm have all necessary equipment?
   c. How responsive was the firm to last-minute requests?
   d. Was the final bill equal to the original competitive bid?

2. Look for an AV service contractor with communication technology specialists certified by the International Communication Industries Associa-

tion. An AV firm with these specialists on staff is committed to continuing education within this highly technical and ever-changing industry.

3. See if the AV firm is in fairly close proximity to the club.

4. Is the firm available for deliveries and installations after normal business hours?

5. How many field representatives does it have?

6. How many delivery vehicles does it have?

7. Do all field representatives and drivers carry beepers or cellular phones so that they can be contacted quickly?

8. What are the rental charges for equipment? Ensure that you are quoted the total charge for delivery, setup, and postproduction.

9. What is the charge (if any) for backup, emergency equipment?

10. Are deposits required?

11. What are the refund policies? For instance, if an equipment order is canceled at the last minute, will some of the deposit be returned? Also inquire about the procedures used to reconcile disputed charges.

12. How much setup time is needed?

13. How much rehearsal time is needed?

14. What is required in the way of staging area(s)?

15. Make sure function assistance is provided. Many hosts will need assistance in planning their AV needs. The approved AV service contractor is able to provide sufficient input and assistance in developing these plans. A host may also need some help in computing his or her budget for AV production, equipment, labor, delivery, installation, and postproduction costs.

16. What are the labor charges? This can be the biggest part of a host's AV budget. However, armed with the correct information about the catered event, the AV firm will be able to develop a detailed labor schedule that complies with union contracts and give the host realistic expectation of total labor costs.

Unfortunately, actual labor charges tend to exceed the budgeted ones because the host and the AV service contractor cannot anticipate everything about the scheduled function. For instance, there may be a problem getting into the facility to set up sound equipment because another catered function is running late. Delayed access to function rooms, as well as tight turnarounds, last-minute on-site changes, and incomplete agendas are the most common reasons for labor cost variances.

These cost variances may increase if union labor must be scheduled. Many clubs and AV companies have contractual agreements requiring union labor for AV services. With complex, elaborate setups, more than one union may be involved. Since most labor contracts include hourly minimums, meal penalties, overtime rates, and show calls, the actual labor charge can be significantly greater than the budgeted one.

The more your AV service contractor knows about the catered function, the easier it will be to predict accurately the final, actual labor cost. Furthermore, the event's show coordinator will then be able to select and schedule a crew capable of handling the event properly.

17. Is the firm able to coordinate with other service contractors? For instance, if a separate lighting service contractor is required, both firms will need to work together smoothly to avoid glitches that can add to final costs and cause guest dissatisfaction.

18. What other services can the AV firm provide? Some hosts appreciate a one-stop shopping opportunity. It is good practice to be able to recommend to them AV firms that can perform other related services. For instance, some AV service contractors offer a wide variety of services, such as theme parties, laser and pyrotechnics shows, video conferencing, personalized Power Point presentations, and simultaneous translation.

Accommodating a Client's AV Needs

If a host is using AV services, the function must be held in a room where sound can be transmitted effectively. The walls should have absorbent panels and be at least 1 inch thick. If air walls (moving partitions) are used, they should be metal or fiberglass and about 2 to 4 inches thick. Be sure that seals and gaskets are intact and tightly secured to prevent sound leaks.

Wool or thick-pile rugs are excellent floor coverings. These will absorb unwanted sounds, such as those created by footsteps and moving equipment.

The function room's ceiling should not be too high or else sound can reverberate. If the local building codes require very high ceilings, you will need to have some sort of acoustical material installed to reduce this effect or, if the host allows, position the speakers appropriately so that this problem is minimized. If there is any potential for sound reverberation, you can quickly overcome it by installing temporary fabrics, tiles, or other acoustical material.

If you have anything to say about room decor, avoid using permanent acoustical tiles. While they represent an effective and efficient way to minimize sound reverberation, unfortunately they are not very attractive. Permanently installed acoustical tiles may detract considerably from the function room's attractiveness.

If a host is using an outside AV service contractor, be certain that the firm is apprised of the club's logistics. For instance, the firm must be aware of accessibility, freight elevators, height and width of the doorways, and so forth in order to plan and implement the project correctly. Also inform the firm of other events in the club that could interfere with installation and teardown procedures. These are very important factors that the AV firm must know about ahead of time or else a satisfactory AV budget cannot be prepared.

Since AV service requires additional electrical power, and if your club's policy is to charge extra for it, be absolutely sure that the host realizes this. Do not point this out at the last minute. Experience shows that most hosts are unaware of these subtle, hidden charges. It is up to you to disclose them up front so that they can plan accordingly.

Finally, make certain the host realizes that all outside services will be billed at the actual cost, which may or may not be the same as the competitive bids submitted. You do not wish to dwell on the negative, but experience shows that the least little thing can throw off an AV schedule and drive up its labor costs.

ENTERTAINMENT

Many catered events offer some type of entertainment. The offerings run the gamut from the mundane to the spectacular. At one end of the spectrum is the one-man keyboard player, while at the opposite end are internationally famous singers headlining major show productions.

As with any outside service contractor, the club could develop an approved supplier list for potential hosts to use. This would be relatively easy for those clubs that offer entertainment in their restaurant and bar outlets or have a corporate entertainment director.

If a host requires entertainment, though, usually the responsibility for booking, scheduling, and coordinating it falls on his or her shoulders. Generally speaking, hosts get in touch with booking agents and work closely with them and the catering executive to plan and implement the desired production.

The club's major involvement in the entertainment decision is to take it into account when planning the catered event. For instance, if a dance band is scheduled, everything from banquet setup to work scheduling will be affected. Considering the major impact that entertainment will have, the catering executive cannot work effectively unless he or she is privy to this information.

The club must also know if there are any additional services that must be provided. The entertainment contract will indicate what they are and who is responsible for securing them. Generally speaking, the key variables the club must consider are

1. *Lighting requirements.* Will the entertainment provide its own? Will there be a separate outside lighting service contractor? Will the club's permanent system suffice?

2. *Number of dressing rooms needed.* Also note where they must be located.

3. *Sound systems.* Many entertainers have their own systems and technicians. Your responsibility is to provide sufficient space and electrical power. Club policy may require you to charge the client for this extra space and electrical power.

4. *Rehearsal time and facilities needed.* If you need to hold the function room space for a day or two before the event so that rehearsals can be held, you will probably need to charge the host extra for this accommodation.

5. *Setup time.* In lieu of rehearsal time or in addition to it, you may need to hold a function room for an extra day or two so that the entertainment production can be set up properly.

6. *Security.* Some entertainers have their own security guards. Others may depend on the club for all security or for additional security to supplement their own.

7. *Staging requirements.* In addition to setting up a stage and runway, you must know if you need to dovetail with the lighting and AV service contractors.

8. *Dance floor.* You also want to know if one or more dance floors are needed.

9. *Buffer area.* This is the space between the entertainers and the audience. Some big-name acts want quite a distance between them and their fans, primarily for security purposes.

10. *Liability.* A glance at the contract will tell you if there is any potential liability concern. For instance, some magicians use unusual and potentially dangerous props that could expose the club to a lawsuit if guests are injured.

    You also need to know if the club will be responsible for the entertainer's personal property. If so, you must control the handling of these items.

11. *Complimentary food, beverage, and/or sleeping rooms.* You may want to offer entertainers the hospitality of the house as a goodwill gesture. Alternatively, you may let them run a tab and then charge it back to the host. Or you can arrange for the booking agents to pay for these services and bill it back to the hosts. Before making a decision, though, you will need to get the host's permission up front.

12. *Operational restrictions.* Some entertainers have demands that may impact the rest of the club's operations. For instance, a singer

may require a smoke-free ballroom, sleeping room, and dressing room. Or an entertainer may request special foods and beverages.

LIGHTING

Lighting is most commonly used to provide safety and security. It is primarily used to illuminate public and work areas properly so that they meet local building code requirements as well as create a relaxed atmosphere.

Lighting can be much more than this, however. Lighting is magic. It can be used to overcome a plain, pedestrian environment; highlight persons, products, and specific function room decors; illuminate speakers and other entertainers; focus attention on a particular spot; create a more exciting and dramatic dance floor; frame an area; and provide other decorative touches.

Lighting can also be used to tell a story. For instance, you can use laser equipment to project company logos, pictures of awards recipients, names of VIPs, and so forth on a wall so that guests can view them when they enter the facility.

Depending on the host's needs, he or she can obtain lighting service in at least three ways: use the club's permanent lighting system; rent lighting equipment and personally install, operate, and tear it down; or employ an outside lighting service contractor.

Club Lighting System

The typical club does not own specialized lighting equipment that can be used to create light shows or any other type of unusual production. Normally it can provide a few spotlights and other similar equipment. However, usually its in-house system is not set up to accommodate unusual requests.

The typical club, though, is capable of accommodating the outside service contractor. Sufficient electrical power, space, overhead beams, and so forth are normally included in the original building design in anticipation of these needs.

If a host requires only enough lighting to illuminate the function room, then no additional lighting service is required. But, if lighting will be used as a form of decoration, few clubs can provide a complete service package.

Rental Lighting Equipment

If a host has unusual lighting demands, he or she can save a considerable amount of money by renting and handling the equipment personally in lieu of employing a lighting service contractor. Rental rates are usually very competitive, whereas this is not usually the case with contractor fees. Additional savings can be had if a host can coordinate and share expenses with a preceding or succeeding group who has similar lighting needs.

Your hosts should not choose to handle lighting equipment personally unless they are familiar with the use of this equipment. They also should avoid it if local unions prohibit this type of work. Furthermore, you should warn them that the potential savings could prove illusory if, for example, they need to hire additional labor to handle the work. In some cases, it may be more economical and convenient to select an outside lighting service contractor.

If a host prefers this option, be certain that he or she signs insurance and/or liability waivers indemnifying the club. Furthermore, make sure the club's insurance carriers and local building codes permit you to allow unlicensed and inexperienced clients to do this type of work on your premises. If there are any liability concerns, you should not let hosts do their own work.

Employment of a Lighting Service Contractor

An outside lighting service is an extremely labor-intensive, capital-intensive service. Consequently, hosts will pay a pretty penny for it. Nevertheless, the results of professionally developed light shows are very attractive and will certainly guarantee a memorable affair.

Lighting shows can be very expensive for several reasons, including

1. Most designs are unique and, therefore, will take some time to perfect.
2. Highly skilled, expensive union labor is typically used.
3. The club design may inhibit efficient installation.
4. The lighting service contractor must house an inventory of very expensive equipment that is subject to rapid obsolescence.
5. Liability insurance that service contractors must carry is very expensive.
6. Rehearsal time must be paid for.
7. The temporary installation may be subject to inspection by the local government's building codes agency.
8. Portable electrical power generators may be needed if the club does not have sufficient electrical power or if the electricity cannot

be drawn from the main power panel and redistributed to the proper locations.

9. When the system is being installed and tested, other club departments, such as banquet setup, may have to postpone their work.

10. Coordination with other club departments and outside service contractors can be expensive and time consuming.

11. If the lighting show requires a lot of electrical power, the club may charge extra for it. There may also be a surcharge if a function room must be shut down for a day or two so that installation and testing can be completed.

If the club decides to develop an approved supplier list, it should use selection criteria similar to those noted for AV and entertainment services. As with all outside services, you are primarily interested in the firm's ability to provide timely, adequate service.

OTHER SERVICES

Functions occasionally will require other services the club is unable to provide. If outside service contractors must be used, once again, the club may have an approved supplier list for the host's convenience. If not, it is up to the host to secure the necessary services and coordinate them with the club catering executive.

The most common types of other service contractors used by hosts are

1. Decorator
2. Designer
3. Florist
4. Photographer
5. Transportation services
6. Media coverage
7. Specialized security
8. Religious services
9. Host/hostess
10. Amenity/souvenir manufacturer

INTERMEDIARIES

At times, the catering executive will not work directly with a host. Instead, he or she will be dealing with an intermediary hired by the host to arrange a catered function.

Intermediaries are sometimes referred to as *10 percenters*. This name is based on how they charge for their services. Generally, they charge 10 percent of the host's total bill for catered events. If the client schedules a large affair, the percentage fee may be reduced.

Hosts typically use intermediaries when the catered event represents a major undertaking. For instance, if there will be several meal and beverage functions and many outside service contractors, a potential host may feel more comfortable employing a seasoned professional experienced in producing these types of detailed affairs.

Intermediaries are often used for civic and political fundraising events where it is necessary to solicit financial support and to sell tickets. Fundraising fashion shows, theme parties, charity auctions, and art shows are typically planned and implemented by professional intermediaries.

Intermediaries may also be used by hosts planning the following types of events:

1. Theatrical production
2. Pyrotechnics show
3. Laser show
4. Video conference
5. Festival
6. Fair
7. Testimonial roast
8. Reunion
9. Awards program
10. New-product introduction
11. Company party
12. Training program
13. Exhibition

The catering executive typically has mixed feelings about intermediaries. Their professionalism is certainly welcome. For the most part, they know what they are doing. Unlike some hosts, they do not need to be educated about every little detail. Furthermore, the host is paying for their work. On the other hand, intermediaries generally are more astute shoppers than the typical catering host. They tend to drive harder bargains. They sometimes want more control over events than the typical catering executive is willing to surrender. It is sometimes inefficient to funnel your proposals and comments through a third party. And there may be some uneasy moments if, in addition to getting a fee from the client, an intermediary solicits a commission from the club for including the property in the event. Because some properties will not pay this type of commission, a host may not be exposed to all potential clubs capable of handling his or her needs.

Some catering executives feel that it is too difficult to work with intermediaries. For instance, some of them will never let you talk directly to the host, which presents problems when you are trying to produce an event as seen through the eyes of another. Without direct host contact, there is no way of knowing if your proposals are consistent with the host's wishes. If the host is disappointed, he or she will more readily blame the caterer, not the intermediary.

Another potential problem with intermediaries occurs when hosts contact you directly instead of going through their intermediaries. If the contact involves a discussion of prices, you have a particularly significant dilemma if the intermediaries are marking up your prices and rebilling hosts. Before talking to any host who is represented by an intermediary, you should meet with both of them so that these potentially troublesome occurrences do not arise.

Independent Meeting Planner

Professional meeting planners, sometimes referred to as *contract planners* or *multiple management companies,* are probably the most common type of intermediary used by hosts. A host can hire them to plan and implement the entire function, or they can be used to perform specific services, such as site selection, negotiations, or registration of function attendees.

Independent meeting planners specialize in producing convention programs, business meetings, training programs, and other similar events. They are capable of coordinating all necessary business functions, meal functions, beverage functions, and outside service contractors. They usually meet the needs of small- and medium-sized companies that require professional assistance, but do not have the resources to hire in-house planners. Most government hosts also engage these types of intermediaries.

Special Event Planner

These intermediaries are sometimes engaged by corporations to plan and implement company parties and other similar affairs. They usually have a select clientele and serve their clients on a periodic, predictable basis. For instance, a special event producer may plan a particular company's annual picnic every year. Hosts tend to prefer this type of long-term arrangement because it ensures continuity and variety.

Professional sports teams typically use special events planners to coordinate after-game parties, halftime events, parades, and so forth.

Major events, such as the Olympics, corporate centennial celebrations, building openings, presidential inaugurations, and so forth, usually use several planners. For instance, the Coca Cola Company's 100th birthday celebration in Atlanta required the services of several special events specialists, with each one responsible for one specific part of the event.

If several special events planners are used, one of them may be responsible for overseeing and coordinating everyone's efforts. He or she may also need to develop a master plan for the event and decide how each planner will be used.

Independent Party Planner

This intermediary is similar to the special event planner. The primary difference is that he or she tends to work more often with noncorporate clients. For instance, a small group of persons wishing to organize a 20-year high school reunion will tend to use this type of intermediary to help publicize, plan, and implement the function.

Professional reunion planners are the most rapidly growing segment of the independent party planning community. According to the National Association of Reunion Planners (NARP), by 2000, one of three high school reunions will be planned, organized, implemented, and supervised by a professional planner.

High school reunions are the most common type of reunion function. However, other reunions, such as family, military, and company alumni, are quickly becoming commonplace as clients realize how easy it is to accomplish what was once thought to be an impossible task.

Independent party planners usually take over all aspects of the function. They usually book the site, handle mailings, book entertainment, prepare a memory book, and so forth. Many of them also lend hosts the deposits required by club caterers, thereby allowing hosts to avoid paying out of pocket for up-front expenses; hosts can wait until their guests pay before they have to pay the planners.

Many independent party planners are brokers who subcontract most or all portions of the function. For instance, if a group wants to hold a prom function, it may contact a prom function intermediary who will then select the club caterer, help plan the menu, hire a decorator, and engage the appropriate entertainment.

10

Staffing

One cannot overestimate the importance of staffing in the service industry. The catering department's reputation rests on its ability to prepare and serve a consistent quality of food and beverage. Without the proper amount and type of personnel, the club cannot hope to develop or maintain a sterling reputation.

What motivates a host to book business at a particular club? What is the difference between one club's catering department and another's? Certainly each club lays claim to some sort of unique benefit that it alone can provide to hosts. However, if you scratch the surface of any club's reputation, chances are you will find that its perceived level of service is its most salient feature.

There is an old saying in the foodservice business that supermarkets sell food, and restaurants sell service. The same thing can be said about the typical club catering department. Conceivably a host could rent a hall and perform all the shopping, cooking, serving, and cleaning chores. And he or she could probably do it at less than half the cost of hiring a caterer. Why then, would he or she agree to book a catering function knowing full well that it will not be cheap?

The obvious answer is that hosts are willing to pay for someone else to do the work. But, more than that, they are willing to pay a premium for someone who can do the work in a timely and efficient manner, and who can certainly do it better than they could do it themselves.

One of the best things that can happen to a club is for hosts to say, yes, they did spend a great deal, but they got their money's worth. In other words, they received value for their dollars.

Conversely, one of the worst things that can occur is for hosts to perceive that they did not get a good value. No matter how low the price is, if a host does not perceive value, it is too high.

Staffing is critical. It is an organization's life blood. Experience shows that customer satisfaction and repeat patronage are influenced primarily by food and beverage quality, service, and sanitation and cleanliness. An inadequate, undermanned, undertrained staff is incompatible with the successful club operation.

EMPLOYEE RECRUITMENT

The wise catering executive does not rely solely on the club's human resources department to secure adequate staffing. You cannot merely pick up the phone and call the employment manager whenever you have a job opening. Rather, it is very important to adopt a proactive stance in order to satisfy your staffing needs.

Staffing is an ongoing activity primarily because the typical club catering department's staffing requirements fluctuate widely. This is especially true for the group of employees who work part-time and/or work very unpredictable schedules.

There is a critical core of permanent, fixed-cost, full-time and part-time managerial and hourly staff members. Many of these people are career oriented and/or satisfied with their current positions. Consequently, they are apt to remain with you. This does not mean that this core will never change. As with anything else, it is subject to change at a moment's notice. For instance, a permanent part-time head bartender may suddenly leave you to take a full-time bartending job at a competing operation.

The majority of your staff are variable-cost employees who tend to work for more than one operation. While many of them prefer part-time status, some of them are looking for full-time employment. If they secure something permanent, chances are they may leave you on short notice.

Many variable-cost employees may be busy when you need them. For instance, some of them may be working their regular jobs and cannot break away to help you, while others may be working at another operation's catered function that day.

Your variable-cost employees also tend to move into and out of the industry. It is not unusual for food and cocktail servers and buspersons to qualify for employment in other segments of the service industry. For instance, the people skills and customer-contact skills that food servers develop are the major prerequisites for many job positions in department stores, supermarkets, and boutiques.

An unfortunate fact of life in the service industry is the labor shortage that frustrates your efforts to build and maintain an adequate staff. Not only must you compete with other foodservice operations for a diminishing labor pool, you also need to fight other retailers. For instance, a recent trend in foodservice is for qualified, experienced chefs to leave the restaurant industry and join the supermarket industry. It seems that many supermarket companies are making a major investment in deli operations and are willing to employ expensive chefs to develop prepared foods for customer takeout. Complicating your efforts to compete with the supermarket industry is the fact that it generally will offer more attractive work schedules and pay more than the typical foodservice operator. For instance, several foodservice publications report that entry-level wages and discretionary employee benefits in supermarket delicatessens exceed those paid in the food and beverage industry.

To say the least, maintaining an adequate number of qualified employees is no easy task. No one likes to encounter severe employee turnover. However, the fluctuating demands for staff members in the catering industry have resulted in a certain amount of structural (that is unavoidable) turnover.

Experience shows that, if a foodservice operation has normal employee turnover, the manager may spend as much as one-fourth of his or her working hours recruiting, interviewing, and training new staff members. This time investment can be reduced slightly if the club has a human resources specialist. However, you must resist the temptation to lean too heavily on the human resources specialist because it is risky to completely delegate this responsibility. Unless you are intimately involved with staffing procedures, chances are you will be unable to handle your host's needs effectively.

The catering executive must be willing to constantly cultivate potential employees. This is especially important for your hourly staff. Your A-lists and B-lists can never be too long. You do not want to get to the end of them and find that you still do not have enough people to staff the upcoming catering events.

You also need to cultivate and develop your fixed-cost employees. In addition, it is important to spend as much time as possible recruiting entry-level variable-cost employees and promoting them to fixed-cost status when they are ready and when these positions open up.

Job Specification

For management positions, a job candidate must have technical work experience along with the requisite people skills. For many hourly positions, you also prefer job candidates with a reasonable amount of catering work experience. However, it is conceivable that you could hire persons for many positions who have minimal or no work experience in our industry, which may be a good way to hire catering staff because you won't have to break any bad service habits. If a person has the willingness to do the work and possesses customer-contact skills and a positive attitude toward the catering industry, you can train him or her to perform capably. With patience and understanding, you can turn energetic people into excellent food and cocktail servers. Conversely, the lack of technical skills can place an additional burden on you and the rest of your staff because of the extra training that must be done. Nevertheless, many managers in the foodservice industry are accustomed to hiring and training neophytes.

It is one thing to hire someone without catering work experience, but quite another to hire a person who has no work experience in customer-contact positions. There is no way to predict how someone will react when put into a high-pressure situation where guests are blowing off steam. Experience shows that the various personality tests available do not adequately predict a newcomer's initial reactions.

Likewise if you contemplate hiring someone who has never worked a paid job outside the home. If you hire such a person, you encounter all the problems associated with hiring someone with no catering work experience plus those that crop up whenever someone is introduced to the realities of the workplace. Not only must you teach these novices how to perform their jobs, but you must also teach them the protocols of working for an employer.

When recruiting job candidates, you must see to it that they possess the appropriate credentials. For instance, some positions may need to be staffed solely with union members. A few may require college degrees or similar training. Secretaries should be certified in word processing, computerized record keeping, and other related tasks. Other positions may require persons who have current training certificates in alcohol server awareness. And some employees may need current health cards issued by the local health district.

Minimum age is another job specification for job candidates who prepare, sell, and/or serve alcoholic beverages. In most parts of the United States, these persons must be at least 21 years old. As a general rule, clubs may hire minors for kitchen preprep, food runner, and other similar jobs. These clubs must bear in mind, however, that there are laws pertaining to the number of hours and times of day younger employees can work. Most catering departments usually will not hire minors because it is almost impossible to keep them away from alcoholic beverage service.

Job Description

It is imperative to maintain up-to-date job descriptions so that job candidates know exactly what to expect if they come to work for you. You do not want to be put into the position of relating inaccurate information. This will cause unnecessary grief, job dissatisfaction, and unnecessary employee turnover.

The job descriptions should paint accurate pictures of all job duties that must be performed. Experience shows that job candidates often misinterpret job parameters because the job descriptions are too vague. The recruiter may exacerbate this problem further by failing to address the specific job needs during the interview process.

It is thought that job misinterpretation is one of the key variables responsible for excessive employee turnover. Generally speaking, if you can keep an hourly person for 30 days and a management person for one year, chances are that he or she is satisfied with the job and the company and is likely to remain for a while. If you paint a realistic picture up front and then see to it that reality does not vary significantly from this description, your employee turnover will probably be much less than the industry average.

Labor Pool

The catering executive should work closely with the club's human resources specialist to develop an adequate labor pool. He or she should inform human resources of potentially fruitful areas to seek job candidates so that efforts are not wasted. For instance, if you feel that the local college would generate adequate job candidates, encourage the human resources specialist to recruit on campus.

The catering department also should not be afraid to adopt a proactive stance. It should have a long-term staffing plan that notes expected terminations and resignations, as well as anticipated total staffing needs. It should take the lead whenever possible and seek out job candidates and send them to human resources for interviewing and possible hiring.

It is important to note that experience shows we are guilty of trying to convert our part-time employees, especially seniors, into full-time employees. Since this is an unattractive option for many of our part-time employees, you should avoid this temptation lest you lose valuable part-time personnel.

The catering manager will find a number of labor sources that can yield capable job candidates.

1. *Promotion from within the catering department.*   Employees like a promotion-from-within policy since this gives them an opportunity to move up in the company. Experience shows that career ladders and career scaffolds attract potential employees who would otherwise not perceive your club as a good place to work.

2. *Use of the club's job bidding process.*   Usually a club will post job openings on the employee bulletin board. Interested employees can then bid, or apply, for them. For instance, a person currently employed in the club's grill room may want to apply for a full-time catering position.

3. *Job referral.*   Current catering employees may have friends or relatives who might wish to apply for job openings. This could be a win-win situation in that the current employee might receive some type of bonus while the catering department gets another good employee who knows what to expect. Unfortunately, some conflict-of-interest and nepotism problems could arise whenever this sort of inbreeding occurs. Because of these problems, some clubs severely restrict this hiring practice.

4. *Employees from other club departments.*   A part-time employee in another department may be a good addition to your A-list or B-list. This can be another win-win situation, assuming it does not violate club policy. You must be careful when doing this, though, because some jealousy and hard feelings can develop. For instance, it could be rather ticklish if a part-time grill room employee finds your department more inviting and requests a transfer.

Using other club department employees also could cause overtime problems. For instance, if in one week an hourly employee works five full days in the grill room and one full day for you, he or she would have to be paid overtime premium pay for the sixth day. Federal regulations mandate that an hourly employee must be compensated 1.5 times his or her regular rate of pay for all hours worked in excess of 40 per week. Furthermore, in some states an hourly employee may be entitled to overtime premium pay for all hours worked in excess of 8 per day (if the normal work week is 5 days, 8 hours per day) or 10 per day (if the normal work week is 4 days, 10 hours per day).

5. *Union hiring hall.* A unionized club may need to use the union hiring hall for permanent and temporary hires if the job positions are unionized. In some cases, the union may sponsor internships and apprenticeships that can provide you with a steady, albeit ever-changing, supply of young, enthusiastic workers.

6. *Culinary schools.* This is a good source of permanent, full-time employees. It also represents a good pool of part-time workers who need to earn work-experience hours to complete their degree requirements. The instructors themselves may be interested in working part-time. Or they may be willing to work for you during their summer vacations.

7. *Colleges and universities.* You should concentrate your recruiting efforts on the many universities and two-year colleges offering hospitality management training. You may be able to attract graduates for full-time positions. In addition, since most college programs require students to earn a minimum number of work hours in the hospitality field, you should try to set up a system whereby your part-time staff is continually replenished with underclassmen.

Many other college majors might be willing to work part-time. Our industry is flexible enough to work around most young persons' school schedules. Students are usually favorably disposed to part-time club work because of your ability to satisfy almost anyone's personal schedules. You should call the schools' placement offices and ask them to post job openings on their job bulletin boards.

8. *High schools.* This labor source is similar to colleges and universities. The major difference is that, while some college students are underage, almost all high-school students are too young to work around alcoholic beverages. They also may be too young to work past curfew. Usually catering departments will not hire anyone under 21 years of age. However, you might consider working with vocational schools to develop catering internships and other similar job opportunities. When the interns reach majority age, they may look favorably on your current job offerings.

9. *Other retail establishments.* Some retailers, such as department stores and supermarkets, employ part-time persons who may be interested in adding more work hours to their current personal work schedules. You may be able to help them do this by giving them one or two days of work per week. At the very least, you can put them on your A-list or B-list.

10. *Manufacturing plants.* Some persons working in these industries may be interested in moonlighting activities. They may want to extend their current part-time earnings, or they might want to work a sixth day. You can accommodate them with a regular day each week, or you can put them on your A-list or B-list.

11. *Homemakers.* This segment is one of the best for A-list or B-list people. Experience shows, though, that you will need to be extremely flexible with them because they will not work if your needs conflict with their personal family responsibilities.

12. *Seniors.* Many retired persons want to keep active in the work world. They are becoming more and more of a fixture in many retailers'

part-time labor pools. Several types of foodservice operations are anxious to hire them on a part-time basis. They usually bring a favorable combination of work experience, enthusiasm, patience, personableness, and dedication that makes them extremely valuable employees. Be particularly careful not to pressure these employees to become full-time workers. They are usually happy with their part-time status.

13. *Private industry councils.* Many businesspersons support institutes and other similar organizations that can be good sources of full-time and part-time labor. For instance, groups such as the Urban League are very active in sponsoring employment job fairs, apprenticeship programs, and other job training opportunities that can dovetail very nicely with your employment efforts.

14. *Employment agencies.* Public and private employment agencies may yield full-time job candidates. Public agencies operated by the state unemployment security departments can be good sources of hourly wage earners. They may be preferable to private employment agencies because they do not charge fees for their services. Because of the fees involved, employers tend to use outside employment agencies (or private head-hunters) only when it is necessary to hire middle- and top-level management personnel.

15. *Government job training agencies.* There may be one or more local government agencies sponsoring job training programs on their own or with the cooperation of the federal government. For instance, the local workers' compensation insurance program may sponsor several rehabilitative training programs for injured employees who cannot go back to their old jobs. You could be part of these training efforts by providing jobs for the trainees. In some cases, your cooperation can result in payroll savings since some programs grant tax credits and/or pay part or all of the wages during the training periods. Moreover, a successful trainee could end up taking a full-time, permanent position with your club.

16. *Day-labor operations.* These organizations are similar to public and private employment agencies. The major difference is that they usually lease personnel to you on a daily basis. For instance, if you need a few extra hands to set up an outdoor tent, a call to the local "manpower" agency could yield the exact amount of labor required. You get only the amount of help needed. It is more convenient to pay one price for it rather than putting everyone through the normal, expensive hiring procedure.

17. *Other clubs and hotels.* While it is not neighborly to steal employees from your competitors, you should not let this stop you from spreading the word about job opportunities at your property. Furthermore, since all food and beverage operations use many part-time persons, there is ample opportunity to offer someone one or two work days at your property while

allowing him or her to keep the other job. Some of your employees are most likely working for several food and beverage operations anyway. For example, a few of them may be on the B-list of every major property in town. You might as well take the initiative and maximize the potential of this labor source by publicizing your job opportunities (tastefully, of course).

18. *Professional associations.* This is one of the most prolific sources of sales and management personnel. Many hospitality managers belong to one or more professional associations. For instance, many club managers belong to the Club Managers Association of America (CMAA) and may also belong to the National Association of Catering Executives (NACE).

One of the benefits association members enjoy is being kept apprised of current career opportunities available in their field of expertise and interest. You should use these built-in grapevines to advertise current job vacancies.

19. *Reduction of employee turnover.* The seeds of employee turnover or employee retention are planted when a job candidate is interviewed and take root when the new hire gets a chance to experience reality and compare it to your promises.

Turnover and retention are also directly related to the type and amount of job training and development provided to employees. Studies show that the lack of training and development is one of the main reasons people leave their jobs.

It has been said that, depending on the type of job position, it costs at least several hundred to several thousand dollars to replace a hospitality industry worker. The costs of hiring, orienting, training, putting up with lower productivity for a while, and so forth, can add up very quickly. If you can reduce turnover, the potential payroll savings are very handsome. Moreover, a reduction in employee turnover relieves the pressure for you to cultivate other labor sources.

Job Application

The job application is the most common method used to screen potential employees initially. Walk-ins—persons who respond to classified ads or who merely stop by to see if you need help—are the usual applicants who fill out these forms.

The job application can be an excellent prescreening device. The employment manager can use it to quickly weed out unqualified job candidates who do not possess the requisite experience, education, and other pertinent background characteristics.

If you find someone to fill a job position yourself, you may still need to send him or her to the human resources specialist to complete a job application and go through the rest of the job processing procedure. Chances are that, since you found the person, the total procedure will be expedited.

Job Interview

If a walk-in seeks a job, usually he or she is given a prescreening interview if the job application reveals some promising information. Typically, the prescreening interview involves a discussion of things such as: When can the person report for work? What is the depth of his or her work experience? Will the person feel comfortable working under your club's particular rules and regulations?

A prescreening interview is also an excellent opportunity to determine if a job candidate is likely to succeed at your club. For instance, you can use a prescreening process to determine if a job candidate has the proper attitudes, skills, and work habits needed to perform effectively. Managers might ask job candidates questions, the responses to which are compared to those of current successful club employees. A statistically significant positive correlation of responses suggests that the job candidate will excel with the club.

If a job candidate survives the prescreening interview, the interviewer should take the time to check references before moving him or her along in the job processing procedure. Telephone calls should be made to verify information indicated on the job application and during the prescreening job interview.

A reference check may also include some testing procedures. For instance, your club may have a policy of giving all job applicants integrity tests, drug tests, physical exams, job-skills tests, and so forth before they can qualify for the next step in the employment process.

If the reference check yields favorable information, the job candidate usually is then interviewed by you and/or someone on your staff. In some cases, he or she may be interviewed by you and other management personnel in the catering department. This is especially true if the person is applying for an entry-level sales or management position.

After this interview, it is usually up to you to determine if the club should offer the position to the job applicant. If you want to hire the person, a formal job offer should be made. You should then complete the employment process and schedule the new hire's first workday.

ORIENTATION

At most clubs, a human resources specialist is responsible for orienting all new hires. This procedure normally takes the better part of one workday.

Orientation usually involves providing new hires with nonjob-related information. For instance, new hires are:

1. Introduced to the club's philosophy
2. Fitted for uniforms
3. Given an employee handbook and explanation of the information it contains
4. Given a welcoming by the club's general manager and other major department heads
5. Exposed to general lectures dealing with property security procedures, club history, career opportunities, and so forth
6. Given a property tour
7. Assigned locker room space, parking place, name tag, and so on
8. Introduced to supervisor and coworkers

TRAINING

A human resources specialist and the catering department generally share training efforts. For instance, human resources may provide general training in life safety, customer courtesy, complaint handling, telephone procedures, drug and alcohol awareness, and so forth, with catering taking responsibility for the initial and ongoing specific job-related training.

The Food & Beverage Committee of the Hotel Sales & Marketing Association International (HSMAI) developed training guidelines that can be used to familiarize a catering department's new hire with all pertinent operating and nonoperating activities. Depending on the position, a new hire should be exposed to one or more of the following systems:

1. *Banquet sales manual.* All catering sales representatives should be familiar with your catering policies and procedures. New entry-level salespersons who are unfamiliar with the general sales systems used in the hospitality industry should pay particular attention to the following:
   a. Catering files and filing procedures
   b. Tracing procedures
   c. Solicitation procedures
   d. Catering sales analysis

    e. Booking procedures

    f. Procedures used to prepare BEOs, prefunction sheets, and convention resumes

    g. Dates and space reservation procedures

    h. Confirmation procedures

    i. Cancellation procedures

    j. Specific job responsibilities

    k. Sales techniques

    l. Credit procedures

    m. Guarantee procedures

2. *Food and beverage department.* If relevant, the new hire should be exposed to some or all of the following food and beverage operating procedures:

    a. Food and beverage controller's office

        (1) General banquet food and beverage cost requirements

        (2) Exposure to banquet food and beverage cost calculations

        (3) General food and beverage accounting procedures

        (4) Food controls

        (5) Beverage controls

        (6) Guarantee and attendance calculations

        (7) Variance analysis

        (8) Profit-and-loss statement analysis

        (9) Total banquet costs computation

      (10) Percentage analysis

      (11) Payroll cost analysis

      (12) Profit ratios

    b. Kitchen

        (1) Executive chef's responsibilities

        (2) Banquet chef's responsibilities

        (3) Banquet menus

        (4) Banquet change orders

        (5) Staffing

        (6) Stock requisitions

        (7) Food preprep

      (8) Food prep

      (9) Banquet dish-up

    (10) Evaluating potential menu items

    (11) Month-end inventories

    (12) Portion control

c. Steward

      (1) Payroll forecasts

      (2) Review of banquet menus

      (3) Staffing

      (4) Stock requisitions

      (5) Equipment preparation

      (6) Equipment inspection

      (7) Equipment storage

      (8) Coordination with kitchen and service

      (9) Salvage procedures

    (10) Sanitation procedures

    (11) Refrigeration

    (12) Equipment par stocks

    (13) Equipment inventories

    (14) Supplies storage

    (15) Equipment and supplies purchasing

d. Banquet manager

      (1) General service procedures

      (2) Coordination with kitchen and steward

      (3) General supervisory procedures

      (4) Banquet rooms

      (5) Function room setups

      (6) Premeal service meetings

      (7) Seating charts

      (8) Function room maintenance

      (9) Menu meetings

    (10) Preconvention meetings

    (11) Coordination of tableware and napery

        (12) Payroll forecasts

        (13) Rehab meeting (forecasted repair and maintenance needs)

        (14) Work scheduling

        (15) Housekeeping work sheets

        (16) Styles of service

  e. Beverages

        (1) Banquet menus

        (2) Coordination with steward and banquet manager

        (3) Stock requisitions

        (4) Change orders

        (5) Guarantees

        (6) Sales and cost data

        (7) Prefunction meetings—roll call and briefing

        (8) Banquet bar stocking

        (9) Bar teardown

        (10) Beginning and ending bar inventories

        (11) Cash reconciliation

        (12) Drink ticket reconciliation

        (13) Month-end inventories

        (14) Work scheduling

  f. Room service (if rooms are available)

        (1) Hospitality suites

        (2) Liquor control

        (3) Room service checks

        (4) Coordination with room setup

        (5) Amenity service packages available

  g. Food and beverage manager

        (1) Daily revenue and payroll report

        (2) Filing system

        (3) Restaurant outlets

        (4) Bar outlets

        (5) Forecasting

(6) Payroll analysis

(7) Menu analysis

(8) Coordination with the district or regional director of food and beverage (if applicable)

(9) Coordination with the corporate vice president of food and beverage (if applicable)

3. *Purchasing*

a. Product availability

b. Seasonal variations

c. Special items not commonly used

d. Banquet menu reviews

e. Banquet order sheets

f. Order sizes

g. Purchase price trends

h. Plant visits

4. *Front office* (if rooms are available)

a. Reservations

b. Front desk procedures

(1) Check-in

(2) Check-out

(3) Baggage handling

c. Coordination with sales departments

d. Room and suite tours

e. Bell desk

f. Concierge

5. *Credit/accounting*

a. Credit procedures

b. Deposit requirements

c. Collections

(1) Procedures

(2) Problems

(3) Outside collection agencies

(4) Types of accounts

6. *Human resources*
   a. General personnel procedures
   b. Coordination with hotel departments
   c. Compensation packages
7. *Engineering*
   a. Sound
   b. Lighting
   c. Utilities available in function rooms
   d. Charges for utilities, labor, and equipment
8. *Safety*
   a. Recognizing safety hazards
   b. Slippery floor procedures
   c. Customer safety
   d. Proper utilities hookups
   e. Crosswalk area setup
   f. Fire codes
   g. Health codes
   h. Evacuation routes
9. *Laundry and valet*
   a. Napery controls
   b. Stock requisitions
   c. Soiled napery storing procedures
   d. Usage charges
   e. Uniforms and costumes

The department head should use these suggested training guidelines to develop an appropriate training program for each new hire. The new hire's progress should then be monitored, with the department head submitting a training report to the director of catering at the conclusion of the training period.

The training report should be reviewed with the trainee before preparing the final draft. For instance, each time an entry is made in the report, the trainer and trainee should visit together for a few moments to discuss the entry and determine if any changes need to be made in the program. This is also a good time to discuss the trainee's progress and clear up any problems.

For some new hires, it would be useful to have them prepare a personal report at the end of their training period. For instance, if you are training a new catering sales representative, you may want to ask him or her to submit a written report detailing what was learned after visiting and working in all other pertinent hotel departments. This report can give you a valuable insight into the trainee's communications skills. It can reveal if additional training is needed. It can also tell you if the training programs need to be modified.

COMPENSATION

The typical compensation package includes a combination of some of the following: salaries, wages, gratuities, commissions, bonuses, tips, required employee benefits, and discretionary employee benefits. All compensation packages are developed and coordinated by a human resources specialist. You should know specifically the types and amounts of compensation allowed for each job position so that potential job candidates will not be misled when you are cultivating them.

Management positions normally receive predetermined salaries unrelated to the amount of time worked. Some managers may receive performance bonuses and/or commissions. For instance, a catering sales representative may receive a modest fixed salary plus a percentage of all business booked.

Nonmanagement, wage-earner positions are usually compensated on an hourly basis. Some of them may also receive a preset split of the gratuities collected for each catered event. If a host leaves a tip, the wage earners typically will share it as well.

Required employee benefits are usually referred to as payroll taxes. They include primarily the club's contribution to the federal government social security, medicare, and unemployment tax programs. Some states also require employers to contribute monies to their unemployment tax programs and the state-operated workers' compensation program.

As a general rule, the minimum cost of required employee benefits is equal to about 15 to 18 percent of your total payroll expense. For instance, if you pay a server $10.00 per hour, the club's out-of-pocket expense for this employee is about $11.50 to $11.80 per hour after factoring in these payroll taxes.

In some parts of the country, the club's total payroll tax expense is much higher because the tax percentages will be applied to the payroll expense plus the amount of gratuities and declared tips. For instance, if a

$10.00-per-hour server averages an additional $5.00 per hour in gratuity and tip income, the hourly payroll tax expense for this employee will be about $2.25 to $2.70 (15 to 18 percent of $15.00). The hourly out-of-pocket expense for this employee, then, is about $12.25 to $12.70.

Typical discretionary benefits are health, dental, optical, and life insurance paid for by the company or offered to employees at a reduced rate. Some clubs also provide pension plans; free meals; matching contributions to selected charities; paid vacations, holidays, personal days, and sick days; insurance coverage for dependents; formal training; career opportunities, such as promotion from within; reimbursement of educational expenses; flexible work scheduling; uniform allowances; and reduced-cost meals and beverages.

Only full-time employees qualify for the full range of discretionary benefits, although some clubs offer a limited number of discretionary benefits to part-time employees who work at least 20 hours per week. Employees working 19 hours or less per week usually do not qualify for discretionary benefits.

Some clubs, especially unionized properties, have generous overtime-pay policies that exceed those mandated by federal and state labor regulations. They may also have very generous holiday-pay policies. For instance, union and/or company policy may require you to pay double time instead of time and a half for all overtime worked, straight time for all state and federal holidays not worked, and double time for all state and federal holidays worked.

Discretionary benefits are not cheap. It is estimated that the least-expensive, bare-bones health insurance package costs a minimum of about $2500 per year for each covered employee.

It is also estimated that the cost of required benefits, discretionary benefits, and administrative expenses needed to operate the human resources function is approximately 40 percent of your total payroll cost. An employee earning $10.00 per hour, then, actually costs you approximately $14.00 per hour after factoring in all payroll-related expenses.

11

Financial Controls and Reports

....

Control procedures must be used to ensure that actual performance is in line with planned performance. The control cycle begins when a potential host considers booking business at your club, and it does not end until the catered function is completed to everyone's satisfaction.

Before a control system can be implemented, you must set standards of performance. If you book a beverage function and you expect each bottle of liquor to yield approximately 15 drinks, the actual number of drinks served per container must be consistent with this standard. If your bartenders pour more or less than 15 drinks per container, you may have a control problem. If they pour too many drinks per container, usually the customers are receiving a reduced portion size. If they pour too few drinks per container, chances are there is excessive waste or customers are receiving excessive portion sizes.

It is management's duty to set the required standards and policies by which all catered events will be run. All operational procedures—from booking the business to purchasing, receiving, storing, issuing, producing, and serving the finished products, to function room selection and setup, to final bill tabulation and collection—must be standardized. If all employees follow the standard operating procedures, chances are you will reach your cost-control and quality-control goals with minimal difficulty.

One of management's primary responsibilities is to see to it that actual results are in line with the standards. To do this, management must develop data-gathering and data-analysis procedures that can be used to compute actual results and compare them to the standards. If there are variances between the standards and the actual results, management must move to identify and solve the underlying problem(s). Experience shows that this correction phase of control is the most difficult one because it is not always easy to diagnose what went wrong. If you cannot get at the root of the problem, it is impossible to solve it.

For example, if your bartenders are consistently pouring more drinks per container than you expect, there are many potential causes for this variance. Unintentionally underpouring each drink is the most logical cause, although mechanical problems with the liquor-dispensing machinery, inadequate record keeping, and failure to account properly for those guests who ask for short pours are also possible reasons.

Another difficult aspect of the control process is the potential to overcontrol everything. You should not cost-control yourself out of business. You must not spend a dollar to control a dime. There comes a point where some controls are not cost effective. For instance, computerized automatic liquor-dispensing units will increase your ability to control drink service. Unfortunately, the expensive investment in these systems may never be recovered in a reasonable period of time.

Overcontrol can also put a manager in the position of concentrating solely on inanimate objects and ignoring hosts and guests. You cannot dwell so much on cost-related matters that you begin to lose sight of the customer. You must satisfy your members, hosts, and guests. However, if you are spending too much time gathering and processing cost data, you may be neglecting them.

It is very difficult to strike just the right balance between effective control and customer service. Experience shows that, if you take good care of the guest, your expenses and profits will fall into line. But, if you concentrate solely on every penny, eventually you will not have to worry about control because you will have no business left to control.

Michael Hurst, past president of the National Restaurant Association (NRA), summed it up best when he remarked that you can achieve maximum control by *closing your business;* this is the only way to avoid control problems. If you want to stay in business and build it into a profitable enterprise, Mr. Hurst suggests that you manage from the front door, not the back door. Taking care of the members and guests and providing consistent value is the best recipe for success in the club industry.

The purpose of this chapter is to discuss the generally accepted control procedures used in the club catering industry. By adopting them, the director of catering takes a giant step toward minimizing variances and maximizing club member and guest satisfaction.

BANQUET EVENT ORDER (BEO)

The BEO, sometimes referred to as the function sheet, is the basis of the club's internal communication system between departments. It is also the basic building block upon which the club catering department's accounting and record-keeping systems are constructed (see Figure 11.1).

A BEO is prepared for each meal and beverage function, and copies are sent to the departments noted in Chapter 4 that will be directly or indirectly involved with the events.

Usually all club departments receive a copy of each BEO about two weeks before the catered function is held. This ensures that all department heads have enough time to schedule and complete their necessary activities that support the events.

Most BEOs are numbered sequentially for easy reference. It is important to assign an identifying number to each BEO so that department heads can resolve any discrepancy easily and quickly. For instance, if banquet setup is unclear about a particular event's requirements, it can call the catering office for additional information regarding BEO 175. This is certainly easier and more accurate than using the hosts' names or other forms of identification, all of which can be garbled and misinterpreted after two or three phone calls.

The typical BEO contains:

1. BEO number
2. Function date
3. Type of function
4. Host name
5. Host address
6. Member contact or person in charge
7. Person who booked the event and authorized signature
8. Name of function room
9. Beginning time of function
10. Expected ending time of function

HOUSTON COUNTRY CLUB
Function Sheet

Pop Up   Time Issued: _____

Replaces Original   Date: _____

Function
Page # ....

Party Info

Party Day Date ....

Name of Function ....

....

Type of Function ....

Location ....

Contact ....

Phone (Fax) Number ....

Member Sponsor .... # ....

Phone (Fax) Number ....

Misc. Time ....

Cocktail Time ....

Misc. Time ....

Meal Time ....

Approx. Number .... Guarantee ....

Bar Arrangements

Tab [ ]   Locker System [ ]

Beer [ ]   Perrier [ ]

Brands Available ....

....

....

Wine Service ....

....

Table Diagram/Set Up

Linen/Napkins

Color

Decorations/Entertainment

Entertainment/Decor ....

....

....

Votives [ ]   Hurricanes [ ]   Mirrors [ ]

Canopy [ ]   Extension [ ]

Florist .... P.O. # ....

Phone # ....

Menu

Hors d'Oeuvres

....

....

....

Sit Down [ ]   Buffet [ ]

Special Instructions

Billing

Charges ....

....

20% Service + 8-1/4% Tax

Security @ $35hr/min 3hr	[ ]	Linen @ 3.50/5.50	[ ]
Party Services $2.50/$3.00pp	[ ]	Hurricane @ 5.00	[ ]
Doorman	[ ]	Votive @ .67 ea.	[ ]
Cloakroom	[ ]	Mirrors @ 3.50	[ ]
Maids	[ ]	Bartenders @ 40.00	[ ]
Shuttle	[ ]	Waiters @ 30.00	[ ]
Valet	[ ]	Chef @ 40.00	[ ]
Set Up @ 7.50/8.50	[ ]	Typeset Menu @ $2.75	[ ]
Corkage @ 7.50/8.50	[ ]	Other:	[ ]

Completed By ....

Billing Sent To .... # ....

Address ....

Figure 11.1. Club function sheet (reprinted with permission of the Houston Country Club).

11. Number of guests expected
12. Number of guests to prepare for
13. Menus
14. Style of service
15. Function room setup
16. Special instructions (such as sleeping room blocks (if applicable), centerpieces, table sets, bar arrangements, unique underliners, VIPs, and other special amenity orders)
17. Prices charged
18. Member billing account number
19. Billing instructions
20. Reference to other BEOs or other relevant records
21. Date BEO was completed
22. Signature of person preparing (or approving) the BEO
23. List of departments receiving a copy of the BEO

PREFUNCTION SHEET

Some clubs want to warn all departments well in advance of future catering activity. For instance, management may want everyone to have a good idea of the amount and types of catering business booked for next month. This can be done by preparing a monthly prefunction sheet that briefly notes the types of groups and number of guests expected the following month.

The prefunction sheet serves many purposes. Its major advantage is that it allows each department head to preplan his or her staffing needs for the long term. Other advantages are: kitchen and purchasing can use this information to plan tentative ordering, prepreparation, and preparation schedules; the storeroom can plan its inventory management procedures more effectively; the steward will have plenty of time to secure additional furniture, equipment, and tableware if needed; and housekeeping can plan its heavy cleaning routines much easier if it knows what to expect.

CHANGE ORDER

Usually hosts have opportunities to make alterations in their booked functions. For instance, they may be able to order changes in the menu a week before the event is scheduled, switch from table service to buffet service 3 days before, and decide to add extra bars 24 hours in advance.

At times, several changes must be made at the last minute. For example, if a function that initially expects 200 guests suddenly expands to 300 guests, the catering department may need to move the buffet line into the prefunction space in order to accommodate additional seating.

Sometimes a change may be suggested by the catering executive. For instance, if the purchasing agent has a problem getting a particular wine, the catering sales representative will need to meet with the host and discuss alternate brands that can be served for the same price.

These types of alterations must be communicated to all of the club departments that are involved with the catered event. The most efficient way to do this is to prepare an addendum to the original BEO.

The BEO addendum is customarily referred to as a banquet change order or banquet change sheet (see Figure 11.2). It contains the original BEO's identification number as well as other pertinent identifying factors. It also notes very specifically the changes that must be made. The department head must note unequivocally what must be eliminated and what must be added to the scheduled catered event.

To avoid confusion, the club should use a simple color-coded system to ensure that changes are recorded accurately. For instance, one property uses a three-color system: white—original BEO; green—revisions; pink—guarantees. In this case, if a change must be communicated, all relevant departments will receive them on green or pink paper, update their original BEOs, and reduce the paper flow so that only one document is retained.

FUNCTION CHANGE SHEET

Party Name:		Function Page #
Day of Week:	Date of Function:	

Message Received By:		Message From:	
Day:	Current Date:		Time of Conversation:

Figure 11.2. Club function change sheet.

CATERING AGREEMENT

Some clubs may require hosts to sign formal catering agreements before the events can be scheduled to take place. This is especially true when dealing with large functions and nonmember functions.

Sometimes a club will forego the use of formal contracts and instead rely on signed BEOs or signed letters of agreement. These documents may be every bit as legally binding as formal contracts, although they usually do not include the typical boilerplate language (that is, standardized legalese) found in most formal contracts.

Never book and confirm a catered event without a signed agreement. Usually an unwritten contract cannot be legally enforced in a court of law unless you are dealing with an agreement worth $500 or less. But even with small parties, it is good business practice to detail in writing both your and your host's responsibilities and obligations.

If you have standardized agreement forms, you can give a copy to a potential host to read and study before progressing any further. This gives the host enough time to examine the terms and conditions and to ask questions about anything unclear.

Experience shows that many hosts are unfamiliar with the language of the food and beverage industry. For instance, several years ago there was a dispute about the meaning of the term *chicken*. Since it was not defined in the purchase order contract, the supplier shipped hens. But the buyer wanted to purchase broiler (or fryer) chickens. The dispute ended up in litigation where, unfortunately for the buyer, the court found for the seller since the term *chicken* encompasses several types and varieties and the seller was able to interpret its meaning loosely.

Many clubs develop standardized agreements that contain a considerable amount of boilerplate clauses with enough blank space available to write in specific details as needed. For typical functions, the standard boilerplate contract will usually suffice. But if there is anything unusual that must be addressed, the club's legal counsel or other representative must add it.

Some club catering departments do not have to get involved with contract preparations. The director of sales may handle all contract negotiations. He or she may take care of adding clauses, explaining club policies, detailing the club's responsibilities and obligations, and so forth. Only occasionally would you need to participate in these developments.

The basic catering contract usually includes the following details:

1. Contract date
2. Function date(s)

3. Function time(s)
4. Appropriate signatures
5. Function room(s) tentatively assigned
6. Menus
7. Style(s) of service
8. Function room setup(s)
9. Other host services, such as
   a. Audiovisual
   b. Lighting
   c. Sleeping rooms (if applicable)
   d. Transportation
   e. Security
10. Head-count guarantees (and/or dollar-amount guarantees)
11. Estimated cost summary:
    a. Food and beverage charges
    b. Consumption taxes
    c. Gratuities
    d. Labor charges
    e. Room charges
    f. Cancellation penalty
    g. Deposits
    h. Other charges
12. Billing procedures
13. Procedures that must be used if changes are necessary
14. All club catering policies (see Chapter 1)
15. Host's responsibilities and obligations
16. Other standard contract language, such as:
    a. Person signing contract represents that he or she has full authority to legally bind the host.
    b. The contract shall be binding upon the parties, as well as their heirs, administrators, executors, successors, and assigns.
    c. Host has read the contract and completely understands its contents.
    d. Host stipulates that he or she is not signing the contract under duress.

CREDIT MANAGEMENT

Deposit

Deposits are rarely required of members for smaller catered functions, but many clubs require a deposit for functions costing over a certain amount. Nonmember hosts are always required to make a deposit on the function, generally at the time of booking, with a percentage of it nonrefundable if they cancel.

Billing Procedures

On the night of the function or the day after the event, the club generally will review the function bill with the host to ensure that there are no discrepancies in the charges. When dealing with member functions, the club generally bills the catered event on the member's monthly statement. If the function is a member-sponsored event, the club can bill in various ways—for instance, the nonmember may be responsible for paying for the function in full on the day of the function, or the member may be billed for the function and be responsible for payment. The former billing option has been instituted by clubs that do a significant amount of member-sponsored catering events in an attempt to make payment convenient for the member. The function would still appear on the member's monthly statement, but there would be a zero balance due.

Other Credit Procedures

The club may need to be involved with other credit-related issues. The club manager, either alone or in conjunction with the catering executive, could be faced with the following:

1. Tax-exempt clients must demonstrate this status by providing evidence of tax-exempt numbers and any other related documentation.

2. If hosts are promised complimentary products and/or services, the final billings must be adjusted accordingly.

3. Some clubs pay referral fees or other types of commissions. If your club does this, the club manager may need to provide the data necessary to compute them correctly.

4. If a host cancels the catered event after the cancellation grace period expires, the club will need to determine if he or she will forfeit the entire deposit or if part of it can be refunded. In some cases, particularly when hosts cancel at the last minute, the deposit may be insufficient consideration for

work you have already done. If so, the club will need to compute the appropriate charges and institute collection procedures.

5. Some hosts may have refunds due. For instance, you may want a host to put up a refundable deposit for AV equipment. When the equipment is returned on time and in acceptable condition, the club may credit the deposit to the final billing, or it may process a separate refund check.

6. Returns and allowances may need to be factored into the final billing. If, through no fault of the host, you had to make a last-minute menu substitution that is less expensive than the original selection, the club may need to adjust the final billing; conversely if the club had to use a more-expensive substitute. In this case, the club may not wish to pursue the matter because it is not the host's fault that the original item could not be procured. However, the host and catering executive may meet and perhaps split the difference. If so, the club may need to take this into account when processing the final billing.

FOOD AND BEVERAGE COST CONTROL

Effective product cost control is based on standardized operating procedures. To ensure consistent, predictable business results, top management must establish budgetary, quality, labor, and layout and design standards, among others—the list is endless.

If there is one major, overriding problem afflicting many businesses in the food and beverage industry, it is the lack of standards. This is understandable due to the fact that standards are difficult to establish, implement, monitor, and revise. The poorly trained manager has only so much time. When rushed, he or she may neglect club standards and permit unacceptable practices.

Even those establishments that have complete sets of standards can fall prey to the inability or unwillingness of managers to apply them consistently. The best control procedures are worthless if they are not used correctly and consistently.

Management must develop and implement a consistent cycle of control. Moreover, it must monitor the control system continually so that needed changes can be made quickly and efficiently.

The food and beverage operation's cycle of control begins with the purchasing function. It continues through receiving, storing, issuing, producing, and servicing. Checks and balances need to be inserted throughout the cycle in order to pinpoint responsibility and reveal any problems.

The main purpose of product cost control, or any other expense control, is to ensure that actual costs parallel standard (that is, budgeted) costs.

Unlike the typical restaurant business, catering is in a better position to minimize variances between standard and actual costs. After all, you know what to expect and when to expect it. Consequently, it is easier to forecast your needs and prepare for them accordingly.

Experience shows, though, that catering's advantage over the typical restaurant operation is not as large as it may initially appear. For instance, even though you know what to expect, guests are notorious for arriving late, leaving late, and/or requesting special attention at the last minute.

The potential to minimize variances between actual and standard costs is generally a bit easier for the typical catering department. But, while this may be true, the system is not error free. It can be as close as possible to being error free, however, if you pay close attention to every major operating activity.

Purchasing

The food and beverage cycle of control begins in the purchasing agent's office. This person is responsible for selecting and procuring the needed products at the most economical prices. Prices obtained by the purchasing department establish initially the ultimate costs of doing business.

Probably the most critical cost-control tool used by the purchasing agent is the product specification (see Figure 11.3). Food and beverage costs, as well as the quality of finished menu items, cannot be predicted accurately unless you are using standardized, consistent product specifications. You must use the same ingredients time after time or else the finished products' costs and culinary qualities will vary unpredictably.

Intended use	Packaging procedure
Exact name	Degree of ripeness
Brand name	Product form
U.S. grade	Color
Product size	Trade association standards
Expected yield	Chemical standards
Package size	Inspection procedures
Type of packaging	Instructions to suppliers
Preservation method	Quantity limits
Point of origin	Cost limits

Figure 11.3. Typical information included on food, beverage, and nonfood supply specifications.

Another major cost-control technique is to identify appropriate suppliers who can handle your needs adequately and include them on an approved supplier list. When ordering, use only these approved suppliers. Only top management should authorize exceptions.

The purchasing agent also contributes to cost and quality control by preparing and entering the optimal order sizes for each ingredient purchased. If you underorder, you risk stockouts and unhappy guests. If you overorder, you risk spoilages and excessive inventory carrying charges.

Catering lends itself nicely to computing optimal order sizes because, unlike typical restaurant service, most catered events are very predictable. If, for instance, you expect 100 dinner guests and you normally prepare for 105, you then order enough merchandise to prepare and serve 105 meals. In most cases, you do not have to anticipate customer demands because you know about them well in advance. Furthermore, if the ingredients used for catered events are also used in the club's other dining outlets, you can even order a little additional safety stock and not worry about it going bad in storage.

Receiving

Unlike the typical large restaurant operation, large clubs usually do a very good job receiving their shipments. They usually assign at least one full-time receiving agent to ensure that deliveries are consistent with purchase orders and the club's product specifications.

Clubs generally follow the invoice receiving technique. This system requires the receiving agent to:

1. Compare the delivery slip (the invoice) to the purchase order to be certain that the shipment is the correct one and that it contains all the items originally ordered.

2. Compare the products delivered with the invoice and the purchase order. All three must match.

3. Inspect the quality of each item. The shipment must meet the product specifications. If it doesn't, it should not be accepted unless a superior authorizes receipt.

4. Inspect the quantity of each item. Weights, volumes, counts, and so forth must be accurate.

5. Arrange for credit from the supplier, if applicable. If there is any problem with product quality or quantity, the receiving agent must

get a credit slip from the driver. If the driver is an independent trucker, you will need to send a request for credit memorandum to the supplier's credit department. Before your accounting department's accounts payable division pays the bill, it must account properly for any and all credits.

6. Sign the invoice, retain a copy to send to accounting, and arrange to store the shipment.

Storage and Issuing

The major purpose of storage is to protect the merchandise from theft and spoilage. Theft is minimized by keeping everything under lock and key, restricting access to the storeroom facilities, and using a standardized issuing system whereby anyone wanting merchandise from the storeroom must complete and sign an authorized stock requisition and take responsibility for the products (see Figure 11.4).

Spoilage is minimized by maintaining appropriate sanitation standards and rotating the stock correctly. Products must also be stored in the appropriate temperature and humidity environment.

Canned goods and other dry-storage groceries are usually stored at about 60 to 70 degrees F (50 degrees F is ideal), with approximately 50- to 60-percent relative humidity.

Frozen foods should be stored at 0 degrees F or less. Ideally, the freezer thermostat would be set at −10 degrees F so that, when someone opens the door to get something, the interior temperature will not rise above 0 degrees F.

Refrigerated meats, seafood, and poultry should be stored at the coldest temperature possible without freezing. Dairy products are best kept at about 38 to 40 degrees F. Fresh produce should stay at about 40 degrees F. Each of these product categories requires approximately 75- to 85-percent relative humidity. Ideally, you will have at least three separate walk-in refrigerators so that these recommended temperatures and humidities can be maintained.

Products in the typical club storage facilities normally do not spoil to the point where they are inedible. Usually they lose just enough culinary quality to render them unfit for service. For instance, flaccid lettuce could be eaten without risking food-borne illness; however, you cannot expect a guest to pay for it. The challenge of maintaining culinary quality is a little more daunting in the food and beverage industry than it is, say, in a homemaker's kitchen.

No. XXXXX FOOD REQUISITION

FOOD REQUISITION

No. XXXXX

Dept.: _____ Date: _____ 19 ___

Quantity	Unit	Description	Issued	Unit Price	Amount

Ordered by: _____

Issued by: _____

Received by: _____

Distribution

White Copy: Controller _____

Yellow Copy: Storeroom _____

Pink Copy: Chef _____

Figure 11.4. Sample food requisition form.

Production

Preprep and prep procedures offer several opportunities for cost overruns. To combat this tendency, the catering executive should work with the chef and/or food and beverage director to develop adequate production controls. The major production controls that should be emphasized are:

1. *Always use standardized recipes.* Standardized recipes are just as important as product specifications (see Figure 11.5). It is useless to purchase

STANDARD RECIPE FORM

Product Name:

Equipment Needed:

Yield:

Serving Size:

Preparation Time:

Temperature(s):

Ingredients	Quantities	Method

Figure 11.5. Sample standard recipe form.

the same quality merchandise every time if you do not use consistent preprep and prep procedures.

2. *Develop a standardized production plan.*   The timing of preprep and prep activities is another crucial factor impacting product costs. This is particularly true for foods because, if you produce foods too far in advance, chances are you will have a lot of finished items past their peak of culinary quality that cannot be served.

Since you have a good idea of how much to produce and when the finished items will be served, you can develop a very accurate production plan. It is this knowledge that gives you a cost-control advantage over the typical restaurant operation; predictability minimizes cost variances.

3. *Supervise portioning procedures.*   Experience shows that we tend to overportion foods. Guests who help themselves tend to take more than they can eat. And employees have a tendency to put a little more on the guest's plate, especially if the guest is witnessing the dish-up process.

It is also true that we have a tendency to create excess scrap, or waste, during the production process. This is especially the case if we are rushed. Since you usually have sufficient lead time and know what to expect, chances are correct production planning can virtually eliminate this problem.

Many foodservice experts believe that, if you use standardized product specifications and recipes, if you make a conscious effort to reduce avoidable waste, and if you maintain portion control, the odds are excellent that your actual costs will be in line with your standard costs. Minimizing or eliminating cost variances should be one of the food production manager's major goals.

Service

If you have enough servers, you should not encounter any significant service problems that could cause cost and quality variances. However, good service does not just happen. Someone must supervise and monitor the service function to ensure cost and quality standards are met and that all guests are satisfied.

The most critical aspects of service control are:

1. *Dish-up should be done as close as possible to service time.*   Culinary quality suffers if finished items have to sit any longer than necessary. Products past their peak of quality cannot be served; usually they end up in the garbage, with your product costs increasing accordingly. Service costs may also increase if you need to plate and serve quite a bit of food to replace products that cannot be served.

2. *An expeditor should be used to coordinate production and service.* This person usually sees to it that servers' needs are communicated properly

to production people and that foods are delivered from the kitchen and served to the guests in a timely manner. Usually a supervisor or manager fills this critical role as part of his or her overall responsibilities.

3. *A food checker should be used to inspect the quality of finished menu items.*   He or she should also be responsible for ensuring that only the correct amount of meals and beverages are served. As meals are carried from the kitchen to the banquet room, the food checker will keep a running tally of them and compare the total served to the expected number of guests noted on the BEO. As with the expeditor position, this role may be filled by an existing supervisor or manager.

In some cases, the expeditor could also perform the food checker's duties. For small catered events, he or she could keep the tally as well as maintain coordination between production and service.

Food and Beverage Cost-Control Record-keeping System

Your cost-control efforts are incomplete if you do not have some way of gathering and analyzing cost data. You will need an effective data-gathering and data-analysis procedure for at least two reasons—you must have some way of calculating standard and actual product usage; and these data might be needed to calculate a client's final billing.

If you are primarily interested in calculating standard and actual costs, you should use the *standard-cost* record-keeping system. The standard-cost system is a rather long, arduous procedure that is not usually performed in the typical foodservice operation unless that operation is fully computerized. It is usually too difficult and time consuming to operate this system by hand.

The system requires you to calculate the standard cost for each menu item. You must precost each menu item; that is, you must determine the exact standard cost for each one. This requires you to cost out each recipe and calculate the expected (or potential) product cost per serving (see Figure 11.6). Once you have the potential product cost for each serving, multiply it by the number of servings used. This gives you the total standard cost.

To determine the total actual cost, you must take a physical inventory of all foods and beverages left at the end of the catered function and cost it out. This ending inventory is then inserted into the following formula in order to compute the total actual cost.

> Beginning inventory (the previous ending inventory)

plus: Issues from the storeroom

plus: Direct purchases (that is, deliveries that bypass the storeroom and go directly to production)

<table>
<tr><td colspan="4" align="center">PRODUCT COST ANALYSIS</td></tr>
<tr><td colspan="4">Product: _____</td></tr>
<tr><td align="center">Ingredients</td><td align="center">Unit
Price</td><td align="center">Amount
Used</td><td align="center">Ingredient
Cost</td></tr>
<tr><td></td><td></td><td></td><td></td></tr>
<tr><td></td><td></td><td></td><td></td></tr>
<tr><td></td><td></td><td></td><td></td></tr>
<tr><td></td><td></td><td></td><td></td></tr>
<tr><td></td><td></td><td></td><td></td></tr>
<tr><td></td><td></td><td></td><td></td></tr>
<tr><td></td><td></td><td></td><td></td></tr>
<tr><td></td><td></td><td></td><td></td></tr>
<tr><td></td><td></td><td></td><td></td></tr>
<tr><td></td><td></td><td></td><td></td></tr>
<tr><td></td><td></td><td></td><td></td></tr>
</table>

Total Product Cost: _____

Number of Servings: _____

Cost per Serving: _____

Target Cost Percentage: _____

Menu Price: _____

Figure 11.6. Sample product cost work sheet.

minus:	Ending inventory
equals:	Total actual cost

The total standard cost is compared to the total actual cost. If there is a significant variance, you need to go back through the cycle of control and see if you can spot the problem(s). In other words, you must examine your purchasing, receiving, storing, issuing, preprepping, prepping, and servicing procedures to see what needs to be corrected. You then make the necessary correction(s) so that future catered events do not suffer the same fate.

Most foodservice managers cost out recipes only once in a while. It is not an ongoing effort because it is very difficult to revise costs that are apt to change frequently. Of course, when submitting a competitive bid to a host, the catering executive may want to calculate current recipe costs. Likewise, you may need the current standard costs if you book an event that will be priced according to the amount of food and beverage consumed. There are numerous computer programs that can streamline this process.

Another way of gathering and analyzing cost-related data is to use the *product-analysis* record-keeping system. This system (sometimes referred to as the *critical-item inventory* system) concentrates on food and beverage usage, not on the costs.

This system is not as accurate as the standard-cost system, but it is much easier to use. However, while it exchanges a bit of accuracy for time savings, the information it yields is sufficient to control product costs. Experience shows that it is the most common type of product cost record-keeping system used in the foodservice industry.

In summary, this system involves a comparison of banquet room counts to production counts. For instance, if the kitchen plates 125 steak dinners, the banquet records should reveal that 125 guests were served. The kitchen usage should compare favorably with head counts, plate counts, or any other service records used. Any variance must be investigated and the underlying problem(s) corrected.

The products counted are usually only the critical or expensive items. If you book a party for 100 T-bone steaks, you tend to concentrate your food cost-control efforts solely on the meat. You should take the time to compare kitchen counts with banquet room counts. In addition, you should match these data with the stock requisition records and check for consistency. If everything works out right, there will be 100 T-bone steaks noted on the stock requisition, 100 prepared, and 100 served.

Some foodservice experts are critical of this system primarily because you neglect other product costs. However, the product costs you neglect are not nearly as high as the ones you monitor. While not infallible, the system does provide a reasonable measure of product cost control. Furthermore, this system provides enough information to calculate the final billings of those catered functions that are priced according to the amount of guest consumption.

Other foodservice experts criticize this system because, if you rely on it exclusively, you will ignore raw-product purchase prices and edible-portion costs. If this happens, you may not have sufficient data upon which to base menu prices. You also do not know if your month-end actual cost calculations reflect reality, because you have no standard cost with which to compare them.

It would appear that the product-analysis system will be with us for some time since the standard-cost system cannot effectively be used unless the food and beverage property is fully computerized or a large central accounting staff is maintained. An integrated property computer system is expensive and may not be cost effective for the small club operation. However, without a computer system, it is difficult and time consuming to maintain accurate, current recipe costs.

A form of product analysis that is used exclusively for beverages is sometimes referred to as the *ounce system* of control. Under this procedure, the manager establishes a standard number of drinks that should be poured from each container, and the actual number of drinks served should be consistent with the standard.

For instance, if you use 1-liter containers of vodka and the average drink size is 1.5 oz, the potential number of drinks per bottle is 22.5 (33.8 oz/1.5 oz = 22.5 drinks). At the end of the beverage function, if you note that 2.7 bottles of vodka were used, the sales records for vodka should reflect approximately 60 drinks served (2.7 bottles × 22.5 drinks = 60.75 drinks). In this example, after taking an ending inventory and calculating the expected number of drinks served, you should have approximately 60 drink tickets in the ticket lockbox. You expect 60 drinks to be served (standard usage), so you should collect about 60 drink tickets (actual usage).

Usually at the end of the beverage function, the manager will calculate the usage of each brand of liquor and determine the total number of potential drinks served. This total serves as your basis of comparison, the standard to which is compared the actual number of drink tickets collected.

You expect the actual number of drinks served to be a bit less than the standard. If the bartenders do not use a liquor-dispensing machine and have to free pour, chances are there will be some overpouring. Furthermore, with free pouring, you cannot get all the liquor out of the bottle; some of it will remain on the sides of the bottle since you usually do not have time to wait for every drop to drip out. Faced with this situation, you may need to adjust your standards. You may plan to lose, say, 0.5 oz of liquor per container and revise your standards downward. For instance, in the vodka example noted earlier, you might expect 22 drinks per container instead of 22.5.

For complete control, you will need to relay the beverage usage data to the head cashier so that he or she can audit the performance of the cashier assigned to the beverage function. The basic comparison here is between the number of drink tickets sold, the number collected by bartenders, and the amount of cash collected. The cash collected and the number of drink tickets sold should match exactly. However, you expect the number of drink tickets collected to be a little less than the number sold and the cash collected because a few guests may not use each drink ticket purchased.

If the bartenders collect cash from guests, you might want to use the *standard-sales* record-keeping system for beverage functions. This system (sometimes referred to as the *potential-sales* system) is very similar to the ounce system in that it concentrates on usage and not on product costs. The major difference is that it allows you to control cash as well as product usage.

To use this system, you need to calculate a bottle value for each container of liquor stocked in inventory. The bottle value represents the amount of sales revenue a container of liquor should generate. For instance, if the 1.5-oz serving of vodka noted in the example above sells for $3.75 per drink, the bottle value of a liter of vodka is approximately $84.38 (33.8 oz/1.5 oz = 22.5 drinks; 22.5 drinks × $3.75 = $84.38). If you note at the end of the function that 1.7 liters of vodka were used, the cash collected should be approximately $143.45 (1.7 bottles × $84.38 = $143.45).

At the end of every beverage function, you must calculate usage rates for each brand of liquor. Each brand's usage rate must then be converted to its standard sales revenue. After calculating each brand's standard sales revenue, a grand total of standard sales revenue must be determined. This grand total serves as your overall standard sales figure, which is then compared to actual sales revenue, that is, total cash collected. The comparison should show very little variance.

A variation of the standard-sales record-keeping system is to keep track of disposable glassware usage. For instance, if you use 9-oz cups for mixed drinks at $3.00 apiece and there are 100 cups missing at the end of the event, the cash collected should equal $300, and the beverage inventory usage should be consistent with the preparation and service of 100 mixed drinks.

Although most clubs will not use disposable ware instead of glassware for beverage functions, there may be some occasions when it is appropriate. For instance, plastic cups may be preferred in the pool area, parties on the club grounds, and other off-premises sites.

Controlling Product Costs for Buffets, Receptions, and Open Bars

If guests are able to serve themselves or can order drinks without using drink tickets or other forms of documentation, your cost-control procedures need to be adjusted to take into account average usage figures. Since you do not control portions or guest usage rates, your purchasing, production, and service strategies must be based on historical averages. This requires you to analyze previous catered events periodically in order to keep up to date on average customer usage in your property.

Another key area that will need revision is the record-keeping system used. If you use the product-analysis system, you must be sure to use relevant averages or else you will have no control over the critical items. For instance, if you are serving veal cutlets on an all-you-can-eat buffet line for 100 guests, and if in the past you note that each guest takes an average of 1.5 servings, at the end of the event, the kitchen and banquet room counts should balance at around 150 servings.

Unfortunately, when working with averages, there is a greater opportunity for inventory shrinkage. For instance, in our veal example, you have no way of knowing if 5 of the 150 servings were pilfered by employees unless you use additional subtle cost-control procedures designed specifically to thwart this activity. This is particularly troublesome if the client's final billing is based on guest consumption.

Unfortunately, in our industry there are many opportunities for undetected pilferage and shoplifting if you must work with average cost data. Mystery shoppers, extra supervision in the function room and kitchen, and other similar techniques usually must be used to minimize them.

Product Cost-Reduction Techniques

While cost reduction is not technically the same as cost control, many people see no difference between them. The typical food and beverage operation spends about one-third of its sales revenue on product costs. Any little decrease, therefore, will have a major favorable impact on net profits.

Some of the more common product cost-reduction techniques used in the foodservice industry are:

1. *Seek long-term competitive bids from suppliers.* This allows you to maximize your purchasing power. Suppliers may be willing to offer price concessions if they can count on your business.

2. *Qualify for purchase price discounts.* Many suppliers will grant quantity discounts if you purchase a huge amount of one type of item. Furthermore, a volume discount is sometimes offered if you purchase a large dollar amount of several types of items. Before agreeing to a huge purchase, though, make sure that the club has enough storage space and cash or trade credit available to handle it.

Some suppliers also offer promotional discounts, whereby they may reduce the purchase price if you agree to promote their products in your operation. If you allow them to put table tent-card advertisements on your dining room tables, you might receive a 1- or 2-percent price reduction.

Cash discounts may also be lucrative alternatives. These are granted by some suppliers if you pay your bills before the due dates. Purchasing agents will routinely ask suppliers if they offer any type of discount for prompt payment.

3. *Other purchasing opportunities.* Suppliers occasionally offer other cost-reduction opportunities the club may find attractive. You may be willing to take advantage of:

a. *New products.* These usually carry some sort of temporary introductory price that is much lower than normal. You could stock up on some of these things and use them to accommodate a few catering functions. For instance, a new frozen chicken entree may come on the market. You may be able to get two free cases for every one you purchase at the regular price. If you have the storage room and the budget, you could stock up on this product and offer it as a low-cost alternative to some of your members who are on tight budgets.

b. *Stock discontinuation sales.* Similar to the new-product introductory prices, these money-saving items can increase your net profits or allow you to be more competitive when soliciting cost-conscious functions.

c. *Trading.* Consider trading for products instead of paying cash. Some clubs have trade-out arrangements with certain suppliers. For instance, instead of paying cash for your canned groceries, you might find a supplier who is willing to accept payment in kind. While trading is not commonly done for food commodities (it is more common with services), it is worth pursuing because bartering can save a good deal of money. It is cheaper to pay a $100 invoice with $100 worth of club services and menu items because your out-of-pocket costs are much less than $100. Furthermore, if you allow these trade credits to be used only during your slow periods, there will be no extra pressure on your production and service staffs. The club board *must* approve any plans to trade club services for outside items.

4. *Use more raw food ingredients.* These are much cheaper than prepreprepared convenience items. Unfortunately, you will usually spend more for labor and energy since you will need to do most, if not all, of the preprep and prep work. Generally, though, unlike the typical restaurant, the typical club has sufficient production space and labor on hand to make raw-ingredient use an economical option.

PAYROLL COST CONTROL

Foodservice experts agree that the manager's first line of defense against pay-roll cost variances is the work schedule. Your work-scheduling skills will have a major impact on your ability to minimize variances between the standard and actual payroll costs.

The work schedule represents the standard payroll cost. It is based on the club's staffing guide, and the staffing guide is based primarily on the number of guests expected. As the guest count increases, the number of pay-roll hours and staff members needed also increases.

Unfortunately, the relationship between the number of guests and the number of work hours and staff members needed is not easy to predict. For instance, there is no neat formula that tells you how many work hours you need for each guest, nor is there a calculus that reveals the additional num-ber of work hours that should be scheduled if 5 more guests show up. Fur-thermore, you cannot always predict whether you need more staff members to handle a few more guests; for example, if 1 server can handle 14 guests, he or she may be able to handle 16 with no additional trouble.

The optimal payroll cost is a very illusive figure in the foodservice busi-ness. Unlike food and beverage costs, payroll costs are not completely vari-able. They have been tagged with several descriptions, such as semivariable costs, semifixed costs, and stepwise variable costs. The fact remains, however, that, if you plot payroll costs against sales revenue on a graph, you will not get a straight line.

Factors Affecting Payroll Cost

The optimal payroll cost is a bit unpredictable because there are so many fac-tors affecting it. While some factors are controllable, many of them are not. The degree of control that can be exercised can vary considerably from club to club. Indeed, if you manage a particular property and have mastered its payroll cost-control vagaries, you may find that a move to another club will cause you to regress temporarily to the bottom of the learning curve in that some of your experience at the old property cannot be effectively applied to the new one.

The key factors that affect the amount and cost of payroll needed are:

1. Menu
2. Style of service
3. Guest count

4. Guest arrival patterns

5. Facility layout and design

6. Type of equipment

7. Employee tenure

8. Employee turnover

9. Local labor market conditions

10. Hours of operation

11. Union regulations

12. Federal and state labor department regulations

    a. Minimum wage

    b. Tip credit

    c. Meal credit

    d. Child labor restrictions

    e. Overtime premium pay

Payroll Cost-Control Record-keeping System

As with any type of cost-control record-keeping system, the primary objectives are to compute standard and actual costs, compare them, and evaluate and correct any unacceptable variances.

The standard payroll cost is computed by costing out the work schedule. If you are lucky, a healthy part of the work schedule will be fixed. But if the bulk of your work schedule is variable, you might have to calculate standard costs daily.

The club caterer must expect the typical work schedule to lean heavily in the direction of variable-cost employees since many catered functions booked in your property may need completely different crews. Furthermore, if the host is paying separately for labor, you will need to cost out the work schedule.

You *cannot* avoid calculating standard payroll costs. Competitive bids rely on accurate cost estimates. Since payroll is a considerable chunk of the total cost needed to prepare for and serve a catered event, chances are the catering sales representatives will continually ask you for current payroll cost estimates.

Actual payroll costs are computed by costing out the time records. Some time records are fixed; for example, secretarial, supervisory, and managerial salaries may not vary. However, variable-cost employees normally use a time clock and/or sign a time sheet.

The fixed costs and variable work hours are converted to a total, actual payroll cost. This actual is then compared to the standard. As always, if there is a significant variance, the problem(s) must be uncovered and corrective action taken.

Payroll Cost-Reduction Techniques

The typical food and beverage operation spends, at the very least, 25 percent of each sales revenue dollar for payroll, with about another 5 percent or more going for employee benefits. Payroll, employee benefits, and payroll-related administrative costs can easily exceed one-third of a foodservice operation's sales revenue. As a result, no payroll cost-control procedure is considered complete unless it includes one or more cost-reduction techniques.

Some payroll cost-reduction techniques used in the hospitality industry are:

1. *Employee leasing.* Instead of hiring employees, you lease the entire staff from a leasing company. This can save money because the leasing company consolidates and handles all the human resources administrative details, thereby relieving the club of this costly burden. The leasing company can also consolidate several small employers' employee benefits needs, qualify for large-employer discounts, and pass on some of the savings to its clients. According to the employee leasing industry, clients typically save between 2 and 4 percent of their current labor costs by using leased employees.

2. *Hiring rehab employees.* In some instances, if you agree to participate in rehabilitative efforts by hiring the handicapped, allowing the local workers' compensation agency to place trainees in your property, or hiring individuals in certain targeted social or income groups, you may receive a monetary reward. For instance, the workers' compensation agency may pay part of a trainee's wages for a few weeks. Or you might qualify for an income tax credit if you hire the handicapped.

3. *Use independent contractors in lieu of employees.* For some tasks, you may be able to employ independent contractors instead of hiring employees to do the work. For instance, instead of hiring cloakroom attendants, you might want to hire an independent service. This can be more convenient in the long run since you do not have to maintain extensive personnel files, process payroll checks, or handle all the other relevant administrative details. You merely send a check once a month to the service and use the time saved to pursue other more profitable activities.

4. *Use part-time employees in lieu of full-time employees.* Usually part-time employees working 19 hours or less per week do not receive discre-

tionary benefits. Hiring part-timers also gives you a great deal of flexibility. The down side, though, is the fact that you need to have more employees on the payroll, which can significantly increase uniforms, employee meals, and other personnel-related costs.

5. *Use more preprepared convenience foods.* When using convenience foods, you do not need as many employees, nor do you need very many highly skilled (hence, costly) employees. The drawback is the increased food costs. Prices are much higher for convenience products because they include the cost of food, production labor, and energy needed to produce them. Generally, frozen-food entrees can be used to maximize the productivity of current production labor because it allows food handlers to significantly increase the number of portions that can be prepared.

6. *Eliminate overtime premium.* The labor laws, as well as union regulations, require you to pay overtime premium pay under certain circumstances. For instance, an employee may need to be compensated one and one-half times the regular rate of pay for any hours worked in excess of eight hours per day.

At times, you may fall victim to this problem because some catered events are bound to run over and you will need to keep some employees on board to take care of the stragglers. If these overruns are common, you would be much better off scheduling one or two persons to come in later during the event who can stick around and take care of closing down. This way, instead of being stuck with overtime premium pay, you would be able to pay the more economical straight-time wage.

Another way to prevent overtime premium pay is to negotiate with hosts and ask them to agree in advance that, if the events run over, they will be responsible for paying the additional labor charges.

Alternatively, you could schedule a supervisor or manager to handle any unpredictable last-minute overruns. Usually management employees do not have to be compensated at overtime premium rates. They normally receive straight salaries that do not vary with the amount of hours worked.

7. *Reduce costly employee turnover.* Proper employee selection, orientation, and training should help reduce employee turnover and the subsequent costs of hiring replacement personnel.

8. *Use labor-saving equipment.* Under some circumstances, you may be able to reduce your payroll costs by investing in labor-saving devices. For instance, a computerized automatic bar may increase worker productivity enough for you to reduce the number of bartenders needed. However, the expensive investment that usually must be made in this type of equipment may not be recovered easily. Chances are you will not see enough of a payroll cost reduction to justify any major investments. However, if an

investment can pay for itself in about three years or less, it is generally considered a good choice.

Be careful when estimating the cost savings that supposedly accompany labor-saving equipment. Our industry has been unable to take full advantage of many labor-saving technological advances since, after all, we are in the personal service business. It is easy to overestimate cost savings, particularly if we rely on enthusiastic equipment salespersons for these estimates.

CONTROL OF OTHER EXPENSES

Usually the catering executive concentrates on controlling product and payroll costs primarily because these costs represent a very large chunk of the sales-revenue dollar. This *prime cost* (that is, product cost plus payroll cost) is about 60 to 70 percent of the typical foodservice operation's sales revenue. Consequently, it is understandable that a manager's cost-control efforts will be aimed in this direction.

But there are a handful of other controllable expenses that deserve some of your attention. Generally speaking, these are direct operating expenses such as napery, tableware, soaps, chemicals, and paper products; utilities, repairs, and maintenance; and administrative and general expenses such as telephone, postage, and office supplies. The key to controlling these expenses is to be on the lookout for waste, pilferage, and incorrect equipment use.

Waste is a typical problem when using paper products, production equipment, soaps, chemicals, and other similar items. For instance, it is not uncommon for employees to use too much chemical in the rinse water, to be overly generous with the use of paper napkins and doilies, to turn on the oven long before it is needed, and to neglect sorting soiled napery correctly. While these actions do not necessarily cause significant decreases in net profit, they add up quickly if you do not monitor them closely.

Office supplies and telephone use are subject to employee pilferage as well as to waste. Subtle controls, including taking frequent inventories of office supplies and restricting long-distance telephone use, should be applied in order to minimize these problems.

Employees must be trained adequately in equipment use before allowing them to operate it. If they do not know how to use equipment correctly, they may injure themselves and the equipment. In addition to increased workers' compensation costs, experience shows that incorrect equipment use is the major cause of exorbitant repair and maintenance expenses. Moreover, incorrect equipment use drastically reduces the equipment's useful life. One of the paradoxes of the food and beverage business is that we would never allow someone to drive a car without a driver's license, yet we are willing to let someone operate a $40,000 dish machine without proper training.

COMPUTERIZED CONTROL PROCEDURES

The club catering department can gain many benefits by computerizing its operations. However, since computerization is an expensive undertaking, to justify its investment, a computer system must offer substantial benefits to the hotel property and to its guests.

Club catering departments may be able to reap these potential benefits:

1. Improved guest service
2. Streamlined handling of paperwork and data
3. Improved control over day-to-day operations
4. Generation of complete, timely reports
5. Reduced cost of paper supplies
6. Increased sales revenue
7. Increased employee productivity
8. Reduction of clerical staff
9. Job enrichment due to the reduction of repetitive tasks
10. Ability to keep current sales and expense data on file

Selecting a Computer System

Take your time to carefully consider all available options before making a computer-investment decision. Some catering executives suggest that you let the following rules guide your decision:

1. Never be the first buyer of a new computer system. The first user is usually placed in a high-risk position. Benefit from others' experience.
2. Avoid purchasing or leasing a computer system from a firm that has many large clients unless you are one of them. The largest clients will receive priority service from the computer firm.
3. Before buying a system, always observe someone else using a similar system at a similar club property. Interview the users and seek their opinions.

4. Decide specifically what you want the system to do for you. This tells you the type of software you will need to purchase or rent.

5. Once the software is selected, look for the appropriate hardware. Be certain that the hardware is compatible with other computer systems used at your property. If possible, never select hardware that requires you to take data from one machine, reformulate it, and enter it into another machine. Data reentry tends to significantly reduce the benefits of computerization.

6. Select an adequate computer service firm. The firm should provide sufficient training and technical backup. The company should have a help hotline. Furthermore, the firm must be able to adapt the standard software to coincide with your property's overall system.

Computer Uses

Software available to the food and beverage industry can be purchased to perform the following tasks:

1. Desktop publishing for menus, brochures, and other similar promotional materials
2. Sales analysis
3. Bookings analysis
4. Cancellation report
5. Group booking log
6. Daily tracer list printout of current and previous clients
7. Sales call report
8. Group profile sheet
9. Banquet event order (BEO)
10. Function resume
11. Lost business report
12. Prefunction sheet
13. Catering contract
14. Daily event schedule
15. Forecast
16. Daily function room schedule
17. Work schedule
18. Room layout

19. Space management
20. Link to outside suppliers and service contractors
21. Payroll processing
22. Recipe costing
23. Menu pricing
24. Inventory management
25. Recipe nutrition analysis
26. Invoice control
27. Product cost analysis
28. Payroll cost analysis
29. Equipment scheduling
30. Word processing
31. Time clock
32. Production schedule
33. Break-even analysis
34. Menu planning
35. Tip reporting
36. Tip allocation
37. Server analysis
38. Stock requisition
39. Department-by-department comparison
40. Open-guest-check report
41. Cashier analysis
42. Communication with other club departments
43. Link with corporate headquarters
44. Billing
45. Inventory reorder
46. Yield management
47. Web research/Web resources
48. E-mail

*Index**

* *Note:* Page references to figures are in italic.